Managing Human Resources

An Introduction to Public Personnel Administration

Managing Human Resources

An Introduction to Public Personnel Administration

N. Joseph Cayer
Texas Tech University

St. Martin's Press   New York

Library of Congress Catalog Card Number: 80–50125

Copyright © 1980 by St. Martin's Press, Inc.
All Rights Reserved.
Manufactured in the United States of America.
43210
fedcba
For information, write St. Martin's Press, Inc.
175 Fifth Avenue, New York, N. Y. 10010

typography: Caliber

ISBN: 0–312–51244–9

To
Muriel M. Morse

Preface

Public management and public managers are going through a period of intense public scrutiny, and this scrutiny is stimulating a great deal of change in the way public personnel administrators conduct their activities. The election of a president in 1976 who stressed in his campaign the need to reform the bureaucracy brought about the first major reorganization of the way the national government conducts its personnel activities since the establishment of the civil service system in 1883. Taxpayer disenchantment with public service, and with public servants, is fostering many changes in personnel practices at the state and local levels as well. In short, the 1980s may be the most challenging decade ever for public personnel managers.

The aim of this text is to offer students and practitioners of public administration a broad introduction to the function, process, and effect of public personnel management. To understand and respond to the challenges of the 1980s, it is necessary to understand the foundations on which the public personnel system is based. It is also necessary to understand the forces of change and the processes by which change occurs in our system of government. To that end, this book integrates historical background with an evaluation of the dynamics of the decision-making processes which produce personnel policy and practice. Personnel administration is viewed here as a part of the larger political process responding to pressures from the political environment. Like the rest of the political system, public personnel management is ever changing as it reacts to new values and conditions and as it attempts to move in new directions.

My debts in preparing this text have been numerous. Lee Sigelman, formerly a colleague at Texas Tech University and now at the University of Kentucky, deepened my understanding of many developments in personnel management, and his critical perspective forced me to sharpen my analysis of a number of issues. My students at both Texas Tech and the University of Maine deserve much credit for being good critics of my ideas and approaches. Their interest and their evaluations of my efforts were an encouragement. Several people reviewed the manuscript in its successive drafts and provided thoughtful suggestions for improvement. I greatly appreciate the efforts of James S. Bowman, University of Wyoming; James Carroll, Syracuse University; Irving O. Dawson, University of Texas at Arlington; Dianne N. Long, Michigan State University; and James M. Banovetz, Northern Illinois University. Alison J. Davidow, Research Associate, Center for Public Service, and Glenn J. Jaspers, Jr., M.P.A. student and Teaching Assistant, Texas Tech University, were invaluable in editing the manuscript and helping me state my ideas clearly. Brenda Hoyle deserves much credit for an excellent typing job under great pressure. The editorial staff of St. Martin's Press, particularly Bert Lummus, Carolyn Eggleston, and Michael Weber, have my gratitude for their patience and efficient work.

Finally, a special note of appreciation to Muriel M. Morse, recently retired manager of the Los Angeles Department of Personnel, to whom the book is dedicated. On many occasions she has shared with me her rich insight into public personnel management.

Although many colleagues made this book possible, I bear sole responsibility for its shortcomings.

In 1975 St. Martin's Press published my brief book entitled *Public Personnel Administration in the United States*. Readers of that volume—which will continue to be in print—will recognize some of the same ideas, presented here in considerably expanded form.

NJC
Lubbock, Texas

Contents

Chapter **12**   Forces for Change: A Look Ahead   217

Managing Human Resources

An Introduction to Public Personnel Administration

Chapter 1

The Environment of Public Personnel Administration

Personnel administration is a major and multifaceted component of managing any organization. Personnel managers need to know how to recruit, select, evaluate, promote, train, discipline, and dismiss employees. They must be adept at motivating, counseling, and bargaining with workers. They are called upon to classify positions, map out compensation plans, measure productivity, and handle grievances and complaints. In short, personnel management involves all aspects of managing the human resources of an organization. Public personnel administration refers to that function in governmental entities.

Personnel administration is also a universal management activity. Every supervisor is, in effect, a personnel manager. While personnel offices normally develop and monitor personnel policies, supervisors are responsible for carrying them out. They are the crucial links in the personnel process, since they deal with employees from day to day. The effectiveness of the organization hinges in part on how well supervisors perform their personnel functions.

Those who perform personnel activities in the public sector do so in a political environment, and their actions are thus shaped by political forces. Among these forces is, first, the competition among interests which have anything to gain or lose from developments within public bureaucracies. Second, the bureaucrats themselves have stakes in the process and engage in politics to assure their status. The reactions to civil service reform at the national level in 1978 attested to the political involvement of bureaucracies.

Finally, politics includes policy issues which affect and are affected by public personnel administration. Some of these issues are:

1. How collective bargaining (employee organizations participating in decisions affecting employment conditions) and merit (personnel decisions based on ability and performance) can coexist.
2. Whether the public service should be used to solve social problems, e.g., be an employer of last resort, take the lead in affirmative action, or satisfy the demands of myriad special interests who have convincing claims.
3. How to reconcile continued demands for a high level of services with demands for reduction in taxes and budgets.
4. How to maintain responsive bureaucracy without endangering the concept of merit.

More generally, the public service itself is an issue. The support that Jimmy Carter gained for his election as president by promising reform of the public bureaucracy is one indication of the concern people have about government. While public policy issues affect the personnel function, it is also clear that pubic employees have a great impact on policy as they help shape and implement it, giving the policy substantive meaning.

In examining the personnel process in government, this book will analyze the specific responsibilities of supervisors, personnel officers, and the personnel policies which characterize the process. In particular, it will evaluate the effects that each of the elements have on democratic government and on the delivery of services to the taxpaying public.

Public Personnel as a Field of Study

As a field of study, public personnel administration has not had a particularly illustrious history. It has had difficulty in differentiating itself from general personnel administration. David Rosenbloom suggests that public personnel administration suffers from three problems:

1. Identification—because it has not focused sufficiently on its public nature.
2. Narrowness of scope—because it has ignored the political implications of personnel policies and activities in government.
3. Lack of methodological sophistication and theory.[1]

These problems resulted in large part from slavish attachment to principles which seemed appropriate in developing civil service systems to replace the abuses of spoils systems in the nineteenth century.[2] In the zealous effort to remove partisanship from the personnel process, administrators focused almost exclusively on techniques, such as testing and selection methods, which could be applied to personnel activities. As a result, personnel administration was viewed as a nonpolitical, technical service to management rather than being considered as management per se. This perspective, widely adopted by the profession and academics, led to the isolation of public personnel management from the real environment in which it takes place. The approach is also largely responsible for public personnel administration's lagging behind public management generally in the realization that management must adapt to a wide diversity of situations, environments, and available resources. As Klingner and Nalbandian argue, different organizations and environments have different impacts on the personnel function.[3] Public personnel administrators should recognize that fact as they deal with personnel issues and problems.

Likewise, it must be recognized that personnel systems differ. Public systems may be based on civil service, merit, or spoils and patronage. Civil service refers to a system in which personnel activities are governed by rules and regulations insulated from partisan political activity. Merit means that good performance is rewarded and poor performance is penalized. Patronage and spoils refer to systems in which those loyal to the person in power are rewarded with jobs while opponents are purged from or denied employment.

A more fundamental way of differentiating personnel systems, however, is according to whether they are management dominated or labor dominated. Historically, public personnel systems have been management dominated with strict legal limitations placed on the role of labor in the personnel process. Private systems, by contrast, have had a long history of active labor participation. In recent years, of course, the public sector has undergone extensive change in the relationship of management and labor. Management prerogatives have given way to bilateral decision making in the federal government, and the same is gradually happening in most states. Many states, however, continue to view labor relations as the prerogative of management.

Today the civil service and merit concepts prevail in public personnel management. The growth of public-sector labor unions, however, has led to many changes in personnel practices. What these changes are and how they affect the personnel process will be examined in chapter 10. In general, however, the development of unionism in the public sector has sharpened the identification of competing interests in the personnel process. The fortunes of management, employees, elected public officials, citizens, and the bureaucracies themselves are all affected by the changing manner in which personnel is managed.

Although different groups with differing values influence personnel management, personnel administrators have been exhorted to apply "value-free" principles. In reality, however, personnel administrators cannot avoid making value judgments as they attempt to implement policies such as differing employee selection systems, affirmative action programs, and performance evaluation. Someone stands to gain and someone to lose with each decision made. For example, how is an agency to respond to a cut in its budget? Are the newly hired let go? Are older employees urged to retire early? Are those hired under affirmative action programs protected? Are all departments required to contribute to the reduction? All of these and many other concerns affect the final decision, and each involves a value judgment. Decisions involving competing value judgments are also political decisions. Modern personnel literature will pay increasing attention to these facts of management life and to the administrator's role as active participant in the political process.

Public Versus Private-sector Personnel Administration

Public and private-sector personnel administration have much in common. For instance, the technical processes used for selecting, interviewing, evaluating, and training employees may be the same in public and private organizations. Administration of personnel in the public sector differs from that in the private sector in four important ways:

1. Public employees are subject to more legal restrictions.
2. Lines of authority are less clear in the public sector.
3. Labor-management relations have followed different paths.
4. The political environment affects public personnel to a greater extent.

These differences will be examined briefly, although the reader should keep in mind that they are being blurred by the interaction of the public and private sectors and constant changes in society.

LEGAL RESTRICTIONS

Public employees are usually governed by numerous legal limitations on their activities. Legislation or executive orders require them to refrain from even the appearance of a conflict of interest, that is, the possibility that their official actions will serve their self-interests, economically or otherwise. Personnel administrators and supervisors must monitor the activity of employees to implement conflict-of-interest provisions.

Government employees are often prohibited from engaging in political activities. At the national level the Hatch Act of 1939 prohibits most partisan political participation by federal employees. State and local government employees are usually covered under state statutes. These restrictions are aimed to make the delivery of services less partisan and to protect employees and citizens from abuses of the spoils system.

After many years of relaxing regulations on personal appearance and dress, governmental units, especially on the local level, have been reinstituting such rules, for example, on haircuts and beards. Employees have challenged these restrictions but have met with little success. The United States Supreme Court seems disinclined to interfere in such matters at the present time.[4]

Also being reinstated in many jurisdictions are residency requirements for obtaining or keeping state and local government jobs. Cities adopt this policy so that employees will be readily available to respond to emergencies, so that the tax base does not erode, and so that employees will identify with the community in which they work. At present, the Supreme Court sanctions such restrictions as fulfilling legitimate needs of the jurisdictions.[5]

The national government tends to be less concerned with personal behavior as long as it does not affect job performance. In fact, the federal government is now relaxing its restrictions. Nevertheless, a stricter standard of behavior is generally applied to public employees than is applied to private-sector workers. Because citizens pay the taxes which pay government employees' salaries, managers and personnel administrators are sensitive to the image public employees project. Their concern leads them to attempt to curtail behavior which could create a negative public reaction. When public displeasure is aroused by employees who are intoxicated in public, engage in extramarital sexual activity, or become involved in controversial causes, elected political leaders often put pressure on managers to do something about the "problem." The same pressures are not so likely to occur in the private sector.

LINES OF AUTHORITY

The lines of authority for public employees are much less clear than for those in private enterprise. While the public agency organization chart may suggest a clear line of authority, it does not show all the outside pressures brought to bear on the activities of public employees. Theoretically, they must respond to the "public interest" and a variety of representatives of the public and of interested parties. The agency employees may be asked to do something different by the chief executive, an influential member of the legislature, a clientele group, or a consumer group. Such multiple command points often make it difficult for public employees to sort out exactly what they should do in a given situation.

For instance, Deputy Comptroller of the Currency Robert A. Bloom testified that he feared loss of his job if he made available to a Senate committee information which would have been harmful to the confirmation of Bert Lance as director of the Office of Management and Budget in the Carter administration.[6] The dilemma faced by Bloom is a common one for public employees—is their responsibility to their superiors or to the legislative body, clientele, or general public? While the general public is supposed to be the ultimate benefactor of the civil service's activities, it is seldom possible for employees to act strictly on the basis of such an assumption. Not only the individual employee but the personnel system as a whole must respond to the confusion produced by multiple commands. The response normally takes the form of personnel rules and regulations, codes of conduct, and the like. Some of these prescriptions often permit little flexibility for administrators to adapt to differing situations and needs of the organization.

LABOR-MANAGEMENT RELATIONS

The public sector has traditionally differed from the private sector in being almost totally management oriented. There have been exceptions in both sectors: some governments, such as New York City and Milwaukee, Wisconsin, have had rather long histories of public-sector union activities; and many corporations in the Sun Belt are fervently anti-union. In general, however, the public sector only recently began to share personnel decisions with employees through the bargaining process. The implications for public personnel management have been and will continue to be many; these will be discussed in chapter 10.

POLITICAL ENVIRONMENT AND SCRUTINY

Perhaps the most significant factor peculiar to public personnel administration is that the public service is closely scrutinized by the general populace and its representatives. Since the taxpayers foot the bill for the government, they are entitled to know what is being done with their money. In recent years freedom-of-information acts and open-meetings legislation have become common across the country. With passage of such legislation most activities of agencies have become subject to public examination, and personnel management must accommodate such scrutiny. While personnel decisions themselves are usually exempted from these "sunshine" laws, personnel policies are affected in many ways. The elements of the political environment important to public personnel management include the executive, legislative, and judicial branches; the media; interest groups; political parties; and the general public.

The Executive Branch.   The chief executives of all governments have general responsibility for the performance of public servants, although their power to influence individual employee behavior varies greatly. As the elected leaders of their jurisdictions, mayors, governors, and the president are supposed to guide the rest of the executive branch. In reality, the powers of chief executives are often limited. Most of them complain about their inability to affect the behavior of the bureaucracies they theoretically control. At the national level, for example, President Richard Nixon undertook an extensive effort to make the federal bureaucracy more responsive to his administration's political values. Concerned that the Kennedy and Johnson administrations had shaped the bureaucracy to reflect liberal Democratic philosophy, the Nixon administration developed a detailed procedural manual, "The Malek Manual," outlining ways in which the administration could "establish political control" through influencing the recruitment and selection of personnel throughout the national government.[7] Of course, in patronage or spoils systems, as still exist in some state and local governments, control over personnel rests in the hands of chief executives and their staffs. In civil service systems, however, patronage appointments are usually few.

The appointment power of chief executives is one part of their ability to affect personnel. Usually they appoint the department head (cabinet member) and boards and commissions. These appointees shape policy but also supervise the rest of the bureaucracy; thus they have a direct role in personnel management. Among the most important appointments relative to personnel matters are those to civil service or personnel agencies, such as the appointment of the director and deputy director of the Office of Personnel Management. These kinds of appointments affect the orientation of the agency and thus affect personnel policy. The power to control personnel agencies in state government is much more limited. In only twenty-one of the fifty states does the governor appoint the major personnel official—the personnel director or merit system director.[8] Moreover, in only sixteen of those states does the personnel director report to the governor. Thus governors, on the whole, have even less control over the personnel system than does the president.

Among local governments the power of the chief executive to appoint personnel is varied. Most larger municipalities have highly developed personnel systems operating under civil service rules or under merit systems, although patronage may still be important in some places, for example, Chicago. Small cities usually have less formal systems, and policies are often less fully developed. County governments operate under patronage systems for the most part.

Chief executives may also have the power to issue executive orders affecting personnel policy. President Johnson's order on ethics of federal employees, for example, outlined acceptable and unacceptable standards of behavior for national government employees.[9] Wide-ranging effects for national government personnel functions resulted from executive orders of presidents Kennedy and Nixon permitting collective bargaining by federal employees.[10] Similarly, reorganization efforts by presidents have implications for transfer, retention, and morale of public employees. At the state and local levels, the constitutions and charters greatly affect the powers of governors, mayors, and other chief executives to use executive orders in mandating personnel practices. Compared to the president, state and local officials tend to have limited powers in this regard.

Within the executive branch the way in which agencies affect one another has implications for personnel management. Some agencies, such as the Department of Labor and the Equal Employment Opportunity Commission, have specific personnel responsibilities, while others affect the process more generally by competing with one another for resources. Still others, such as the Office of Management and Budget (OMB) or the General Accounting Office (GAO), have monitoring roles which in turn affect personnel management. An OMB request that an agency trim its budget usually requires a change in staffing plans, just as a critical report on an agency's performance by GAO is likely to change the way in which employees perform.

The Legislative Branch.   The role of legislative bodies in the personnel process is diverse. Legislatures normally create the governmental personnel systems, although state constitutions or city charters may provide for the system in some instances. Personnel policies are also developed by legislative bodies, as are other policies which may impinge on personnel. A decision to reorganize an agency, for example, requires personnel managers to plan for such eventualities as employee transfers, reductions, or new hiring.

The legislative committee system also has implications for personnel management. Committees dealing with personnel management, such as the U.S. House Committee on Post Office and Civil Service, take a direct interest in personnel policy. The substantive committees also take special interest in the personnel of the agencies over which they have jurisdiction. Thus the Senate Committee on Foreign Relations examines closely the activities of employees in the Foreign Service and other agencies dealing with foreign affairs.

The Judicial Branch.   Traditionally the courts have been the least active branch of government in personnel activities, but recent court decisions have dealt with numerous issues affecting public personnel. One area in which the courts have taken great interest is in insuring due process procedural rights when personnel decisions are made affecting individual employees.[11] Public personnel systems have been forced by such decisions to develop fairly elaborate appeals procedures and to insure that employee rights are not trampled upon by employers. Equal employment opportunity issues have generated much litigation in public personnel management, resulting in decisions on such matters as examination, selection, performance evaluation, compensation, promotion and discipline.

Courts have started to exercise considerable restraint where public employees are concerned and thus appear to be giving fairly wide discretion to public jurisdictions in personnel matters. The United States Supreme Court, in particular, has been reluctant to intervene in personnel activities of state and local jurisdictions. It has allowed to stand residency requirements, dress and conduct codes, and dismissal of homosexual public employees.

The Media.   It is difficult to imagine a force in the political environment with greater potential for influencing public personnel administration than the communications media. Because of the Constitutional guarantees of freedom of the press and speech in the United States, the media can keep the public well informed about the public service and its activities and problems. The public, as well as the political actors themselves, depends upon the media for much of their information. While the press often focuses on the negative aspects of the public service, it is frequently responsible for many improvements. Many problems in the public service are brought to light and scrutinized by the media, whereas the private sector rarely undergoes such close examination of its staff or personnel policies and practices. The media cannot, however, insure that agency personnel perform effectively on a continuing basis. They are unlikely, for example, to expose unenthusiastic performance of duties (which is an important part of an evaluation of the public service).

Interest Groups.   Many interest groups exert pressure on public personnel operations. Among them are clientele groups, minority and women's groups, public interest groups, professional associations, civic groups, and public employee associations and unions. While interest groups generally focus on issues other than personnel management, they recognize that having some say about which people make decisions affects the agency's response to their concerns.

Some groups tend to concentrate on relatively narrow issues of self-interest. Thus clientele, minority and women's, professional, and public employee groups are likely to seek policies which will assure that their particular welfare be given as much consideration by the agency as possible. Public interest and civic groups such as civil service leagues, good government associations, the League of Women Voters, and the Center for the Study of Responsive Law take a more general approach. They pursue policies beneficial to the "public interest" and usually promote personnel systems which reduce the potential for partisan political input. They also tend to favor policies which require public employees to disclose personal financial interests and which control conflict-of-interest situations.

Political Parties.   Political parties and politicians have always had an interest in public personnel operations. The politician often views patronage as a means of exerting control over and insuring responsiveness of public employees. Furthermore, politicians often find public bureaucrats easy targets for political rhetoric and exploit public service problems and inadequacies for political purposes. It must be noted that public personnel reform came about partly because politicians did use corruption and inefficiency as issues; therefore, personal political gain may not always be the overriding concern behind such appeals. Too often, however, the criticism of the public service does little to improve it and serves merely to denigrate it.

Certainly the exploitation of the public service for political demagoguery is not as extensive today as it once was, but one still hears references to the "incompetent" or "oversized" public bureaucracy. Jimmy Carter and many other political candidates in 1976 based much of their campaigns on promises to reduce the size of government, and the implications for personnel administration would be obvious. Governors using such issues in their campaigns included Jerry Brown of California, Michael Dukakis of Massachusetts, and James Longley of Maine. All have had serious difficulties with state employees over their attempts to streamline state bureaucracies.

The political parties traditionally depended upon government jobs as a way of building up party strength, but the continued trend toward use of comprehensive merit systems has greatly diminished this source of support. Indiana and New Jersey, however, demonstrate that patronage is alive and well in many state bureaucracies. Local government still indulges in political favoritism too, as is illustrated by the recent experiences of cities such as Chicago, Boston, and Philadelphia.

The General Public.   In a democracy the public service is supposed to serve the interest of the general public. The problem is in defining what the "public interest" means. Responsiveness to the public and its wishes—which are rather difficult to determine—is one aspect of serving the public. Some prefer to consider that a responsible public service is one that is effective in achieving the long-range goals of the system. However, this approach sometimes runs counter to the public's wishes.[12] What is important for the administration of public personnel is that the public expects responsiveness. Many political leaders exploit this expectation by promising attractive but impractical solutions to voters' problems. Other individuals and groups, particularly public interest groups, direct their attention to long-range objectives. Public administrators, including personnel administrators, are caught in the middle.

Images of the Public Service

The image people have of government, particularly of public service as a career, is of concern to personnel administrators because it affects their ability to attract top-quality employees. While jobs in the public sector have generally lacked the prestige of private-sector employment, attitudes shift over time and vary from one person to another.[13] Many factors contribute to a person's receptivity to public service work. The Watergate scandal undermined Americans' confidence in government and had ill effects on public service recruitment. Additionally, social and ethnic backgrounds appear to influence a person's likelihood of entry into the field.[14] Different levels of government appeal to different people as well.[15]

Finally, the public's view of bureaucracy is determined by the general societal value system. The assumptions people have about the work ethic, self-reliance, and individualism affect their response to the public service, especially as they weigh the effects government programs and employees have on these values. Common lore has it that the public service is composed of indolent, secure employees who have too much power over people's lives and consume tax money with little beneficial effect. These views, along with the belief that the bureaucracy is over-sized and uncontrollable, make it difficult for the public service to recruit.

After Watergate the public's image of government was poor, but the steadiness and decency of President Gerald Ford seemed to renew people's confidence in the political system,[16] although his pardon of Nixon heightened many Americans' distrust of government. However, the 1976 scandals involving members of Congress and the investigations into illegal activities of agencies such as the FBI, CIA, and IRS caused a resurgence of cynicism on the part of much of the public. The election of Jimmy Carter to the presidency heralded new hope for clean and efficient government because people believed his promise to set very high standards for judging employees in his administration. The Lance affair mentioned earlier undermined Carter's credibility, serving once again to tarnish the image of public service. The General Services Administration scandals of 1978–79 only reinforced the feeling of distrust.

Summary

Public personnel management takes place in a complex environment and is part of a larger governmental system. Because the system in the United States involves a variety of interests competing for position and power, the personnel system becomes entwined in the political process. The various political actors and forces outlined in this chapter obviously have different interests in the personnel process. For example, although both the president and members of Congress insist that they want only the most efficient and responsive public service possible, they may be primarily concerned with maintaining or bettering their political positions. Thus expressions of outrage from either side regarding personnel actions are often calculated more to political advantage than to the improvement of personnel practices. Conflicts between the executive and legislative branches are inevitable. Similarly, the other actors in the political environment have conflicting interests regarding personnel policies and decisions. These varying interests lead to compromise and accommodation in public personnel management. No longer can the personnel function be viewed as a neutral instrument of management. It is at the center of the decision-making process and can easily become a pawn in the struggle for political power and influence.

This chapter has identified the role of public personnel management in the governmental process. Additionally, it has introduced the major forces which affect public personnel and the issues which are of concern to personnel managers. The remaining chapters elaborate on these topics. Chapters 2, 3, and 4 focus on political considerations in the development of public personnel systems. Chapter 2 traces the evolution of public personnel management, while chapter 3 examines some of the enduring political forces shaping the management of human resources, especially in state and local government. Chapter 4 discusses the structures of personnel systems produced by the forces considered in chapters 2 and 3.

Chapters 5 through 8 evaluate the processes—the various tools and techniques—used by personnel managers. Chapters 9 through 11 consider some of the major issues which challenge traditional government approaches to personnel management, and chapter 12 attempts to view what challenges lie ahead.

NOTES

1. David H. Rosenbloom, "Public Personnel Administration and Politics: Toward a New Public Personnel Administration," *Midwest Review of Public Administration*, 7 (April 1973), 98–110. For a discussion of the lack of theory, see Donald E. Klinger and John Nalbandian, "Personnel Management by Whose Objectives?" *Public Administration Review*, 38, no. 4 (July/August 1978), 366–372; and H. Brinton Milward, "Politics, Personnel, and Public Policy," book review essay, *Public Administration Review*, 38, no. 4 (July/August 1978), 391–396.
2. Muriel M. Morse, "We've Come a Long Way," *Public Personnel Management*, 5, no. 4 (July/August, 1976), 218–224, analyzes these issues.
3. Klingner and Nalbandian, "Personnel Management," 366–367.
4. *Kelley v. Johnson*, 425 U.S. 238 (1976).
5. *McCarthy v. Philadelphia*, 96 U.S. 1154 (1976).
6. AP Wire Service report, September 12, 1977.
7. The manual can be found in U.S. Senate, Select Committee on Presidential Campaign Activities, Executive Session Hearings, *Watergate and Related Activities: Use of Incumbency-Responsiveness Program*, book 19, 93rd Cong., 2nd Sess., pp. 8903–9017. It is also reprinted in its entirety in "Federal Political Personnel Manual: 'The Malek Manual,'" *The Bureaucrat*, 4, no. 4 (January 1976), 429–508.
8. Bureau of Intergovernmental Personnel Programs, U.S. Civil Service Commission, *Statistical Report on State Personnel Operations*, January 1977, p. 4.
9. Executive Order 11222, May 8, 1965.
10. Respectively, Executive Order 10988, January 1962; and Executive Order 11491, October 29, 1969.
11. *Greene v. McElroy*, 360 U.S. 474 (1959), was a major precedent in due process rights of employees.

12. See Francis E. Rourke's excellent discussion of responsiveness and effectiveness in *Bureaucracy, Politics, and Public Policy* (Boston: Little, Brown, 1969), pp. 3–6.
13. Franklin Kilpatrick et al., *The Image of the Federal Service* (Washington, D.C.: The Brookings Institution, 1964), is the seminal study, but more recent analyses include James S. Bowman and David L. Norman, Jr., "Attitudes towards the Public Service: A Survey of University Students," *Public Personnel Management*, 4, no. 2 (March/April 1975), 113–121; and Robert D. Lee, Jr., "Watergate and the Image of the Federal Service Revisited," *Public Personnel Management*, 3 (March/April 1974), 111–114.
14. See Harold M. Barger, "Images of Bureaucracy: A Tri-Ethnic Consideration," *Public Administration Review*, 36 (May/June 1976), 287–296.
15. Ibid.
16. In addition to Ford's influence, there were other actions by government which also aided in bringing about changes in attitude. See "Watergate in Perspective: The Forgotten Agenda," *Public Administration Review*, 36 (May/June 1974), 306–314.

SUGGESTED READINGS

Golembiewski, Robert T., and Michael Cohen, eds. *People in Public Service —A Reader in Public Personnel Administration*. 2nd ed. Itasca, IL: Peacock, 1976.
Lee, Robert D., Jr. *Public Personnel Systems*. Baltimore, MD: University Park Press, 1979.
Levine, Charles H., ed. *Managing Human Resources: A Challenge to Urban Governments. Urban Affairs Annual Review*, vol. 13 (1977).
Mosher, Frederick C. *Democracy and the Public Service*. New York: Oxford University Press, 1968.
Nigro, Felix A., and Lloyd G. Nigro. *The New Public Personnel Administration*. Itasca, IL: Peacock, 1976.
Selznick, Philip. *TVA and the Grass Roots*. Berkeley: University of California Press, 1949.
Shafritz, Jay M., Walter L. Balk, Albert C. Hyde, and David H. Rosenbloom. *Personnel Management in Government*. New York: Marcel Dekker, 1978.
Shafritz, Jay M., ed. *The Public Personnel World*. Chicago: International Personnel Management Assoc., 1977.
Stahl, O. Glenn. *Public Personnel Administration*. 7th ed. New York: Harper & Row, 1976.
Thompson, Frank J., ed. *Classics of Public Personnel Policy*. Oak Park, IL: Moore, 1979.
Thompson, Frank J. *Personnel Policy in the City*. Berkeley: University of California Press, 1975.

CASE 1.1

Brian Koko

Brian Koko was employed by the city of Kindred Heart as a budget analyst in the Budgeting Office. He started out three years ago as a clerk responsible for checking the accuracy of figures in the budget requests by other departments and in the final budget recommendations presented to City Council. After only six months in that position, Brian was promoted to analyst because his superior, Mike Holt, was impressed with Brian's ability to understand the concepts in the budgeting process and because of his conscientious approach to his work. Then the position of supervisor of budget analysts became vacant, and Holt decided to suggest to Brian Koko that he apply for it. Brian's performance and knowledge of the work were such that he could be perfect for the position. Holt planned on talking to him within the next week.

Kindred Heart is a medium-sized city in a politically conservative area. People in the city have a strong moral conservativism as well. They have always prided themselves on not having the problems of large urban areas with their greater social and cultural diversity.

Brian decided to go to San Francisco over the weekend. There he visited friends who were preparing to march in the Gay Pride parade. Working with them, he decided to march in the parade. He carried a banner demanding that his gay life style be accorded the same rights and respect as heterosexual life styles.

The next day the *Kindred Heart Tribune* ran stories about the Gay Pride demonstrations around the country and included photos from the San Francisco parade. Some residents and city employees recognized Brian in one of the photos and called Mike Holt to report it. One member of City Council was called, and she demanded that Brian be fired.

Assume you are Mike Holt. You are called in by the City Manager to discuss the Brian Koko matter.

1. What recommendations are you going to make to the City Manager?
2. What factors will influence your recommendations? How?
3. How will you suggest that the City Manager deal with the council? The following facts may help you in your deliberations:
a. Kindred Heart has no ordinance either protecting the right of gays to hold jobs or prohibiting employment of gays.

b. The state has no such laws.
c. By state statute, homosexual acts are a criminal offense.
d. The city has no formal personnel policies or procedures; thus employees have no protected tenure or appeals rights on personnel actions.

Chapter 2

Evolution of the Personnel System

All governments face the problem of how to staff and maintain a public service which is consistent with national political culture, competent, loyal to management, and responsive to the public all at the same time. There has been constant conflict among these competing criteria for the establishment and operation of a personnel system. During the history of the United States public service, numerous and dramatic changes have taken place as political values have responded to changing political, social, and economic realities.

As noted earlier, the major premise of this book is that public personnel administration can best be understood in terms of its relationship to political values and processes. Therefore, the brief historical overview of the development of the public service presented in this chapter emphasizes the influence of political values on the public personnel operation. Three periods are outlined: the period of early development, 1789–1829; the period in which spoils predominated, 1829–1883; and the period in which the merit system developed and became predominant, 1883 to the present. Within each of these time spans there are significant events which might be used to further categorize the development of public personnel administration, but the breaks suggested here involve the points at which major new perspectives on the public service emerged.[1] The last section of the chapter evaluates the legacies of each period.

The Early Roots

President George Washington is usually credited with development of a competent public service. Since there was, of course, no established bureaucracy when he assumed the presidency, he was in the unique position of being able to build a public service from scratch. Although political considerations are not usually attributed to Washington in his personnel actions, he did in fact make numerous concessions to political reality.[2] He was not so politically partisan, however, as many of his successors.

One of the realities with which Washington had to contend was that political power in the early years of the United States was held almost exclusively by the aristocracy. Although Washington established fitness and ability as requirements for holding a position in the public service, he usually meant social status or prestige rather than technical competence.[3] Washington was free to use such a definition because the tasks of the public bureaucracy were not highly specialized, as they were to become when our social and political systems became more complex. (As government activities expanded and technological expertise became essential, fitness had to be defined in quite different terms.) The point is that Washington chose public servants from the politically powerful sector of society.

Washington was influenced by other political considerations as well. He had the awesome task of integrating a new nation of previously independent-minded units. To do so he had to plan and act carefully. A significant requirement for public service employment under Washington was support of the new federal political system. Although support for the political system does not seem particularly radical today, it was a controversial issue at the time. Many people hoped the new system of government would fail. Thus, oddly enough, a political position with which many citizens strongly disagreed was a requirement for holding a public job.

There were also regional considerations. President Washington wanted to insure that local programs were administered by members of each community and that all regions of the country were represented in the high echelons of the public service. He thereby hoped to gain nationwide support for and identification with the new political system.

Still another political move by the new president was to defer to the wishes of Congress on many appointments. Recognizing that members of Congress could greatly affect his administration's success, Washington conferred with them even though he was not legally required to in most instances. Presidents still consider congressional wishes in their appointments. Another group accorded special attention by Washington were the Revolutionary army officers. They were often hired in preference to others, although Washington was careful to limit the extent of such appointments. Preferential treatment of veterans, now common in the national as well as state and local merit systems, derives in part from Washington's policies.

That Washington's decisions were often politically motivated should not come as a surprise. In a democratic system it is expected that public officials respond to political forces. What is surprising is that until recently many scholars have described Washington's public personnel policies strictly in terms of competence and integrity, paying little attention to the role played by the political environment. As Van Riper notes, it is fortunate that political considerations were consistent with the development of a highly competent public service.[4] Many of the political accommodations were to leave enduring marks on the staffing of public bureaucracies. Regional representation, partisan political support, loyalty, veteran's preference, and consultation with members of Congress have been and often still are significant concerns in filling public service positions.

George Washington's immediate successors made few changes in his approach to staffing the public service. Partisan concerns became more important under John Adams, but Thomas Jefferson was to make the most significant break with Washington's practices. As the representative of a new party in power, Jefferson wanted to reward his Republican followers with appointments. The long years of Federalist control, however, had resulted in the entrenchment of Federalists in public service positions. To obtain a bureaucracy more to his liking, Jefferson removed many government employees, justifying this policy by claiming a need for a balance in partisan viewpoints. He believed that because the people had elected him president, they should have like-minded public servants to help him carry out his policies.[5] Political party affiliation was not his only consideration, however; he also insisted on ability and fitness in the way that Washington did. He was the real father of the spoils system in the sense of bowing to party pressure in appointments, yet he diligently resisted debasing the public service by making it strictly partisan.

Jefferson's successors carried on in much the same tradition, just as Washington's successors accepted his lead in staffing the public service. Although partisan politics became more important after Jefferson's assumption of the presidency, the character of the public service remained virtually unchanged. Despite his Republican philosophy, Jefferson still had to contend with the politically powerful elite. Consequently, the aristocracy retained its hold on public service positions through the administration of John Quincy Adams. The tests of loyalty, regional considerations, preference for veterans, and consultation with Congress remained factors in public service staffing.

Jacksonian Democracy

With a dramatic shift in the center of political power came an equally dramatic change in the public bureaucracy. The election of 1828 brought to a head the political frustrations that had been building up in the populace. During the period 1800–1829 the United States political system became more democratic in that new elements of the society gained the opportunity to participate in politics. The addition of eleven states —nine in the West—brought a new flavor to politics and elections. Previously only landowners and the aristocracy had had the vote, but electoral reforms in the early nineteenth century and admission of new states where the common man ruled broadened electoral participation extensively. The western states led in extending the suffrage, but by 1829 the right to vote was almost universally enjoyed by the white male. The admission of western states also changed the power relationship between the upper and lower classes in favor of the lower. The egalitarianism of the frontier brought its influence to national politics.

The extension of suffrage resulted from political considerations. With added voters, the parties felt that they could increase their ranks and thus saw advantage in extending the right to vote. As the common man participated in the choice of elected political leaders, he also expected some of the fruits of politics, so it is not surprising that resentment toward the aristocracy's monopolistic hold on the public service positions developed. Astute political leaders could not ignore the expectations of their new constituents. They further saw that political patronage could be used to build up their parties. Consequently, the spoils system became a standard feature of public service staffing in state and local governments.

The triumph of the common man reached the national level with the election of President Andrew Jackson in 1828. With his election a revolution occurred in the staffing of the national government bureaucracy. His inauguration celebrations are often cited as an example of the drastic change in the locus of political power. The social critics of the day were aghast at the antics and crudeness of Jackson's followers, many of whom descended upon Washington in search of government employment.[6]

Expectations of Jackson's followers were high, whereas the genteel elements of Washington politics anticipated disaster. As it turned out, the expectations of both groups were exaggerated. Jackson was interested not only in realigning the political makeup of the public service, but also in reducing government activity and hence the size of the bureaucracy. Consequently, the hordes of office-seekers found that Jackson meant to cut back on government jobs. On the other hand, and most important for our consideration, he followed Jefferson's lead in believing that the bureaucracy should reflect the results of the election, and he removed many people from office and replaced them with his own supporters.

Although Jackson did not turn out a significantly higher proportion of employees from the public service than did Jefferson, he is more closely identified with the spoils system because he was more openly partisan and proud of it. He saw his administration as one that revolutionized the American political system. The most important consequence of Jackson's administration was that it broke the aristocracy's political power over both elective and appointive positions. The revolutionary character of Jackson's approach was that the public service was democratized in eventual response to democratization of the electoral system.

The shift in political power caused intense criticism of Jackson's public personnel policies. However, despite his feeling that the work of government was so simple that anyone could perform it (much more true then than today, of course), he still insisted on competence and judicious use of patronage. He would probably have been as uncomfortable as Washington to see the extent to which many of his successors used and abused patronage.

Weakening of Spoils

Subsequent to Jackson's administration, the alternation of political party control of the presidency led to a revolving door for public servants, with the door taking four years to complete a revolution. Even though there were many carry-overs from one administration to another, they were usually assigned different positions. Even the election of a president of the same party, as when James Buchanan succeeded fellow Democrat Franklin Pierce, was insufficient reason for retaining the same public servants. Buchanan represented a different faction with different demands and thus was pressured into changing the bureaucracy.

The election of Lincoln in 1860 represents both the high point of the spoils system and the onset of its demise. Lincoln used the system to a greater extent than any other president. Mobilizing the Union for the Civil War required a loyal public service, and Lincoln felt that the only way to insure one was to use patronage.[7] Lincoln's sweep of the people from office, the most extensive in United States history, was warranted by the political considerations of the time. His concern was to consolidate the Republican party, which had been in disarray, and to execute a major and controversial war. As the Union began to come apart, officeholders from the South were purged and those loyal to the Union put in their place.

Despite wide use of the spoils system, Lincoln must also be credited with initiating its gradual decline. After his election to a second term, he was put under a great deal of pressure to make a clean sweep of appointees. His supporters had become used to a completely new team every four years. Lincoln's refusal to oblige gave hope to critics of spoils and led to an examination of the system that was to produce significant change in the coming two decades. President Andrew Johnson, faced with internal political problems of his own, found it necessary to replace many of Lincoln's loyalists; but the spoils system was marked for destruction, and in less than twenty years it would be dealt a blow from which it would never recover. In the years between Lincoln's administration and 1883, political forces gradually chipped away at the patronage system. Much like the growth of democratic political participation from 1800 to 1829, the growth of discontent with spoils from 1865 to 1883 was to lead to a revolution in the staffing of the United States government bureaucracy.

The Civil War greatly increased the power of the executive branch vis-à-vis Congress, and the end of the war brought an opportunity for Congress to attempt to regain some of its vitality. With Andrew Johnson in office and with his internal party struggles, the stage was set. The area of greatest struggle, and also the immediate issue in the impeachment proceedings, was control over government personnel. The difficulties Johnson had with Congress and his party led him to purge many of Lincoln's appointees in favor of his own. Predictably, such action only heightened congressional opposition to him.

The Tenure of Office Act of 1867 symbolized Congress's attempt to gain control over patronage. The act limited the removal power of the president to the extent that removal required Senate approval in cases involving officers who had previously been appointed with Senate confirmation. Defiance of Congress and the act led to Johnson's impeachment by the House of Representatives. (The Senate acquitted him by one vote.) Appointment and removal power was the immediate issue over which this momentous confrontation developed, but the political issues were much broader. For the student of public personnel, however, it is a significant occasion because it signaled a movement away from presidential control over patronage and personnel policy issues. Congress was to consolidate its power over the general policy in the next decade and a half. Eventually, congressional interest would lead to establishment of the merit system, although its major interest at this point was controlling spoils.[8]

President Johnson's lack of control and the weak administrations of Grant and Hayes produced even greater congressional interest in, and control over, the personnel process. At the same time, efforts for reform were being made. During Grant's administration Congress passed the Civil Service Act of 1871, although its proponents had some difficulty in getting its acceptance and finally had to resort to attaching it as a rider to an appropriations bill.[9] Surprisingly enough, President Grant was a supporter of civil service reform and had actually proposed legislation similar to that passed in 1871. More importantly, to the surprise of many Republicans in Congress, he attempted to institute a merit system. In effect, the act of 1871 reestablished presidential control over the personnel process. Specifically, the act gave the president the power to establish rules and regulations for employees in the public service and, most significantly, to appoint advisers to help him draw up and administer the rules and regulations. Grant did just that by appointing a seven-person civil service commission and issuing executive orders for the limited use of merit concepts.

Political realities were not to permit Grant's experiment with reform to endure, however. Congress was not really willing to give up the control it had. Fearing loss of power through loss of patronage, Congress refused to fund the system after 1873, and it was no longer able to operate, although some commissioners did work without compensation. Despite its short tenure, Grant's commission did have lasting effects; its recommendations form much of the basis of today's personnel system.[10]

Although the act had to be abandoned, the experiment with reform whetted the appetites of reformers, and the issue would not die. The ensuing scandals of the Grant administration only helped make civil service reform a more vital political issue.

Another supporter of reform, Rutherford B. Hayes, became president in 1877 and made some tentative moves toward reform. However, the controversy surrounding his election left him in a weak position, and he was unable to accomplish much. Indications are that what he did do in the way of instituting reform in some departments was more than counterbalanced by his lack of effort in others. His inconsistency in implementing executive orders against assessment (requiring employees to contribute a percentage of their salaries to the political party) and partisan activity leads one to question the sincerity of his commitment to reform.[11]

The issue of reform was attracting an ever-widening group of supporters. During the late 1870s and early 1880s various associations favoring civil service reform organized and became vocal. They attempted to pressure political leaders, but more importantly, they tried to educate the public to the "evils of spoils." They portrayed the spoils system as one that undermines the work ethic and feeds the avarice of the bad citizen. Somehow, the people still had not become intensely interested, although some public concern was manifested in the elections of presidents committed to reform. With the aid of an increasingly interested press, the reformers made their mark on the public and politicians alike.[12]

The assassination of President Garfield became a dramatic symbol of the evils of spoils—it could even lead to murder. The fact that Charles Guiteau, Garfield's assassin, was an unsuccessful seeker of patronage employment gave the reformers the impetus they needed. That Garfield was a supporter of reform only added to their sense of urgency.

Another political factor favoring reform was the Supreme Court decision in *Ex parte Curtis* in 1882.[13] Congress had passed a law in 1876 that prohibited the assessment of government workers. This practice, which still exists in some jurisdictions, involves a "contribution," or kickback, of a portion of the employee's salary to the political party organization or other benefactor. Obviously, when the patronage system is in use, assessment can be easily enforced; if the employee refuses to "contribute," he or she is removed. At any rate, assessment became a scandal when Newton Curtis, a Treasury Department employee and treasurer of the New York Republican party, was brought to trial for violation of the 1876 law. The Supreme Court upheld his conviction and the law. Reform efforts could only gain from the decision.

In addition, the congressional elections of 1882 made the Republicans reflect on the political consequences of reform. Republican fortunes slipped badly in the elections, and continuation of this trend would mean loss of the White House in 1884, loss of the power to appoint public servants, and possible large-scale purges of Republican officeholders. Congressional Republicans saw the wisdom of supporting reform.

As a result of the aforementioned political forces and the persistent efforts of reformers, the Pendleton Civil Service Act became law on January 16, 1883. The act created a personnel system based on the merit concept and required the development of rules and regulations by which all personnel activities would be conducted. It took a long time and the assassination of a president, but Congress had acted. Now the character of public service would undergo another revolution.

Consolidation of Reform Efforts

The most important provisions of the Pendleton Civil Service Act include the following:

1. Authorization for the president to appoint a bipartisan civil service commission to establish and implement rules and regulations for the personnel functions.
2. Establishment of open competitive examinations that would be practical, that is, that would test skills relevant to each position.
3. Apportionment of positions in Washington offices among the states according to population.
4. Entry into the service at any level—known as lateral entry or an open system—as opposed to entry only at the bottom.
5. No age limit for entering at any level.
6. Authorization for the president to extend coverage over previously "unclassified" positions by executive order or to remove classes of positions from the protected service.
7. Several specific provisions such as provision for neutrality of public employees, prohibition of assessments on public employees by political parties, and penalties for tampering with the examination process.

Passage of the Pendleton Act did not bring an end to the spoils system, nor did it mean that reform became a dead issue. The public servants covered by the act amounted to only about 10 percent of public employees in the national government. Apparently, some supporters of reform expected the public service to become the domain of the aristocracy once again.[14] This did not happen, partially because of the provisions of the act and partially because of its gradual application. However, greater attention to educational criteria gave an advantage to the upper classes.

In passing the Pendleton Act, Congress attempted to exert control over the personnel system of the United States government. Because the president is given the executive authority by the Constitution, a question of the constitutionality of congressional control was raised. Consequently, Congress made the legislation permissive, meaning that the president could provide for establishment of the merit system but was not directed to do so.[15] Certainly the political squabbles between the president and Congress had an impact, but the realities of constitutional provisions had to be accommodated.

Each of the act's major provisions had political implications. The first, authorizing rather than mandating presidential action on the matter, has already been discussed in terms of the conflict between the president and Congress. Open competitive exams and lateral entry may be seen as adherence to the democratic tradition of equality. The reformers were actually interested in adopting the British system requiring entry at the bottom and promotion only from within. The egalitarian tradition of the United States was inconsistent with such a provision, so the open system was adopted. Some suggest that the Democrats put the Republicans on the defensive on the open-system issue and forced them to adopt it for fear of being branded undemocratic by the press and public.[16] Certainly, though, the Democrats were not entirely altruistic. They were doubtless concerned with being able to balance the public service in their favor should they win the presidency in 1884 (as they did). It would be difficult to reward Democratic partisans if the current Republican president were to lock in all high-level public servants. With lateral entry, any vacancies at higher levels could be given to Democrats within the limits of the competitive system. Lest this seem too cynical, it should be noted that the issue of egalitarianism was considered along with the realities of partisan political maneuvering.

Apportionment of positions in Washington offices among the states meant that the constituents of each member of Congress had a realistic and equal chance to obtain public employment. In addition, the South was concerned about its inadequate representation in public service positions. Apportionment also helped integrate the nation further through assuring participation by people from all parts of the country.

Both political parties realized the importance of the provisions regarding extending or reducing the extent of coverage of the merit system. Congress could hardly direct that all public employees be covered, given the constitutional question discussed earlier, so the extent of coverage was to be determined by the president. On the other hand, presidents might abuse the power to extend coverage, particularly if the other party won the presidential election. Therefore, the president was also authorized to roll back the coverage—a power that has been used very sparingly. President McKinley exercised the power in his first term, precipitating a bitter reaction, but others have been reluctant to try it. In contrast, presidents have extended the coverage frequently—particularly at the end of their terms—so that approximately 90 percent of federal government civilian employees are under some sort of merit system.

Changing Concerns of the Merit System

Although the Civil Service Commission seemed to have a fairly broad grant of power under the Civil Service Act, it really exercised very little, devoting most of its early years to screening applicants.[17] Considering the political climate in which it was born, it is little wonder that the presidents and the commission moved cautiously. Remember that Congress created the new system more because of public sentiment and reformers' pressure than because it was committed to reform. Gradually, however, the commission gained prestige and influence and became the major force in public personnel policies. When Theodore Roosevelt became president in 1901, the civil service system had a friend in its chief executive. A former commissioner of civil service, Roosevelt did much to improve the service's image and to increase its coverage. From that day on, with minor exceptions, the commission's position was strong.

During the late nineteenth and early twentieth centuries many changes in society and politics brought adaptive changes in the civil service system. In 1883 the jobs of public servants were still primarily clerkships, but the Industrial Revolution had changed technology, and the post-Civil War era brought on a period of intensified development in the economy. Technological advances and their consequences generated new demands on the political system and resulted in an ever larger public service. Jobs became more specialized, and with this development came the need for yet another specialty—the personnel administrator.

The new system was also faced with constantly changing political forces. Worker movements resulting in union organizations had an early impact on the public service—the National Association of Letter Carriers, for instance, was organized in 1889. Concern with the welfare of the employee became another issue to be considered. As a result, a gradual development and extension of benefits has evolved, so that today federal government employees have one of the best benefit packages available.

It was noted earlier that the spoils system at the national level followed its development in state and local jurisdictions. When the federal government instituted reforms, however, most state and local governments were slow to follow its lead.[18] In 1883 New York adopted the first state civil service law, but only one other state, Massachusetts, enacted a civil service law before the turn of the century. In 1884 Albany, New York, became the first city to create a civil service system, and several other cities and one county (Cook County, Illinois) followed suit during the 1880s and 1890s. Coverage usually applied to clerical workers and the uniformed services of police and fire.

With attention of the muckrakers focused on corruption in municipal government in the early years of the twentieth century, the pressure for reform grew. Similar exposure of patronage abuse in state governments had the same effect. Many state and municipal governments developed civil service systems during the period from 1900 through the 1920s.

While the scope of these reforms was usually limited, the actions did herald an era of major change in state and local personnel practices. The Great Depression of 1929, however, brought a precipitous halt to most of the reform efforts. State and local governments cut back their funding of such programs as they attempted to cope with other more pressing problems relating to the physical well-being of their citizens.

The national government was consolidating its reform effort. The United States Civil Service Commission gradually centralized its authority. Established to protect the neutrality of the federal government service, the commission performed the major personnel functions and also monitored the activities of agencies to insure that they abided by the new civil service rules and regulations.

The Depression brought changes to the federal government service just as it did with state and local governments. President Franklin Roosevelt, in his efforts to create programs to deal with the economic crisis, felt that the already established bureaucracy was not flexible and adaptable enough to act quickly. Speedy action was required if people were to receive the help they needed to avoid total disaster. Convinced that the existing agencies were not up to the task, Roosevelt persuaded Congress to create many agencies outside of the civil service. Although most employees of these agencies were blanketed in (extended civil service coverage by executive order), they did represent a loss of control by the Civil Service Commission.

Roosevelt also directed individual departments and agencies to develop their own personnel units. These were eventually to perform the majority of personnel actions for their agencies. Another factor leading to decentralization of personnel activities was the World War II war effort. The Civil Service Commission was unable to keep up with the demands made by new and rapidly growing agencies, resulting in relative independence for the departments.

Although efforts to reestablish the authority of the commission were made, decentralization characterized the personnel function after the war. Individual departments became increasingly responsible for implementing personnel policies. The role of the Civil Service Commission changed. It became a policy maker, a provider of technical and support services, and a monitor of personnel activities. These changes in its role remain today, even though the old commission was abolished and a new organization created in its place.

Other changes were occurring in personnel activities during this period as well. During the 1930s and 1940s, federal government policy began to impose limits on state and local levels. The Social Security Act of 1935 created programs whereby national government funding assisted state governments in some programs. The act required that such programs be efficiently administered, but there were no provisions for enforcing such a vague prescription. In 1940 the act was amended to permit specific federal personnel requirements in state and local programs utilizing federal monies under the Social Security Act. Over the years, Congress has provided for similar regulations requiring merit systems in other federal programs. Currently, a uniform set of merit principle guidelines exists for federally funded projects.

Another 1940 provision, an amendment to the 1939 Hatch Act, prohibited most political activity by employees of state and local government programs funded by federal monies. These provisions were repealed in 1974, but most states adopted their own statutes restricting partisan political activities; therefore, the federal repeal has not resulted in much change for employees.

Restrictions are still applied to state and local government employees by the national government. During the 1960s and 1970s, nondiscrimination and equality of employment opportunity often became conditions for obtaining federal monies.

During the 1930s and 1940s, there was slow but steady growth in the number of states and municipalities adopting civil service systems. During the 1950s, however, the pace quickened, and, partly due to the prodding of the federal government's grant-in-aid restrictions on personnel, thirty-five states now have statewide civil service systems while the remaining fifteen utilize less comprehensive systems. Municipalities have also enacted provisions of civil service systems in increasing numbers. Counties remain dominated by patronage systems, however.

Changes continued to take place in the federal government public service during this period. The Hatch Act of 1939 gave legislative force to Civil Service Commission prohibitions on political activity, and the Ramspeck Act of 1940 prohibited discrimination in the personnel process. Preference was given to veterans in the Veteran's Preference Act of 1944, and the Government Employees Training Act of 1958 focused attention on the need for continued personal growth of employees. In recent years, personnel systems have been challenged by developments in collective bargaining, equal employment, productivity improvement, intergovernmental concerns, and continually changing political environments.

Civil Service Reform Act of 1978

Ever since passage of the Pendelton Civil Service Act there have been suggestions for reform. While many changes were made over the years, no comprehensive reform of civil service occurred until enactment of the Civil Service Reform Act of 1978. Fulfilling an election campaign promise to reform government so as to improve its efficiency, President Jimmy Carter pushed strongly for the adoption of the Reform Act. Along with the Reform Act, two Reorganization Plans were approved by Congress to reorganize the Civil Service Commission and to shift some responsibilities from the commission to the Equal Employment Opportunity Commission.[19] These reforms took effect in January 1979.

The reorganization of personnel functions divided the Civil Service Commission's activities between the new Office of Personnel Management (OPM) and the Merit Systems Protection Board (MSPB). The Federal Labor Relations Authority (FLRA) was also created to monitor federal labor-management relations policies. The division of responsibilities reflects the concerns that many people, especially employee organizations, had about one organization—the Civil Service Commission —having policy-making, implementing, and reviewing authority. Employees often viewed the commission as representing management and did not feel comfortable in approaching it with complaints or for review of personnel actions.

Under the new system the Office of Personnel Management, headed by a director and deputy director appointed by the president, has responsibility for general personnel policy development for federal employees. It also has responsibility for examinations, personnel investigations, evaluation of personnel programs, and training and development. OPM will also provide technical assistance to departments and will administer retirement and benefit programs for federal employees.

The independent Merit Systems Protection Board replaces the Federal Employee Appeals Authority, which was lodged within the Civil Service Commission. The purpose of the MSPB is to protect employees against unfair personnel actions and other abuses. It will also attempt to see that the merit system itself is protected and make annual reports to Congress on the merit system operations. Employees will be able to appeal personnel actions to MSPB, and it has the authority to institute actions to correct abuse. An important feature of the reform is that a Special Counsel established within MSPB has the power to investigate activities of agencies and officials. The Special Counsel can ask MSPB to take action against those who violate merit system laws.

The Federal Labor Relations Authority will monitor federal collective bargaining activity such as establishment of bargaining units and collective bargaining elections, and will work with departments and agencies on labor-management relations activities. A General Counsel within FLRA will investigate and prosecute unfair labor practices. The Federal Service Impasses Panel remains an independent agency to help resolve negotiation impasses.

Several features of the Reform Act deal with personnel policy issues. OPM is authorized to delegate many of its functions to operating departments, thus continuing the post-1933 trend toward decentralization of personnel functions. A Senior Executive Service (SES) created by the act permits some high-level managers to be assigned where needed so as to maximize the use of their talents. They will also be eligible for substantial pay increases for meritorious service. Merit will be the basis for pay increases for other managers in the federal service as well.

The legislation streamlined the process for dismissing incompetent employees. Additionally, so-called whistleblowers, that is, employees who expose illegal activities or mismanagement in agencies, will be protected against reprisals by their superiors.

One of the most important features of the act is that it puts into law items which have previously existed by executive order or Civil Service Commission policy. One such provision spells out and protects the collective bargaining rights of public employees. Another lists specific merit principles and prohibited practices (see Table 2–1).

The Reform Act was intended to improve the federal personnel system in general and the performance of public employees in particular. At the same time action was being taken on the federal level, state and local governments were actively pursuing reform.[20] Most of their efforts were less comprehensive than the national legislation, but the pressures of tax reform groups and the dwindling resources of management highlighted the need for effective public personnel practices.

Numerous political forces combined to bring about the reform legislation. Popular disenchantment with government and a president willing to push for such legislation were among the most important.[21] Also of influence were the problems created by the Nixon administration's attempt to politicize the public service, and changes in congressional leadership which made it more receptive to reform. The appointment of a prestigious task force to study the civil service and make recommendations gave the effort additional credibility.

Continuing Concerns in Personnel Management

Many issues remain that will continue to affect the conduct of personnel management. Three significant concerns are the conflict between legislatures and executives for control of the bureaucracy, the role of professionals, and spoils versus merit.

Table 2–1   Provisions of the Civil Service Reform Act of 1978

Merit System Principles	Prohibited Personnel Practices
Personnel practices and actions in the federal government require:	*Officials and employees who are authorized to take personnel actions are prohibited from:*

Merit System Principles	Prohibited Personnel Practices
• Recruitment from all segments of society, and selection and advancement on the basis of ability, knowledge, and skills, under fair and open competition.	• Discriminating against any employee or applicant.
• Fair and equitable treatment in all personnel management matters, without regard to politics, race, color, religion, national origin, sex, marital status, age, or handicapping condition, and with proper regard for individual privacy and constitutional rights.	• Soliciting or considering any recommendation on a person who requests or is being considered for a personnel action unless the material is an evaluation of the person's work performance, ability, aptitude, or general qualifications, or character, loyalty, and suitability.
• Equal pay for work of equal value, considering both national and local rates paid by private employers, with incentives and recognition for excellent performance.	• Using official authority to coerce political actions, to require political contributions, or to retaliate for refusal to do these things.
• High standards of integrity, conduct, and concern for the public interest.	• Willfully deceiving or obstructing an individual as to his or her right to compete for Federal employment.
• Efficient and effective use of the Federal work force.	• Influencing anyone to withdraw from competition, whether to improve or worsen the prospects of any applicant.
• Retention of employees who perform well, correcting the performance of those whose work is inadequate, and separation of those who cannot or will not meet required standards.	• Granting any special preferential treatment or advantage not authorized by law to a job applicant or employee.
• Improved performance through effective education and training.	• Appointing, employing, promoting, or advancing relatives in their agencies.
• Protection of employees from arbitrary action, personal favoritism, or political coercion.	• Taking or failing to take a personnel action as a reprisal against employees who exercise their appeal rights; refuse to engage in political activity; or lawfully disclose violations of law, rule, or regulation, or mismanagement, gross waste of funds, abuse of authority, or a substantial and specific danger to public health or safety.
• Protection of employees against reprisal for lawful disclosures of information.	• Taking or failing to take any other personnel action violating a law, rule, or regulation directly related to merit system principles.

SOURCE: U.S. Civil Service Commission, *Introducing the Civil Service Reform Act* (Washington, D.C.: Government Printing Office, November 1978), p. 2.

LEGISLATIVE-EXECUTIVE CONFLICTS

Legislators and elected executives constantly strive for control over many aspects of the personnel function. Executives traditionally view government personnel as instruments through which their policy perspectives can be translated into government action. In reality, most elected political executives complain that civil service personnel actually impede efforts at fulfilling campaign promises supposedly desired by the voters. Newly elected presidents or governors customarily deplore the lack of response of the bureaucracy to their policy directives. As such, executives often view the merit system as decreasing their ability to control policy and see the spoils system as augmenting that power.[22]

Legislative bodies, however, wish to control policy matters too. They see influence over the personnel system as one way to do this or at least to weaken the ability of the executive to exercise such power. The close relationship of legislative committees to administrative agencies serves to insure legislative influence over agency personnel. Additionally, wedges are often driven between lower-level officials and their superiors by committees insisting upon hearing personal views of employees as opposed to official policy.[23]

Lower-level bureaucrats are often protected by legislative committees or influential members of the legislative body. The State Department, for example, tried for years to make changes in passport regulations, but Frances Knight, the director of the Passport Office, took a very cautious approach to easing restrictions. Even the hint of replacing her was invariably met by pressure from conservative supporters in Congress who viewed her as an advocate of United States security. Although she did institute some changes, she was able to withstand pressure for most of the Cold War era and beyond because congressional support insulated her from her nominal superiors. J. Edgar Hoover, as director of the FBI, is another example of how such protection can develop.

The discussion of the 1883 Civil Service Act highlighted the concerns of the president and Congress in creation of the civil service system. Through the years, Congress and the president have been at odds as such laws as the Hatch Act and Veteran's Preference Act were considered and passed. Similar concerns arose during consideration of the Civil Service Reform Act of 1978. Many members of Congress were particularly uneasy about the extent to which the new Office of Personnel Management would be controlled by the president. Creation of the independent MSPB helped to allay some of those fears. The different perspectives and roles of executive and legislator will cause the conflict over control of personnel to persist.

PROFESSIONALS: INHERITORS OF THE SYSTEM

President Jackson characterized the work of government as being simple enough for any citizen to perform. He was not far from wrong because at the time most government work involved simple clerical tasks. However, today even clerical work requires complex skills and responsibilities. Even more to the point, modern society requires government activities calling for a high degree of expertise in practically every field of endeavor. The challenge of creating a personnel system capable of satisfying those needs is great. As the public service has become more specialized, it has had to deal with professionalization in personnel activities themselves.

Professionalization occurs with the development of specialized bodies of knowledge and standards for applying that expertise. Modern society has produced many new professions, along with which come professional associations which strive for the best possible performance of the specialty. The associations enable professionals to meet with and learn from fellow specialists and to keep up with recent developments in the field. Professional groups also develop codes of ethics or conduct. The professionalization of public personnel thereby has the potential of benefiting the public service both by disseminating knowledge and establishing standards. But there are costs as well.

Professionalism is normally characterized by (1) decisions being made on the basis of criteria which are universal and not dependent upon the particular situation; (2) specialization; (3) neutrality; (4) success being measured by performance; (5) elimination of self-interest in the decision-making process; and (6) self-control over the professional activities.[24] The first five of these characteristics are beneficial to the public service and consistent with most of its features. The last, self-control, however, is diametrically opposed to the principle that public personnel are accountable to the public and its elected representatives.

Frederick Mosher suggests that professionals have assumed control over the public agencies in which they work; developed an elite core within the agency to exercise that control; dominated many personnel policies; and provided protection for the members of the profession.[25] Let us look at these effects and others.

As professionals became more numerous in public agencies, their efforts turned from striving for the best performance to a contest for power.[26] Thus the emphasis is now often on gaining policy control through domination of the organization. Professional groups tend to establish their own territorial jurisdiction in agencies and develop operating procedures and approaches based on their expertise.[27] For example, the biologists and engineers in an environmental group may compete for control. While expertise is beneficial to the agency, there are also problems in permitting professional organizations to have control. An elite not accountable to the general public controls under such circumstances, and questions arise over the relationship of the public service to the rest of the political system. In public education, for instance, teachers associations have been successful in establishing criteria by which personnel decisions are made and getting school districts and state education agencies to accept them.

Personnel systems are affected to the extent that professional associations dominate various personnel policies as they gain effective control over agency activities. The professional association may influence recruitment or selection in agency employment by dominating the process of establishing qualifications for applicants. Thus recognition or certification of programs and projects as meeting professional standards normally depends upon the agency hiring personnel with the recognized professional training or experience. Such efforts restrict the flexibility and weaken the authority of personnel agencies and administrators.

Professional associations also emphasize the status and autonomy of the profession. The professional tends to respond to the pressure of the professional organization and professional peers rather than the authority structure within the agency. The potential effect is to undermine the agency's hierarchical lines of authority. In many ways the professional associations become protective shields for their members and theoretically ward off the formal and legal control.[28]

Related to the issue of control is the loyalty employees have to their agencies. The more highly professionalized people become, the less loyal they are to their employers and the more loyal to professional associations and standards.[29] Often such employees view the employing organization as an instrument for advancement and move from one organization to another as they advance professionally. In such a case, there may be a tendency to pursue personal interests at the expense of the public and the public service. Additionally, intense specialization often produces a very narrow view on the part of individual employees. They may become so preoccupied with their particular field of interest that the larger work of the organization suffers from a lack of coordination and interchange among different specialties. Personnel activities, particularly effective supervision, are difficult under such circumstances.

With its emphasis on performance and merit, professionalization is antithetical to spoils and patronage and thus helps to further insulate the personnel system from partisan politics. Similarly, professionalization conflicts with preferential treatment of individuals on bases other than merit. For example, veteran's preference policies are inconsistent with basic professional standards.

Partly as a result of professionalization, the public service itself has attempted to improve the performance of public employees. At the national level the Office of Personnel Management, through its executive seminars, federal executive institute, executive assignment system, and intergovernmental training programs, has led the way in developing programs relevant to the demands of modern society. There is also a variety of training programs created within individual agencies or by contract with other institutions such as universities, professional associations, and private consultants. Such programs expose public servants to high-level professional training and help improve the quality of public service. There is little doubt that professionalization will continue. The problem is in insuring that it works in the public interest.[30] One interesting aspect of the professionalization issue is that personnel administrators have their own professional associations and are subject to the same concerns as other professionals.

SPOILS VERSUS MERIT

Another issue which continuously affects the personnel function is the conflict between spoils and merit as bases for personnel actions. The basic distinction between the two systems is that the spoils approach emphasizes loyalty while the merit concept stresses competence or expertise. Each system needs both attributes, however, if it is to work effectively. Presidents Washington, Jefferson, and even Jackson insisted upon both loyalty and competence in public service employees. What happened is that the users of the spoils system eventually became obsessed with loyalty and ignored the need for competence. Reformers charged that spoils was inconsistent with the work ethic, on which the nation was supposedly built; and this argument, along with the abuses associated with spoils, brought about the demise of the patronage system.[31]

Because abuses of the spoils system led to political corruption, it is viewed as an evil, and there is little appreciation of the system's positive contributions. Yet the spoils system was largely responsible for democratizing the public service. By breaking the hold of the aristocracy on government jobs, the system brought people from all walks of life and from all areas of the nation into the public service. It provided a mechanism for integrating and unifying the political system. The epitome of this functional role was Lincoln's use of patronage during the Civil War, when partisan appointments were instrumental in gaining support for a controversial cause.

The spoils system was also instrumental in building and unifying political parties in the United States. Voters were attracted by the prospect of patronage rewards, and party finances were strengthened through the use of assessment. In addition, with the buildup of party machines, the spoils system aided in the political socialization of various ethnic groups in larger cities and provided many of the social services now performed by governmental agencies.

Jacksonian Democracy's focus on egalitarianism somehow became obscured in the quest for patronage positions, and in an ironic twist, egalitarianism also became an important issue in the arguments of the reform movement. The abuse of the spoils system pointed up some of its costs. The constantly changing bureaucracy led to gross inefficiencies, some incompetence, and even chaos and insecurity for the public employee. In addition, the president and Congress found themselves constantly at odds over appointments, meaning that government was often at a standstill. More importantly, the president squandered much time and energy worrying about whom to appoint to what position. Office seekers came in never-ending streams, and whether jobs were available or not, the president wasted valuable time. The quality of social services provided by political machines was lessened by the corruption and partiality of the political and administrative processes.

The spoils system inevitably led to favoritism and inequity in treatment of the public, so the reformers attempted to neutralize and democratize the public service. The civil service system was heralded as the savior of our political order. It made for a neutral public service in which employees are chosen and dealt with on the basis of their competence and ability to perform. The merit system was also supposed to foster egalitarianism in that everyone would have a chance to compete —not just those who happened to support the elected political leaders.

A major concern of the reformers was to bring morality back to the public service. The merit system would free public servants from the control of the evil politicians and the machines and permit the bureaucracy to focus attention on the job of serving the public. The merit system led to vast changes in bureaucracy and aided in reviving the prestige of the public service. Ultimately, however, problems were to be found with it as well.

One of the unintended consequences of the merit system is that it weakens the authority of the supervisor. Because the supervisor does not control the selection and removal process very directly and as protections for employee job security develop, the employee has a degree of independence. This criticism is frequently exaggerated, but it is worth consideration. An allied criticism is that under a merit system the bureaucracy is not as responsive to people because their representatives have less control when they have to consider factors other than loyalty in making appointments. Of course, others argue that the bureaucracy is more responsive because it is more competent and better able to serve the "real" needs of the people.

The major problem with the merit system is that it has strayed from the egalitarian concept, just as the spoils system did. The examination process obviously eliminates some people from consideration and is seen as a positive instrument for selection of the best qualified. However, questions may be raised about the appropriateness of the exams. Do the exams measure qualities required for successful performance? This question has lately been the focus of much attention, and efforts are constantly made to insure that exams are relevant to the position for which they are used. Closely related is the question of what credentials to require. Professional associations might like to insist on particular credentials, effectively limiting access to certain positions. If the credentials are appropriate, there is no problem; but society's concern with degrees often has little application to the tasks being performed.

The fairness of exams and credential requirements is another important issue. Minority groups in particular often argue that exams discriminate against them because of language or other cultural biases. In addition, they charge that they are screened out of many positions because they have had no opportunity to acquire the necessary credentials. The social responsibility of the public personnel system will be an issue for a long time to come.

It is an extreme oversimplification to distinguish between spoils and merit as the difference between evil and good. Unfortunately, many people do just that. Instead, it should be remembered that each is a product of particular political and social forces. Neither can provide effective bureaucracy without some cost. Although the trend in the United States has been to move toward a neutral merit bureaucracy, patronage is still important at all levels of government. The use of patronage has been adapted to changing conditions and demands just as the merit system has been adapted.[32] Some argue that the merit system has created a politics of its own—one that involves seeking support for its programs, agency autonomy, professional association interests, and clientele interests.[33] These interests and groups play the game of politics and insist that the spoils be theirs rather than the political party's. Regardless of how the system is perceived, it is certain to change in response to demands and pressures from the political environment.

Summary

The conflict between spoils and merit principles has been an enduring issue in the public service. Merit systems were developed originally to rid public personnel of political patronage. Consequently, the primary emphasis of merit personnel systems has been on policing personnel actions. Most personnel departments spend much of their time insuring that others comply with personnel policies, rules, and regulations. Although changes are occurring, such a policing function is still prominent in the activities of personnel administrators, particularly at the state and local levels.

While policing is still important, as in equal employment opportunity programs, merit systems are being confronted by many other challenges and in the process are undergoing change. To a great extent, personnel agencies are providing assistance to other agencies so that they can comply with personnel policies and also improve the quality of the public service. Central personnel agencies offer technical assistance, training programs, and services for labor-management relations among others. Through such activities personnel administrators can reduce the tension between them and department managers so that they can work together to accomplish the objectives of government. Actually, cooperation seems to be more evident in recent years as the central personnel function has centered on policy development, review, and technical assistance, while individual agencies have been performing more of the day-to-day personnel functions. The Civil Service Reform Act of 1978 accentuates this trend.

Other new concerns affecting personnel management at all levels of government include collective bargaining, equal employment opportunity, productivity, intergovernmental activities, and demands from the political environment. The rest of the book examines the impact of these issues on public personnel administration.

NOTES

1. Two who emphasize other significant breaks are Paul P. Van Riper, *History of the United States Civil Service* (New York: Harper & Row, 1958); and Frederick C. Mosher, *Democracy and the Public Service* (New York: Oxford University Press, 1968).
2. See Herbert Kaufman, "The Growth of the Federal Personnel Service," in Wallace Sayre, ed., *The Federal Government Service: Its Character, Prestige, and Problems*, 2nd ed. (Englewood Cliffs, NJ: Prentice-Hall, 1965), pp. 7–69, at pp. 12–14; Van Riper, *History of the United States Civil Service*, pp. 20–22; and Mosher, *Democracy and the Public Service*, pp. 55–61.
3. See Leonard D. White, *The Federalists: A Study in Administrative History* (New York: Macmillan, 1948), pp. 257–263. White's analysis provides much of the background for the discussion of Washington and the Federalists. Readers wanting a detailed discussion of the early development of the public service should consult this work.

4. Van Riper, *History of the United States Civil Service,* p. 27.
5. Leonard D. White, *The Jeffersonians: A Study in Administrative History 1801–1829* (New York: Macmillan, 1961), provides an excellent review of public personnel policies in the period under consideration. See pp. 347–368 in particular.
6. For a colorful account of the events, see Carl Russel Fish, *The Civil Service and the Patronage* (New York: Russell & Russell, 1963, originally pub. 1904), pp. 105–113.
7. The information on which this section is based comes largely from Fish, ibid., pp. 169–177.
8. Ibid., pp. 186–197. For the most complete analysis of the movement for reform, see Ari Hoogenboom, *Outlawing the Spoils: A History of the Civil Service Reform Movement 1865–1883* (Urbana: University of Illinois Press, 1961).
9. Fish, *The Civil Service and the Patronage,* p. 213.
10. For a detailed account of the Grant commission's recommendations and actions, see Lionel V. Murphy, "The First Federal Civil Service Commission: 1871–1875," *Public Personnel Review,* 3 (January, July, and October 1942), 29–39, 218–231, and 299–323.
11. Hoogenboom, *Outlawing the Spoils,* pp. 143–178, provides in-depth analysis of Hayes's efforts.
12. For some excellent statements of proponents and opponents of reform, see the collection of periodical articles of the times in Ari Hoogenboom, ed., *Spoilsmen and Reformers* (Chicago: Rand McNally, 1964). The intensity of feeling is apparent in the words of the writers themselves. An interesting account of press interest may be found in Charles J. Nelson, "The Press and Civil Service Reform," *Civil Service Journal,* 13 (April/June 1973), 1–3.
13. 106 U.S. 371; 27 L. Ed. 232 (1882).
14. Ari Hoogenboom, "The Pendleton Act and the Civil Service," *American Historical Review,* 64 (1958–59), 301–318, at 312. Hoogenboom, *Outlawing the Spoils,* p. 278, provides statistics on coverage.
15. Rocco C. Siciliano, "The Federal Personnel System under Scrutiny," in Thomas Page, ed., *The Public Personnel Agency and the Chief Executive,* Personnel Report no. 601 (Chicago: Public Personnel Association, n.d.), pp. 12–18, at pp. 13–14, examines the issue and its effects.
16. See Hoogenboom, *Outlawing the Spoils,* p. 241. Van Riper, *History of the U.S. Civil Service,* has an excellent chapter on the general issue of accommodation of the European import to our political culture, pp. 96–112.
17. Hoogenboom, "The Pendleton Act and the Civil Service," 305.
18. For an excellent review of state and local developments, see Albert H. Aronson, "State and Local Personnel Administration," in Frank J. Thompson, ed., *Classics of Public Personnel Policy* (Oak Park, IL: Moore, 1979), pp. 102–111, based on material from U.S. Civil Service Commission, *Biography of an Ideal* (Washington, D.C.: Government

Printing Office, 1974), pp. 127–135, 138–144. This section draws heavily on Aronson's account.

19. A more detailed description of the effects of the Reform Act is provided by U.S. Civil Service Commission, *Introducing the Civil Service Reform Act* (Washington, D.C.: Government Printing Office, November 1978).

20. For a review of some of the efforts at the state and local levels, see U.S. Civil Service Commission, *Conference Report on Public Personnel Management Reform* (Washington, D.C.: USCSC, Bureau of Intergovernmental Personnel Programs, 1978); and periodic updates in *Intergovernmental Personnel Notes*, published bimonthly by the Office of Personnel Management.

21. For a review of the various forces, see Steven Knudsen, Larry Jakus, and Maida Metz, "The Civil Service Reform Act of 1978," *Public Personnel Management*, 8, no. 3 (May/June 1979), 170–181.

22. This and the following discussion are based largely on Harvey C. Mansfield, "Political Parties, Patronage, and the Federal Government Service," in Sayre, *The Federal Government Service*, pp. 114–162, at pp. 140–149, and Herman Miles Somers, "The President, Congress, and the Federal Government Service," in Sayre, ibid, pp. 70–113 at 73–86.

23. Somers, "The President, Congress, and the Federal Government Service," p. 86.

24. For elaboration of these characteristics, see Peter M. Blau and W. Richard Scott, *Formal Organizations: A Comparative Approach* (San Francisco: Chandler, 1962), pp. 60–63.

25. Mosher, *Democracy and the Public Service*, p. 110. Also see p. 211. The following discussion is based on much of chapters 4 and 5 of this seminal work.

26. See David Schuman, *Bureaucracies, Organization, and Administration: A Political Primer* (New York: Macmillan, 1976), pp. 170–173.

27. Harold Seidman, *Politics, Position, and Power: The Dynamics of Federal Organization* (New York: Oxford University Press, 1975), pp. 144–150, discusses these issues.

28. Schuman, *Bureaucracies, Organization, and Administration*, pp. 172–173. George Frederick Goerl, "Cybernetics, Professionalization, and Knowledge Management: An Exercise in Assumptive Theory," *Public Administrative Review*, 35 (November/December 1975), 581–588, also discusses these issues.

29. Blau and Scott, *Formal Organizations*, pp. 64–67 describe studies which have been done on this issue.

30. Frederick C. Mosher and Richard Stillman, Jr., "A Symposium: The Professions in Government, Introduction," *Public Administration Review*, 37 (November/December 1977), 631–633, traces the professionalism of the service. Richard L. Schott, "Public Administration as a Profession," *Public Administration Review*, 36 (May/June 1976), 253–259, discusses the issue from a more general perspective. In-depth

discussion of the issue can also be found in Don L. Bowen, ed., *Public Service Professional Associations and the Public Interest* (Philadelphia: The American Academy of Political and Social Science, 1973).

31. See Van Riper, *History of the U.S. Civil Service*, p. 84, and Hoogenboom, *Spoilsmen and Reformers*, for discussion of the relationship between public attitudes toward spoils and the onset of its demise.
32. For a particularly good analysis of changing terms of patronage, see Frank J. Sorauf, "The Silent Revolution in Patronage," *Public Administration Review*, 20 (Winter 1960), 28–34.
33. Kaufman, "The Growth of the Federal Personnel Service," pp. 59–69.

SUGGESTED READINGS

"The Federal Personnel Crisis." *The Bureaucrat*, 4 (January 1976), 347–512.

Galbraith, John Kenneth. *Economics and the Public Purpose*. New York: The New American Library, 1973, especially pt. 5.

Gallas, Edward C., and Nesta M. Gallas. "General Problems of the Public Service." *Public Personnel Management*, 8 (March/April 1979), 64–73.

Hoogenboom, Ari. *Outlawing the Spoils: A History of the Civil Service Reform Movement 1865–1883*. Urbana: University of Illinois Press, 1961.

Mosher, Frederick C. *Democracy and the Public Service*. New York: Oxford University Press, 1968.

Panetta, Leon E., and Peter Gall. *Bring Us Together*. Philadelphia: Lippincott, 1971.

Rosen, Bernard. "Merit and the President's Plan for Changing the Civil Service System." *Public Administration Review*, 38 (July/August 1978), 301–304.

Sayre, Wallace, ed. *The Federal Government Service: Its Character, Prestige, and Problems*. 2nd ed. Englewood Cliffs, NJ: Prentice-Hall, 1965.

Sorauf, Frank J. "The Silent Revolution in Patronage." *Public Administration Review*, 20 (Winter 1960), 28–34.

Stanley, David T., ed. "Symposium on the Merit Principle Today." *Public Administration Review*, 34 (September/October 1974), 425–452.

Tolchin, Martin, and Susan Tolchin. *Political Patronage from the Club House to the White House*. New York: Vintage, 1971.

Van Riper, Paul P. *History of the United States Civil Service*. New York: Harper & Row, 1958.

Weisband, Edward, and Thomas M. Franck. *Resignation in Protest*. New York: Penguin, 1975.

CASE 2.1

The Sheriff's Office

Merry County is in a midwestern state with a strong two-party tradition. Sheriff Sayess, a Democrat, had been in office for twenty years, but I. M. Brite, a Republican, was able to defeat him in his most recent bid for reelection. It was a surprising upset because it appeared that everyone liked Sayess and there was no apparent crime problem to alarm people in the county.

When Brite took office, he called in all the employees and told them that he was going to be making many changes in the way the office was run. His intent became clear when he fired all the clerical staff and all the dispatchers. Brite did not offer any justification for his actions beyond wanting to surround himself with people he knew. Many of the employees had been with the office for more than fifteen years.

The county has no official personnel policy and traditionally has permitted the sheriff to staff the office without interference.

1. Is Brite's action justified? Explain.
2. What advice would you offer the employees who were fired?
3. What basic issues of personnel management are raised by the situation?

Chapter **3**

Intergovernmental Personnel Relations

Public personnel management is affected by the federal system of government established by the United States Constitution. It created a structure in which national and state governments have distinct identities and particular functions, making interactions among units inevitable. Those interactions constitute what is known as intergovernmental relations and may be characterized as vertical or horizontal. Vertical relations refer to the interactions of different levels of government, such as between a national unit and a state or local unit, or between a state unit and a local unit. Horizontal relations involve interactions among equivalent levels of government, such as among states, cities, or counties.

Intergovernmental relations may be cooperative or conflictive. The vagueness of many Constitutional provisions leads to differing interpretations of each level's responsibilities and authority but also leaves much flexibility for working together to solve common problems. Personnel administrators are affected by both the cooperative and conflict situations which occur. Significant aspects of intergovernmental relations which affect personnel include federal restrictions through the grant-in-aid process, legislation directed at the personnel function, technical assistance for personnel system development, and judicial decisions affecting personnel practices. State governments impose similar kinds of requirements on local jurisdictions.

As society grows increasingly complex, individual units of government find it difficult to perform their functions independently of other units. Interactions are necessary to share limited resources, especially in this era of taxpayer revolts and the like. The analysis in this chapter focuses on the implications of intergovernmental relations for the personnel process in government.

Financial Assistance and Personnel Management

As the President's Reorganization Project's analysis (the work of the task force President Carter established to study and recommend reform of the civil service system) of the personnel function suggests, the national, state, and local governments form a partnership in carrying out programs.[1] Financial assistance has been a staple of this partnership. While federal government agencies have the responsibility for implementation of policy, the state and local units are often used as vehicles for delivery of services or programs. The national government shares its broad tax base with state and local governments in the form of grants-in-aid. In the same way, state governments provide aid to local jurisdictions for a wide variety of programs. These grants-in-aid enable the lower levels of government to actually deliver the services.

When revenues are shared, restrictions are usually imposed on the unit of government receiving the funds. Personnel guidelines constitute one type of restriction applied to the grants. The intent of the guidelines is to improve the effectiveness of the programs and to insure that good personnel procedures are followed. Making certain that the public's tax money is put to proper use is another reason behind the restrictions. Most public officials and administrators recognize the need for some control by the funding agencies. However, the guidelines have been much criticized for controlling activities in too much detail. Other criticisms concern the overlap, duplication, and multiple requirements made by different granting agencies.[2] In many cases, these restrictions present obstacles to carrying out programs and become burdensome for state and local jurisdictions already facing difficulties in obtaining resources. The constraints often also contribute to the negative image that personnel people have as being promulgators and policing agents of rules and regulations that have much to do with abstract principles and little to do with the realities of administration.[3]

As a result of numerous complaints and a general desire to standardize regulations, efforts have been under way since the late 1960s to develop a uniform system. Since 1940 the national government has restricted personnel policies of state and local governments accepting grant funds. A 1940 amendment to the Social Security Act of 1935 required recipient jurisdictions under the act to establish personnel systems based on merit principles in those agencies receiving the grants. Prior to that time the Social Security Board had encouraged states to develop merit systems but had been powerless to require them. A large part of the intent of the new requirements was to insulate the programs and personnel from direct political involvement so that money could not be used by elected state and local officials to build political machines for their own benefit.

After passage of the 1940 amendment, "Standards for a Merit System of Personnel Administration" were established by the Social Security Board and eventually extended to other grant programs such as child health and welfare, public health, and civil defense programs. The standards represent the minimum merit principles which should be used; individual jurisdictions may adopt stricter standards. The effects of the standards were many because states implemented them in different ways. Some states adopted statewide systems applying to virtually all state and local employees, while others instituted merit systems to cover all those agencies receiving grants under the affected programs. Still others adopted a number of merit systems agency by agency to comply with grant requirements. While the general Standards for a Merit System eventually encompassed the Social Security Board programs and programs in Departments of Labor; Health, Education, and Welfare; Defense; and Agriculture, many grant-in-aid programs developed other, more specific, personnel administration requirements.

Under the Intergovernmental Personnel Act of 1970 (IPA), six merit principles were established to guide personnel systems at all levels:

1. Recruiting, selecting, and advancing employees on the basis of their relative ability, knowledge, and skills, including open consideration of qualified applicants for initial appointment.
2. Providing equitable and adequate compensation.
3. Training employees, as needed, to assure high-quality performance.
4. Retaining employees on the basis of the adequacy of their performance, correcting inadequate performance, and separating employees whose inadequate performance cannot be corrected.
5. Assuring fair treatment of applicants and employees in all aspects of personnel administration without regard to political affiliation, race, color, national origin, sex, or religious creed and with proper regard for their privacy and constitutional rights as citizens.
6. Assuring that employees are protected against coercion for partisan political purposes and are prohibited from using their official authority for the purpose of interfering with or affecting the result of an election or a nomination for office.[4]

As one study indicated in 1973, there were more than 150 personnel requirements imposed on state and local government units by federal granting agencies.[5] With such an array there is little wonder that state and local government officials complain of too many and conflicting restrictions. The 1973 study catalogued many complaints articulated by the President's Reorganization Project staff as objections to the myriad rules and regulations imposed on recipients by federal government granting agencies:

1. Cumbersome and restrictive federal hiring and selection requirements.
2. Difficulty in establishing policy-making jobs that are exempt from federal personnel requirements.
3. Duplicative personnel systems that are necessary to meet the requirements for staffing federally funded positions.
4. Lack of accountability for personnel systems established solely to meet federal requirements.[6]

The objection to detailed procedures regarding hiring and selection stems from the feeling among state and local jurisdictions that they should be able to determine qualifications for those employed and that much of the required record keeping wastes time and money. Such resources could be better used to accomplish the objectives of the program or agency.

Difficulties in exempting policy-making jobs from federal guidelines is a problem to the extent that governors and mayors often find that they must appoint chief assistants under merit systems in program areas funded by grants.[7] Such methods of staffing impair the ability of the chief executive to develop a policy-making staff of his or her own choosing and may prove detrimental to services.

Probably the strongest criticism by recipients of grants is that granting agencies' different systems of rules and regulations duplicate and contradict one another. Recipient jurisdictions find it difficult to satisfy a variety of requirements and waste resources in having to duplicate efforts.

Finally, the issue of lack of accountability of those systems created especially to meet federal requirements is a little different from the others and tends to be a complaint of jurisdictions which do not have comprehensive merit systems. The problem is that employees of the systems in question often operate outside the general personnel patterns of the state or local governments. Procedures may be applied to them which do not apply to other employees, and consequently, morale and other problems arise. They usually identify less with the policy-making leadership of the jurisdiction than with the federal agency benefactors; thus accountability is diffused.

The President's Reorganization Project staff recommended that the role of the federal agencies be to:

1. Provide assistance to state and local jurisdictions requesting help in personnel management.
2. Limit requirements to sound personnel principles.
3. Avoid overlapping and detailed requirements for grantees.[8]

On the basis of these recommendations, efforts to change the standards have reemerged, and finally, in 1979, the Office of Personnel Management published revised standards for state and local governments. The major emphasis of the revised guidelines is on ensuring open competition for jobs and on attracting minorities, women, and other underrepresented groups into the work force. Now grant programs will operate under one system of guidelines based upon the IPA merit principles.[9] They decentralize most of the personnel function as long as general guidelines are followed.

Large government bureaucracy cannot seem to resist getting involved in the minutiae of personnel matters, however. The Equal Employment Opportunity Commission, Office of Personnel Management, Department of Justice, and Department of Labor have jointly issued still another, complex set of guidelines entitled "Uniform Guidelines on Employee Selection Procedures."[10] State and local officials find little in those guidelines to offer relief from detailed controls; in fact, they are even having to hire attorneys and other consultants to explain the meaning of them. The agencies which promulgated the guidelines have recognized the complexity and have tried to enlighten those affected by publishing a series of questions and answers in the *Federal Register* to explain the provisions.[11] So, while some moves toward less restrictive controls have been made, there are also likely to be moves in the opposite direction confronting state and local administrators.

Federal revenue-sharing programs also have implications for public personnel administration. Revenue-sharing funds can be used for management development, although few jurisdictions use it for such a purpose. However, general revenue sharing now carries a provision that funds can be cut off from a jurisdiction which is found by a court or administrative agency to be discriminatory in its program or personnel activities. As such, personnel processes are directly affected. When general revenue sharing was last extended, much discussion revolved around requiring recipients to develop affirmative action plans, but those efforts were rebuffed. Such discussion is certain to come up again in future revenue-sharing considerations.

Just as the states complain about the national government, it is common at the local level to hear county, municipal, and school district officials complain about the state taking over their responsibilities. State governments do not share revenue with local governments to the same extent as the national government. However, in recent years states have increasingly developed programs for granting funds to local jurisdictions. In doing so, the states also tend to impose various restrictions on personnel functions. Aid to school districts has become a major revenue-sharing activity of all states, and with it has come a requirement that certain minimum standards for employees be established. Consequently, teacher certification or similar certification for other professional employees is required of districts receiving state aid. These types of restrictions "dictate" staff qualifications to those jurisdictions accepting such grants. Of course, state accrediting of programs or schools also depends upon certain staffing requirements; thus grants are not the only mechanisms for implementing such restrictions.

General Personnel Restrictions

State and local officials are especially irked by recent federal policies which restrict public personnel functions even in the absence of grant-in-aid monies. As Shapek notes, federal influences on state and local government center on three areas of activity: Department of Labor programs, collective bargaining, and equal employment opportunity policies.[12] Pension reform is another area in which regulation is likely. The federal courts have also had significant impact on state and local government personnel processes.

One of the largest Department of Labor programs to affect state and local personnel efforts is the Comprehensive Employment and Training Act (CETA), which was an effort to consolidate several manpower programs of the national government while at the same time decentralizing the administration and implementation of manpower policies. CETA provides funds to state and local jurisdictions—with a "prime sponsor" general purpose government having the responsibility of carrying out the program. Prime sponsors have included cities, state agencies, counties, and councils of governments depending upon local needs and desires. With few restrictions these prime sponsors run the program for the Department of Labor, although the department monitors its administration to minimize political abuse and insure nondiscrimination.

CETA was developed as a result of the Nixon administration's desire to decentralize decision making and implementation of programs. Therefore, it was popular with the political constituency desiring a return of government to the local level.

While CETA brought together many fragmented efforts in manpower planning, it has also engendered controversy and conflict. One purpose of CETA was to provide funding so that public service organizations and governments could employ people who otherwise would be unemployed. The idea was to subsidize such employees while they received on-the-job training. After a reasonable length of time (usually six months to a year) the organization was expected to find a slot for the employee and pay his or her salary. As often happens in such programs, good intentions somehow went awry. Many jurisdictions or organizations merely looked upon the CETA employees as extra help costing nothing.[13] As a result, plans for continued employment often did not materialize and the employee was left without a job as before. However, the Department of Labor program has been extended to permit continued funding of CETA employees, thus avoiding some of the difficulties. Nonetheless, the training intent of the program has not been met as well as expected.

Controversy has also surrounded the emphasis on minorities, women, and the elderly in some of the CETA programs. Some state and local jurisdictions have been concerned that programs aimed specifically at unemployed persons require them to favor some groups over others and interfere unduly with their decision-making processes. In many cases the local personnel people have felt that CETA employees distort the merit concept. Because CETA employees are not hired in the same way as regular employees, the question of fairness arises.[14] Additionally, many jurisdictions use CETA employees in place of regular employees, thus reducing the number of workers paid for out of local funds. Once again, the intent of the legislation is undermined, while the personnel system is left to cope with the new requirements.

The Fair Labor Standards Act embodies another federal policy that has had significant effects on state and local government personnel functions, although recent Supreme Court decisions have altered its importance. Passed in 1938, the act attempted to insure that employees were paid fairly through establishment of a minimum wage and a maximum number of hours an employee could be required to work without extra compensation. Although originally the act exempted state and local government employees from its provisions, amendments have removed those exemptions.[15] For example, a 1966 amendment applied the act to state hospitals, institutions, schools, and transit companies, because these activities compete with private business operations.

In 1974 Congress went all the way and amended the Fair Labor Standards Act to cover all employees of states and their subdivisions except for executive, administrative, and professional, or elected officials and their appointees. Local governments, in particular, were concerned with the cost of applying the minimum wage to all their employees as well as the cost of overtime when people had to work more than eight hours in a day or forty hours in a week. The result was a suit filed by the National League of Cities challenging the power of the national government to impose such requirements. The Supreme Court agreed that the provisions were unconstitutional, saying that the power of Congress to regulate interstate commerce did not entitle it to regulate the working conditions and wages of state employees.[16] While Congress may use other justifications for limiting activity of state and local governments, the Court also makes clear that it is willing to protect the autonomy of state and local governments from federal interference. Here the Burger Court reflected the political philosophy of President Nixon, who was able to appoint enough members to reverse the direction of the Court on these issues. The decision actually reversed a 1968 decision which had validated the 1966 amendments to the Fair Labor Standards Act.[17]

Another controversial program affecting state and local personnel activities is the Occupational Safety and Health Administration (OSHA) program of the Department of Labor. State and local government employees are exempted from the protection of OSHA, a fact which is greatly appreciated by many public managers as OSHA's rules and regulations have been almost uniformly ridiculed by industry. Public employees are affected, however, by state laws similar to those of OSHA in half of the states.

There seems little doubt that pressure will be brought to bear on all levels of government to regulate safety in public service. The increasing need to reduce expenditures at the state and local levels leads to deterioration of equipment and work places, thus increasing the risk of injury. Ironically, savings in maintenance may result in even greater costs in workmen's compensation and lost time of employees. The evaluations of OSHA and its review of state plans provides an input to state and local government personnel managers concerning safety and health plans. However, OSHA cannot exert formal control.

The second area in which the national government is likely to take steps affecting state and local personnel management is collective bargaining. Many unions favor a general law which would mandate collective bargaining for state and local government employees. Given the decision in *National League of Cities* v. *Usery*, it is questionable whether such a law would be constitutional, although it is likely that the legislation can be framed in such a way as to comply with the Court's decision.

Pension reform is a third area of potential regulation by the federal government. In 1974 the Employee Retirement Income Security Act (ERISA) was passed to protect the investments of private-sector employees in their pension plans. There was some sentiment in Congress for including state and local pension systems in the purview of the legislation, but while employee unions were generally strongly in favor, mayors and governors, along with organizations such as the National League of Municipalities, were just as strongly opposed.[18] As a result, standards were established only for management of private-sector plans.

Since 1974 there has been much discussion of regulating public pensions as well. So far, the public officials have been successful in delaying action, but some regulation seems to be imminent. The 1974 act provided for a study of public-sector systems by the Pension Task Force of the U.S. House of Representatives' Subcommittee on Labor Standards. Hearings on the report began in May of 1978.

The Pension Task Force found several problem areas in state and local government pension systems such as:

1. The liabilities of state and local pension systems exceed funds to pay them by $150 to $175 billion.
2. Use of pension funds is not controlled, and abuses are prevalent.
3. Most pension systems have no knowledge of their assets.
4. Participants in many systems are not provided information about them.
5. Accounting methods are inadequate.
6. Many plans have no independent audits or actuarial reviews.
7. State laws do not adequately regulate the systems and protect the rights of participants.[19]

The Dent-Erlenborn bill—named after its co-sponsors—would remedy the situation by providing federal regulation to cover each of the problems identified. Thus regulations would insure proper funding, reporting, limits on how monies could be used, and establishment of proper accounting measures to protect the investments of participants. Welcomed by employees as a protection of their interests, the proposed legislation has aroused the ire of state and local government officials as just one more intrusion of the federal government into their affairs. The federal government is caught between employee unions and state and local governments. The forces of the political process will determine the outcome. Each side has strong contacts in the Congress.

The final major area of national policy affecting state and local jurisdictions is antidiscrimination policy. Equal employment opportunity and affirmative action policies are discussed throughout the book as they apply to each element of personnel management. Generally, however, these policies apply to state and local governments through the Equal Employment Opportunity Act of 1972. The 1972 act was an amendment to the 1964 Civil Rights Act, which applied to private-sector employers. The act requires state and local employers to refrain from discriminating in their employment practices and to maintain substantial records concerning all aspects of their personnel activities.

Under affirmative action, state and local governments also have to make positive efforts to recruit employees from minority and underrepresented groups and to root out all forms of discrimination in the personnel system. Selection and testing have become focal points of equal employment opportunity issues. The Equal Employment Opportunity Commission has jurisdiction over equal opportunity cases; when a complaint is lodged against an employer, it investigates and attempts to resolve the complaint. Other agencies such as the Department of Justice, HEW, and other granting agencies monitor and enforce equal opportunity policy. State and local jurisdictions complain that such a policy is burdensome in requiring extensive record keeping and the development of lengthy defenses when complaints are lodged. Personnel administrators find themselves spending much time on issues related to equal employment and on evaluating and even changing their whole personnel systems.

The Age Discrimination in Employment Act of 1967 is another legislative attempt to guard against discriminatory practices. The act was passed with the intent of protecting workers between the ages of forty and sixty-five. In 1978 amendments, protection was extended to age seventy, thus prohibiting mandatory retirement before age seventy. Critics of the policy complain that it complicates personnel planning, inhibits innovation, and costs too much. It is widely viewed as one more instance of the federal government's meddling in personnel activities.

While it is clear that more work is created for personnel systems by federal regulations, they must be evaluated in terms of their benefits as well. State and local jurisdictions do not always develop professional and equitable systems, and federal government policy can stimulate them to do so. Federal policy and guidelines can establish minimum standards of merit and fairness with the expected result that government service will be provided at a minimum level of effectiveness. State and local jurisdictions, of course, can go beyond the minimum requirements and create higher standards.

Intergovernmental aspects of personnel are also affected by court decisions, especially those of the United States Supreme Court. As seen in the National League of Cities case mentioned earlier, the Court has restricted the authority of the national government to regulate state and local affairs. It has also required wholesale reorganization of programs and facilities in state and local governments to advance the cause of affirmative action and equal opportunity.[20] The Court has, however, also decided cases requiring back pay and changes in examination and selection procedures used by state and local jurisdictions when discrimination has been established. At the same time, the Court has expanded the discretion which may be exercised by the local jurisdictions in such areas as residency, grooming, and freedom of expression.

Intergovernmental Cooperation

So far the discussion has centered on the coercive nature of intergovernmental relations in which a granting agency imposes personnel practices on the recipient jurisdiction or a higher level imposes policy on a lower level. There are many instances in which cooperation is a voluntary effort, and personnel management is exploring ways in which cooperation can be achieved.

The national government sponsors much cooperation through programs provided for by the Intergovernmental Personnel Act of 1970. The mobility program of IPA is the most well known. It permits local and state employees to spend time in federal agencies and federal personnel to spend time with other units of government. It also provides support for other jurisdictions to exchange personnel. Such exchanges enable units of government to share expertise and to learn of one another's needs and constraints.

The Intergovernmental Personnel Act itself provides financial aid to state and local jurisdictions to help them improve their delivery of services to their citizens. It has been one of the most significant, positive efforts of the national government in stimulating better personnel practices. IPA provides training grants for improving skills of personnel as well as project grants for developing and modernizing personnel systems in state and local governments. The great variety of training development projects has been demonstrated at meetings and conferences of the International Personnel Manager's Association and American Society for Public Administration, among others. Such demonstrations stimulate interchange of ideas among units of government and foster improved personnel practices beyond the specific unit utilizing the grant. Information about projects is also disseminated through Office of Personnel Management publications, and grant recipients are encouraged to share their project results with other jurisdictions. The mobility program of IPA also provides for officials from one level of government to spend time in another level, thus encouraging a sharing of knowledge and expertise.

In addition, the national government conducts many training programs which may be open to state and local governments on a space-available basis. Thus the Federal Executive Institute, Regional Training Centers, and Executive Seminar Centers of the Office of Personnel Management permit managers from all levels of government to receive training as space permits, although the programs are aimed primarily at national government managers. Cooperative programs such as the Southwest Intergovernmental Training Center in San Antonio, Texas, operated by the Department of Labor and Office of Personnel Management, concentrate on training potential and current employees of state and local governments. Other departments at the national level offer a variety of training programs available to other jurisdictions. State governments run programs in law enforcement, water resources, and fire-fighting schools for personnel from local jurisdictions.

Another aspect of training is for preservice personnel, and many departments offer training which has an intergovernmental flavor. The White House Fellows program takes faculty from academic institutions as well as high-quality personnel from other governmental jurisdictions and exposes them to national policy-making processes in hopes all will better understand and be able to contribute to policy efforts. The Urban Fellows Program of the Department of Housing and Urban Development supports training of people interested in careers at the local level.

Other units of government also enter into cooperative arrangements, working together to solve common problems. In California, cities and other local jurisdictions commonly collaborate on recruitment, testing, and wage and salary surveys. In Utah, cooperative efforts involve federal, state, local, and university employers.[21]

Contracting for services, another mechanism for cooperative efforts, reduces the need for personnel in some jurisdictions. Contracting for computer services, health facilities, or water may allow a small jurisdiction to receive services while benefiting from the economies of scale of a larger jurisdiction. Such contracting helps reduce duplication of facilities and benefits all taxpayers.

A recent approach to interjurisdictional cooperation builds upon the idea of the circuit-riding judge or preacher of the past. The North Texas Council of Governments and the University of Colorado School of Public Affairs have successfully experimented with sponsoring circuit-riding managers for local governments. A manager may be hired to work with a few small municipalities which could not afford their own separate managers. Each jurisdiction pays an agreed-upon proportion of the salary. The problem is that disagreements over many aspects of the arrangement may emerge. However, it is one way of dealing with increasingly scarce resources.

Cooperative efforts are becoming more common in the collective bargaining process. Because jurisdictions are themselves pressured to pay employees on a comparability pay or prevailing wage basis, multi-jurisdictional bargaining can help reduce the whipsawing effect of separate agreements which use one jurisdiction's level of compensation as a base for negotiating with another. As each jurisdiction meets the other's wage level, the rates keep going up. Coordinated bargaining aids the jurisdictions and also helps the employees to obtain equitable treatment.

Summary

The operations of governmental units are interconnected. It is inevitable that different levels work together to solve problems which cannot be confined to any one jurisdiction. Costs of services are certain to continue to increase while resources dwindle. As a result, cooperative effort is one method by which jurisdictions can more efficiently provide their service.

NOTES

1. President's Reorganization Project, *Personnel Management Project: Final Staff Report*, vol. 1 (December 1977), pp. 215–228.
2. Ibid., pp. 215–216.
3. See Muriel M. Morse, "We've Come A Long Way," *Public Personnel Management*, 5 (July/August 1976), 218–224, for a discussion of the traditional view of the personnel administrator along with an overview of more current concerns.
4. The Advisory Council on Intergovernmental Personnel Policy, *More Effective Public Service: The First Report to the President and the Congress* (Washington, D.C.: Government Printing Office, January 1973), pp. 7–18.
5. Ibid., p. 75.
6. President's Reorganization Project, *Personnel Management Project* (1977), p. 217.
7. A good historical perspective on this issue can be found in Matthew E. Welsh, "The Hatch Act and the States," *State Government*, 37 (Winter 1964), 8–13.

8. President's Reorganization Project, *Personnel Management Project* (1977), p. 216.
9. See *Federal Register*, vol. 44, no. 34, February 16, 1979, for the detailed guidelines.
10. *Federal Register*, vol. 38, no. 166, August 25, 1978, p. 38290.
11. *Federal Register*, vol. 44, no. 43, March 2, 1979, pp. 11996–12009.
12. Raymond A. Shapek, "Federal Influences in State and Local Personnel Management: The System in Transition," *Public Personnel Management*, 5 (January/February 1976), 41–51.
13. For a critique of these problems, see Juan Cameron, "How CETA Came to Be a Four-letter Word," *Fortune* (April 1979), 112–120.
14. Arthur L. Finkle, "Governmental Economic Intervention and the Merit System," *Public Personnel Management*, 6 (March/April 1977), 78–83.
15. See Thomas E. Gausden, *New Vistas in Federalism: An Analysis of National League of Cities v. Usery* (Chicago: International Personnel Management Association, n.d.).
16. *National League of Cities v. Usery*, 96. S.Ct. 2465 (1976).
17. *Maryland v. Wirtz*, 392 U.S. 183 (1968).
18. Thomas P. Southwick, "Public Pension Plans: Federal Standards?" *Congressional Quarterly Weekly Report*, 34 (May 8, 1976), 1133–1135.
19. Ibid.
20. William H. Steward, Jr., *The Growth of State Administration in Alabama* (University, AL: University of Alabama Bureau of Public Administration, 1978), especially ch. 5.
21. For a good description of the agreement and how it works, see William M. Timmins, "Utah's IPA Center: Report on Cooperative Recruitment and Selection," *Public Personnel Management*, 4 (May/June 1975), 156–159.

SUGGESTED READINGS

Finkle, Arthur L. "The Impact of Federalism on the Merit System." *IPMA News*, October 1977, pp. 4–6.

Gausden, Thomas E. *New Vistas in Federalism: An Analysis of National League of Cities v. Usery. IPMA Special Report.* Chicago: International Personnel Management Association, n.d.

"Intergovernmental Relations: The Federal Influence." *State Government*, 50 (Spring 1977), 62–101.

King, Bruce. "An Array of Tools for Better Public Service." *State Government*, 46 (Autumn 1973), 252–255.

National League of Cities. *State Personnel Requirements Affecting Municipalities.* Washington, D.C.: National League of Cities, 1977.

Shapek, Raymond A. "Federal Influences in State and Local Personnel Management: The System in Transition." *Public Personnel Management*, 5 (January/February 1976), 41–51.

CASE 3.1

Cason City

Cason City, U.S.A., is a small midwestern city which is relatively stable in population and has a solid tax base. During the 1970s it began to search for ways to expand and sought federal grants for a variety of physical improvements. Community Development grants and revenue-sharing funds were used for improving the one deteriorating neighborhood in the city.

The personnel system utilized by Cason City is the merit system. It has been noted by some of the federal funding agencies that only 5 percent of the employees of Cason City are minority group members and 50 percent are female. No minorities or females hold supervisory or managerial jobs. Funding agencies are putting pressure on the city to demonstrate that it is making an effort to provide greater opportunity for minorities and women.

The city council listened as the department heads with projects funded by federal monies related the pressures being applied and appealed for some action by the council to remedy the situation. It then promptly passed a resolution asking the federal government to keep its nose out of Cason City's affairs. No further action on the matter was taken by the council.

Tad Kress, the city manager, received pleas from department heads for assistance in dealing with the federal agencies' demands. Kress asked Lee Glist, the personnel director, to draft recommendations on what could be done. You are Glist's administrative assistant and have to develop a background paper for him to use in making his recommendations.

1. What issues would you investigate?
2. What possible actions would seem available?
3. What consequences would each action entail?

In the Matter of John Gale

Jane Heron was enjoying the party given by the Harrisons for members of the local arts clubs. She was meeting many new and interesting people. As she talked with John Gale, the conversation turned to work. John was employed as a technical projects analyst with a small consulting firm. Jane mentioned that she directed the budget office at city hall and had been looking for a program analyst for over a year. John seemed to have exactly the kind of background she needed. John agreed to apply for the job. The next week, after reviewing John's application, Jane decided to hire him and offered him a salary in keeping with his requirements.

Jane forwarded her decision to the personnel office. She told John to go ahead and resign his present position and be ready to start work.

In a couple of days, Homer Thatcher, the personnel manager, called Jane and said there was a problem on the appointment of John. The city was a member of a cooperative recruiting organization composed of governmental jurisdictions in the area. The members had agreed to apply certain uniform standards to a number of positions. One was a pay ceiling for various jobs. Jane's salary offer to John went over the ceiling, even though the city's own compensation schedule would permit that level of pay. Another agreement among the group's members was that none of them would employ a person who had been newly hired by another within the preceding two years. It turned out that John had been hired by a member city a year and a half earlier but had stayed only two months.

Jane is upset because she has been trying to fill the position for a long time without any success. Now she feels stymied.

1. If you were Jane, what would you do now?
2. What would you have done differently in the first place?
3. What would you do if you were Homer?

Chapter 4

Personnel Systems Management

Although everyone in an organization is involved in the personnel process, supervisors and managers, in particular, have numerous personnel responsibilities. Some particular individuals or units will have the primary function of seeing to the development and implementation of personnel policies. The personnel function may rest with the chief executive officer or may be lodged in a personnel office, ranging from one or a few people to a large complex bureaucracy. This chapter analyzes the various bases on which personnel activities may be organized and alternatives for structuring the personnel function. First, the function of the personnel office is explored.

Personnel offices are often seen as negative policing agencies which ensure that rigid rules and procedures are obeyed by the operating departments. As a result, many department managers view personnel units with suspicion and hostility; rarely have they looked to the personnel office as a source of support and assistance. There seem, though, to be changes in this attitude taking place.[1] Basically, the personnel office is supposed to be a service office to the rest of the organization. It performs what is normally referred to as a staff function, since it facilitates the delivery of services of the line departments which carry out the functions of governments.

The services provided by the personnel office have traditionally focused on the recruitment of employees. The operating department would requisition persons to fill vacancies. The personnel office would then do the necessary advertising and interviewing of applicants and would administer appropriate exams to lead to certification of candidates for selection. Along with these duties, the personnel office would also update the position classification and compensation systems. Its audit and review functions meant policing the departmental activities and often finding problems which would then have to be corrected. Any outside review of activities tends to produce anxieties and suspicion, and personnel offices created both, partly because they tended to emphasize abiding by "good" rules and regulations while ignoring the need for maintaining flexibility and getting things done.[2]

In recent years the role of the personnel office has changed and expanded greatly. One feature of the change is that personnel is increasingly viewed as a provider of support for all aspects of management. In the private sector, personnel management tends to be integrated into the overall management function, but in most public-sector jurisdictions it still has a long way to go. Public-sector managers are becoming more aware of the need for making personnel administration an integral part of general management. Tax revolts, resulting in the need for greater care in the way limited resources are used, prod public managers to include personnel administrators in decisions involving the most expensive resource—the government's personnel. The 1978 Civil Service Reform Act was predicated to a large extent upon President Carter's promise to revamp management at all levels of the federal government. Many state and local jurisdictions are following the lead in such reform.[3]

As a result of the changing attitudes toward the personnel function, many new activities have become the province of the personnel office. Thus, in recent years, training of employees has become of importance as has the emphasis on developing career opportunities and other means of encouraging good employees to remain with the organization. Insuring that pay is equitable and adequate as well as using it as a resource for resolving employee dissatisfaction are other means the personnel office has for retaining employees and improving the quality of service.

Collective bargaining, in which employees negotiate terms of employment with management, is another activity for which personnel offices now have a responsibility in many jurisdictions, including the national government. Along with collective bargaining, productivity improvement projects have gained importance in public employment, and personnel offices are central points in the effort.

The other new responsibility is in the area of equal employment opportunity. In many jurisdictions the personnel office must develop, maintain, monitor, and serve as adjudicator of the equal opportunity program. At the national level the adjudication and general enforcement responsibility rests with a separate agency—the Equal Employment Opportunity Commission (EEOC). The Office of Personnel Management is charged with seeing that agencies develop and encourage equal employment opportunity and affirmative action efforts. All these functions and others are discussed more fully throughout the book.

Types of Personnel Systems

Fritz Morstein-Marx finds four historical patterns in public bureaucracy —guardian, caste, patronage, and merit.[4] Muriel Morse suggests that in the United States there are also four types of personnel systems, namely, spoils, merit, welfare, and affirmative action.[5] These approaches to bureaucracy and personnel systems have many implications for the way in which the personnel function is organized, and serve as the means of organizing this discussion.

The guardian bureaucracy is based on a predestined selection process where the guardians are protectors of good and right. Plato's *Republic* is an example of the guardian approach to the bureaucracy. The bureaucracy of rulers serves to maintain the system which reflects the good society. Determining who is born to rule is not an easy process. The caste bureaucracy, on the other hand, provides an easier method of choosing the bureaucracy. People are born into their social caste and only those of the higher caste rule. Thus the system normally reflects the structure of the society.

The patronage or spoils system of personnel management stems from the model associated with Jacksonian Democracy. In this system a political leader or other patron rewards supporters by giving jobs to them. While merit may be taken into account, the primary consideration is whether the potential employee has worked or will work for the interests of those in power. As explained in chapter 2, many employees in the United States public service are still selected on the basis of spoils. Cabinet members and other high officials are chosen through patronage, as are members of regulatory and other independent agencies and the judiciary in many jurisdictions. In many states, especially in the Southeast, spoils systems still govern many operations of state and local personnel operations.

Merit personnel systems are common in the United States, at least in theory. Under the merit system, personnel decisions are based on specified standards, qualifications, and performance. While most civil service systems are justified as merit systems, as was seen in chapter 2, merit and civil service are not synonymous. The major premises of Weberian bureaucracy (developed by the nineteenth century German sociologist

Max Weber) form the basis of merit personnel systems, especially since a career service with fixed salaries, specified selection and training procedures, rules and regulations for all program activities, and evaluation of performance are parts of the personnel function.

Morse's welfare and affirmative action personnel systems are more recent additions to the bases for personnel actions. The welfare personnel and affirmative action systems are founded on government employment as a resolver of social problems. In the welfare-based approach government serves as the employer of last resort for people who would not otherwise have employment opportunity, who lack skills, or who are the hard-core unemployed. The public service employment programs, such as the Comprehensive Employment Training Act (CETA), are examples of such a system.

Similarly, the affirmative action personnel system is based on accomplishing a social purpose. There is much controversy over whether or not affirmative action is consistent with merit, but normally it does not conflict. It does add another dimension, however, in that the personnel system must take positive action to make opportunities available to members of groups which had previously suffered discrimination. The affirmative action systems may base selection on the best-qualified approach associated with merit systems. Or they may abolish qualification standards and seek people with the potential for training, or give bonuses to protected groups. In some instances, minimum qualifications are established and preference given to those who meet the minimum standard regardless of the qualifications of the other candidates. The relationship of affirmative action to the overall personnel function is examined throughout the book.

Organizing Personnel Activities

The basic structure of the personnel system in any jurisdiction is based in some form of legal framework.[6] In many cases, state constitutional or local government charters spell out the major requirements for the personnel operation. Commonly, such provisions indicate that the public service shall be based on a merit principle and provide for the policy-making and implementation organizations. Whether a civil service commission, single personnel director, or other arrangement will be used is stated, as are details of the powers and duties of such organizations. In the absence of, or in addition to, constitutional or charter provisions, laws or ordinances establish the legal foundation of the system. In addition, executive officers and civil service commissions or the like may issue rules and regulations which affect structure. All these bases for establishing the system are interrelated. Normally the constitutional or charter provision grants authority to the legislative body, which then authorizes the personnel or civil service commission to issue rules and regulations. Thus the various elements of the process complement one another in providing for organization of the personnel activities.

There are basically three organizational questions which must be considered in establishing the personnel system:

1. Is an independent personnel board or commission desirable? If so, what are its powers and functions?
2. Is a central personnel office to conduct personnel functions, or should each department perform its own personnel activities?
3. Should final personnel authority rest with the chief executive, legislature, or independent personnel board or commission?

The answers to these questions depend upon the needs of the individual jurisdictions. The needs of a very small unit of government will not be the same as for one with a large employee force. Similarly, jurisdictions with partisan political elections have needs different from those with nonpartisan elections. Each jurisdiction needs to determine what will work best for it. Here, the basic features of the various approaches are examined.

In 1883 reform at the national government level stimulated a move toward creation of nonpartisan or bipartisan civil service or personnel boards or commissions. The United States Civil Service Commission was created as a bipartisan commission with general responsibility for overseeing the personnel function. Over the years its functions increased as it took on greater responsibility for personnel system development. The commission system was variously copied by many state and local jurisdictions. In many instances, the commissions also have responsibility for conducting the day-to-day operations of personnel. In some larger jurisdictions, such as the national level, the state of Idaho, and the Los Angeles County School District, an executive director or personnel director was appointed for day-to-day operations. An alternative is for the commission or board to have one individual designated as chairperson or president with the administrative responsibilities for carrying out personnel activities. Such is the case in the New York state system.

The major alternative for organizing a central personnel agency is for it to be directly responsible to the chief executive and thus closely integrated into the management operations of the administration. The Civil Service Reform Act of 1978 created such an arrangement at the national level with the new Office of Personnel Management reporting to the president. The Wisconsin state government and the city of Chicago have recently adopted similar systems. Where a personnel office reports to the chief executive and supervises the operational aspects of personnel administration, an appeals board of some sort is normally created to review appeals by employees. In some instances, a personnel board provides advisory services to the chief executive and approves personnel rules and regulations. New York City and Chicago use this approach, which is common in state and local government.

Another aspect of personnel organization relates to whether the function is centralized in one department of personnel or decentralized among the agencies in the jurisdiction. In most systems the approaches are combined. In a few places, such as Texas, individual departments still have a great deal of autonomy over most of their personnel activities. There, despite continuing efforts to centralize the system, politics has insured a highly decentralized operation.

The reform movement stimulated by the 1883 Civil Service Act led to adoption of central personnel offices in most large jurisdictions. In recent years, however, the trend has been toward the decentralizing of many functions, especially policy implementation. After World War II the National Civil Service Commission began delegating the responsibility for operational details to the individual departments. The trend was started in 1938 when the president ordered each department to create its own personnel offices responsible for the technical aspects of implementing personnel policy.[7] The 1978 reform continues the decentralizing process, while the Office of Personnel Management makes policy, develops programs, insures compliance with policy, and provides technical assistance.

Centralization of the personnel functions has many advantages. It provides for uniformity in dealing with personnel activities and permits a high degree of specialization in the technical aspects of personnel. Economies of scale also result when recruiting, examining, and the like are done for the jurisdiction as a whole. With the increasing influence of labor organizations, uniformity of policy and procedures offers a source of support to management as well. A lack of uniformity may lower employee morale and productivity, as employees evaluate their positions relative to that of others in the organization. Table 4–1 lists the suggestions of the Office of Personnel Management concerning the functions which should be the province of the central personnel office.

There are also disadvantages to a central office having all the personnel responsibilities. Critics cite the distance of the personnel office from the work being done by the operating agencies. Many managers view the central personnel office as an outside force and not as a support service. The personnel office also tends to deal with individual problems in any given unit and does not provide an overall management perspec-

Table 4-1   Guide to Establishing Central Personnel Office Functions

Basic functions needed for initial operation of Central Personnel Office	Additional functions to be added when initial operation is well established	Other functions that may be performed by the Central Personnel Office	Personnel functions
			Program services:
▲			• Recruitment
▲			• Selection
▲			• Selection validation
▲			• Certification of eligibles
▲			• Classification
▲			• Pay and benefits
	▲		• Performance evaluation
	▲		• Training
	▲		• Career development services
▲			• Employee-management relations
	▲		• Employee communications
▲			• Equal employment opportunity
▲			• Employee discipline procedures
▲			• Grievance and appeal procedures
	▲		• Employee safety and health
▲			• Layoff procedures
	▲		• Workforce planning
	▲		• Productivity improvement
		▲	• Position management and organizational effectiveness
		▲	• Employee incentive and awards
		▲	• Personnel research
▲			• Program evaluation
			Support services:
▲			• Maintenance of employee records
▲			• Maintenance of related personnel records, statistics, and reporting systems
	▲		• Position control
		▲	• Personal services budgeting
▲			• Personnel policy and procedures issuance system
		▲	• Payroll processing
▲			• Monitoring of personnel transactions for conformance with established policies and procedures
▲			• Benefits administration

SOURCE: U.S. Civil Service Commission, *Organizing The Personnel Function: A Guide for Local Governments* (Washington, D.C.: USCSC Bureau of Intergovernmental Personnel Programs), pp. 6–7.

tive either for itself or the unit. In other words, it lacks an integrated approach to personnel affairs.

Under a decentralized system each department has its own personnel officer and staff. The conduct of the personnel function is likely to be largely autonomous, and policies and procedures not uniform. When each department is permitted to adapt policies and actions to its own needs, the personnel function tends to be closely integrated with the management of the department. The major problems of the departmental personnel office model are the lack of uniformity among departments, the costs of duplicating the activities in numerous agencies, fewer opportunities for specialization, and a lack of objectivity in dealing with the personnel problems.

In most large jurisdictions the extremes represented by the central and departmental systems are ameliorated by the use of a combination. The central office will perform certain kinds of functions, and officials in each department will be responsible for day-to-day activities. Thus the central office can focus on policy development, specialized expertise, monitoring, and review, while the departmental official can focus on the implementation of policy in the relevant setting. The departmental office can seek the assistance of the central office specialist as needed.

Obviously, not all governmental units have the resources to develop a specialized personnel office or staff. As a result, one of the functions of the chief executive may be the personnel responsibility.

In recent years, the personnel function has spawned a host of new agencies dealing with particular aspects of personnel. Collective bargaining developments have led to the creation of numerous special agencies. The central personnel office sometimes has major responsibility for labor relations, as is the case with the national Office of Personnel Management and the State Personnel Board in Alaska. More common, however, is the creation of a separate agency to deal with labor relations. The Public Employee Relations Board (PERB) in Los Angeles, the state PERBs in Maine and Minnesota, or the Office of Collective Bargaining in New York City are examples of this approach. The personnel offices, of course, are still involved in policy matters relating to labor relations, and all their functions affect the collective bargaining process.

Equal employment opportunity and affirmative action have also stimulated the development of separate offices or agencies for implementation and monitoring of policy. The Office of Personnel Management has major responsibility for policy and encouragement of equal employment opportunity in national government, but the Equal Employment Opportunity Commission now handles monitoring and enforcement. Similar arrangements have been made in some state and

local jurisdictions where human rights commissions or equal employment opportunity commissions tend to deal with enforcement issues.
Massachusetts and San Francisco operate under such systems.

Career Systems

Different types of career systems operate within the varied personnel
structures. Certainly political appointees and career civil servants represent two different systems which interact within organizations. Technically the political appointees oversee the career service. During the early
part of every new administration the top-level political appointees
promise major shake-ups in the career bureaucracy. Such changes occur
infrequently. The career bureaucrats provide the information and support needed for programs desired by the agency department head appointed by the administration. In most departments the top administrator cannot risk the opposition of the career servants. Accommodations
are made, and usually the administrator becomes socialized to the career
servant's perspectives. In cases where this does not happen, career
servants lobby for their positions before sympathetic congressional
committees.[8]

The political executive career pattern differs from the career service
in that tenure in a position is dependent upon the election process.[9] If
a new party wins the presidency, governorship, or mayoralty, the political
appointees normally change. Even if a party or administration is re-
elected, there are likely to be changes in emphasis and thus changes in
personnel. Loyalty to the current administration and its policy position
is also characteristic of political executives, and dismissal for disagreement is common.

Even more difficult for political executives is that they may have the
confidence of the chief executive but become a liability because of
political considerations. James Schlesinger, secretary of energy in the
Carter administration, found himself in such a plight. He was the foil
for Carter in the president's difficulties of coming to grips with the
energy crisis. While he was in charge of policy development, he was not
wholly responsible for the lack of a coherent policy. Nonetheless, he
was a major target of the criticism brought about by people's frustration
over energy problems. By taking the heat off of Carter, he appeared to be
getting pressure to resign, again aiding the president by satisfying those
who wanted him out. Of course, top political executives usually have
many other options and may fade into the background for a while only
to reappear in a new administration. Schlesinger is a good example

here as well, having been President Ford's secretary of defense and, after being out of government service for a while, surfacing as chief energy adviser and eventually secretary of energy. Often such departure from and reentry into government service follow the changes in political parties in power. People from the Kennedy and Johnson administrations reappeared in the Carter administration, as did many of those from the Eisenhower administration in the Nixon and Ford cabinets or other high positions.

Career civil servants, of course, have much better tenure prospects and thus carry over from one administration to another. Within that career system, however, are what are referred to as open and closed career systems. Closed career systems are those in which higher-level positions are filled entirely through promotion from below. To become a high-level official within the organization, a person must begin at the bottom and progress up through the hierarchical ladder. The military, FBI, Foreign Service, police and fire departments, and the British civil service use such systems. The military is the strictest, but with some exceptions the others usually require experience at the lower level to attain higher ranks.

An open system means that positions are filled through competition from both inside and outside the organization. Sometimes called lateral entry, it allows employees to enter an organization at any level. Open systems are supposed to make the organization more dynamic by bringing in people with fresh ideas and approaches and thus eliminating the stagnation often created by the socialization process. In actual practice, most systems which are technically open, as is the case in most government jurisdictions, usually tend more toward the closed-system approach. Closed systems are often preferred by employees and employee organizations. Many collective bargaining agreements call for promotion based on seniority, which is a closed-system approach. High-level managers often feel more comfortable with a closed system in that it allows them to deal with known quantities in the selection of staff. People from below can be chosen according to how well they get along and go along in the organization. Someone from outside the organization may pose a risk on such accounts.

Closed systems normally also include an up-or-out feature. Up-or-out, or selection-out, refers to the situation in which a person is expected to qualify for promotion within a certain period of time. If promotion does not occur, the person is dismissed from the organization. The military and Foreign Service use this process, and academic departments in most colleges and universities employ a less strict version of it.

A new element in the national career service is the Senior Executive Service (SES) as provided for in the Civil Service Reform Act of 1978.

It covers high-level managers. Agencies designate positions which will be SES positions, and individuals can choose whether or not to accept such designation. If they do not accept it, they become ineligible for further promotion. Retention in SES is based on performance; thus the risks associated with SES appointments are greater than those in the regular civil service. Those who are removed from SES for poor performance, however, may be placed in non-SES positions at a lower level with no loss in base pay. Thus security still exists. The idea behind SES is that it should provide flexibility in assignment and permit utilization of talented individuals in a variety of areas of activity rather than tie someone to one given task. It also provides incentives through special awards of up to $20,000 for outstanding performance for up to 1 percent of the SES and up to $10,000 for as many as 5 percent in any one year. SES attempts to combine the protection of the civil service with a special inducement to go beyond the basic performance requirements and permit employees to experience new challenges and experiences.

Another variation on the career system is the rank-in-person versus rank-in-job approach. Basically, rank-in-person means the individual is evaluated and ranked according to his or her performance, and compensation and other benefits are based on the person's rank regardless of the duties performed. Qualifications such as education and experience help to determine the rank. In rank-in-job systems the position determines the rank and hence the emoluments. Military organizations and, to a certain extent, academic faculties use rank-in-person systems, while most civil service systems are based on rank-in-job. The SES is yet another example of rank-in-person.

The rank-in-job system and the closed system tend to produce problems in dealing with good employees, because the only way to advance in salary and prestige and to acquire other badges of success is to travel up through the hierarchy. People are rewarded for effective service by promotion to supervisory and managerial positions. These jobs, however, require different skills. Often those good at doing the tasks of the organization are not good at managing or supervising others. As a result, some people have suggested development of a "dual track career system" which would permit the rewarding of individuals for good technical performance while also providing for promotion within managerial ranks for those with management skills. The federal Internal Revenue Service has developed a dual track system which permits technical employees to attain the same grades in the general schedule as do managerial employees.[10] Dual track approaches have not caught on to a great extent in the public service but can alleviate the problems created by the pressures for promotion common in our society.

Summary

The personnel function requires a specified structure which is appropriate to the jurisdiction. The particular form of the structure will depend upon the resources available to the jurisdiction and upon the overall political and governmental framework. Thus no one organizational structure is the best for all jurisdictions. The system must, however, provide for an arrangement which makes the personnel function a central aid to general management if the public service is to be effective.

NOTES

1. For background material, see Elmer B. Statts, "Personnel Management: The Starting Place," *Public Personnel Management*, 5 (November/December 1976), 434–441; and Muriel M. Morse, "We've Come A Long Way," *Public Personnel Management*, 5 (July/August 1976), 218–224.
2. These concerns are effectively dealt with by Morse, ibid. 219–221.
3. For a review of some of the efforts at the state and local levels, see U.S. Civil Service Commission, *Conference Report on Public Personnel Management Reform* (Washington, D.C.: USCSC, Bureau of Intergovernmental Personnel Programs, 1978); and periodic updates in *Intergovernmental Personnel Notes*, published bimonthly by the Office of Personnel Management.
4. Fritz Morstein-Marx, *The Administrative State* (Chicago: University of Chicago Press, 1957), pp. 54–72.
5. Muriel Morse, in a presentation for Center for Public Service, Texas Tech University, April 18, 1979.
6. A good outline of major methods of providing the legal foundation is found in U.S. Civil Service Commission, *Guide to a More Effective Public Service: The Legal Framework* (Washington, D.C.: USCSC, Bureau of Intergovernmental Personnel Programs, 1974).
7. See Frederick C. Mosher, "Features and Problems of the Federal Service: The Management of Merit," in Wallace Sayre, ed., *The Federal Government Service* (Englewood Cliffs, NJ: Prentice-Hall, 1965), pp. 163–211.
8. For an interesting commentary on the process, see Leonard Reed, "The Bureaucracy: The Cleverest Lobby of Them All," *Washington Monthly*, 10 (April 1978), 49–54.
9. For elaboration on elements of the career patterns of political executives, see Dean Mann, "The Selection of Federal Political Executives," *American Political Science Review*, 58 (March 1964), 81–99.
10. For a good explanation of the IRS system, see Carl L. Bellas, "The Dual

Track Career System within the Internal Revenue Service," *Personnel Administration and Public Personnel Review,* 1 (September/October 1972), 4–8, reprinted in Robert T. Golembiewski and Michael Cohen, eds., *People in Public Service,* 2nd ed. (Itasca, IL: Peacock, 1976), pp. 116–122.

SUGGESTED READINGS

Campbell, Alan K. "Civil Service Reform: A New Commitment." *Public Administration Review,* 38 (March/April 1978), 99–103.

"Civil Service Reform." *Good Government* (special issue), 1, (1978), 1–11.

"NCSL's Model Law." *Good Government,* 93 (Spring 1976), 4–9.

"Personnel Management Series." *Bureaucrat,* 7 (Fall 1978), 2–22.

U.S. Civil Service Commission. *Introducing the Civil Service Reform Act.* Washington, D.C.: Government Printing Office, 1978.

U.S. Civil Service Commission. *Organizing the Personnel Function.* Washington, D.C.: Government Printing Office, 1978.

U.S. Civil Service Commission. *Personnel Management Project.* Vols. 1 and 2. Washington, D.C.: Government Printing Office, 1977.

U.S. Library of Congress. *Federal Personnel Management Reform: A Selected Bibliography.* Washington, D.C.: Library of Congress, 1978.

The President's Adviser

The president of the United States has called you in as a personnel management consultant because of your expertise in personnel administration and your excellent understanding of the political realities of life in Washington, D.C. The president finds that many public employees do not respond to his leadership, and he is constantly frustrated in getting things done. Even the Civil Service Reform Act of 1978 did not bring about the desired results.

1. What advice will you give the president concerning further types of reorganization?
2. What education will you provide the president on how the political system affects his concerns with public employees?
3. Is there any way the president can use politics to his advantage in this situation?

Chapter 5

Classification

Administrators must have tools for conducting their activities. Traditionally the processes of public personnel administration have included position classification, compensation, recruitment, examination, selection, promotion, performance evaluation, and discipline. In this and the next three chapters these concerns shall be examined. Later chapters will deal with more recent issues as they have emerged in response to employee demands and societal changes.

Position classification has been the basis of almost all other public personnel activity. At present, the concept is frequently under attack, and changes are being made in its use. The process involves identifying the duties and responsibilities of each position in an organization and then grouping the positions according to their similarities for personnel administration activities.

The major objective of the classification system is to permit management to make the most rational decisions regarding the relationship of duties and responsibilities to the other concerns of personnel administration. For instance, a fair compensation plan requires an understanding of the duties and responsibilities of each position; effective examination and recruiting require knowledge of what the agency is examining and recruiting for; and determining the qualifications necessary for performing the job requires an understanding of what the job entails. Position classification evolved as a convenient and useful tool. It also developed as an extension of the Scientific Management school's focus on efficiency and economy; it offered a rational approach to organizing activities in a hierarchy, resulting in efficient coordination.

The reaction to spoils and the creation of the Civil Service Commission in 1883 aided the development of position classification, since it offered a means of making personnel decisions according to objective considerations rather than on the basis of personal and political factors. In order for the Civil Service Commission to carry out its charge of establishing practical examinations, some idea of position duties and responsibilities was needed. In addition, the chaotic federal pay system of the late nineteenth and early twentieth centuries led to pressure for reform. The democratic tradition of the United States made "equal pay for equal work" a readily accepted slogan. To apply the principle, positions had to be evaluated and classified to give a basis for comparison. Thus the movement toward comprehensive position classification was born of the desire for equality and was reinforced by the increasing complexity of technology and specialization.

The United States originated position classification and still uses it to a much greater extent than most nations. Position classification developed in Chicago in 1909, partly as a response to the "good government" movements and partly from a general reform concern for equity and fairness. Many state and local governments followed suit in succeeding years.[1]

Position classification first came to the national government when Congress passed the Classification Act of 1923, which established the Personnel Classification Board. The act provided for classification of Washington, D.C., offices of the various government agencies. In 1928 the act was extended to field offices. The board was abolished in 1932, and responsibility for classification was transferred to the Civil Service Commission. Further change occurred when the Classification Act of 1949 permitted the commission to delegate responsibility for classifying positions to operating departments and agencies. The commission retained overall supervision and review over classification.

There are two basic approaches to classification—rank-in-job (or whole-job ranking) and rank-in-person. As explained in chapter 4, the rank-in-job approach uses the position and its duties as the basic unit of the organization. The position exists independent of the person who occupies it. Rank is determined by where the position fits in the organizational hierarchy. The rank-in-person system means that the individual person carries a given rank regardless of the duties he or she performs. Rank is determined by credentials, performance, seniority, and the like rather than by what functions the person performs.

Rank-in-Job

To rank positions it is necessary to identify their responsibilities and duties. Three methods are usually used. The employee may be asked to describe his or her responsibilities and duties; the employee may be observed performing them; or the supervisor may be asked to describe the subordinate's job. The three methods are commonly used in combination with one another.

The employee may be asked to describe duties and responsibilities in narrative, open-ended form. Experience with such a technique has demonstrated that it does not produce useful information. Therefore, the most common practice is to develop a specific questionnaire to elicit precise information. In addition to the incumbent's name, title, and department, the employee is usually asked for a brief description of his or her work, a list of specific duties indicating frequency with which they are performed, place and conditions of work, physical difficulty in performance, closeness of supervision by others, supervision of others, and requirements for interacting with other public employees and the public.

Once the employee has completed the questionnaire, the supervisor is usually asked to review it and make additions or corrections to the answers. Often employees neglect to mention things they think of as so mundane or obvious that they do not need to mention them. Supervisors can fill in the gaps.

Occasionally the supervisor is asked to describe a subordinate's position without benefit of the employee's input. Such a description is likely to be inaccurate, as supervisors do not always know every aspect of their subordinate's work or may overlook some activities which are not obvious. Combining input from employees and their supervisors helps to alleviate the problem of inadequate data.

An alternative to the questionnaire method is to observe someone in a position. Obviously such an approach cannot be used for describing a new position; it is most commonly used in reclassifying positions or in writing up descriptions of positions that have never been classified. However, observation of an employee, often called a desk audit, is usually not a good way of discovering what the position is really like. People tend to act differently when they are being watched, a phenomenon known as the Hawthorne effect.[2] Additionally, employees perform different duties at different times, and there is no assurance that an employee will perform all his or her duties in any given day and with typical frequency. One way of controlling for these factors is to also discuss with the employee and supervisor the nature of the job, using elements of the questionnaire technique. Given the problems associated with the desk audit approach, it is not surprising that it is used sparingly.

Once the inventory of the job is completed, the next step is to write up a description of the position based on the duties and responsibilities which are actually performed. For the description to be useful it is imperative that it reflect the job as it really is, not what an employee or supervisor would like it to be.

Positions are grouped into classes involving similar duties and responsibilities and requiring like knowledge, skills, and abilities.[3] Although some subjective judgment must be used, the classifier tries to be as consistent as possible. Individual occupation groups may be divided into more than one class such as Key Punch Operator I, Key Punch Operator II, and so forth.

The position classification plan is developed by ranking classes on the basis of comparisons with one another. Much judgment is involved here, and accuracy is difficult to achieve. Nonetheless, the classification plan establishes the relationship among positions in the organization and is then used to determine compensation levels for each position or class of positions.

POSITION MANAGEMENT

Jay Shafritz conceptualizes the personnel process as one of position management in which work is analyzed relative to the organization's mission and jobs are designed in such a way as to maximize the effectiveness of an agency's human resources.[4] The concept of position management incorporates features of rank-in-job and rank-in-person by recognizing that many factors affect the productivity of employees and organizations.

Job Design. Closely associated with position classification is job design. Job design refers to the way a position is structured, including what duties and responsibilities it involves. Position classification often tends toward very narrowly defined jobs which become extremely boring. Effective job design can insure that such problems do not occur by making the job challenging and giving the employee as much discretion as possible. Recognizing that behavioral concerns, such as needs of employees, motivation, and organizational environment, are as important to job performance as assigned duties, the position management approach attempts to incorporate these concerns in the way work is organized and distributed.

Consider an office with responsibility for monitoring the receipt of sales tax monies. If one position deals only with receiving monies, another with recording receipts, a third with checking records, and a fourth with follow-up investigations, employees are likely to become bored with their repetitive tasks. If, however, the employees are assigned particular accounts with responsibility for all activities associated with them, they are likely to find the jobs interesting and challenging.

Job design has to depend somewhat upon the skills available in the labor market, but training programs can make the agency's response to that market more flexible. Careful job design has the potential of using the available labor supply efficiently and of producing more highly motivated workers by providing them with an interesting combination of duties.

Qualification Requirements.   A direct result of the classification and job design processes is the development of qualification standards. These are the qualities an individual must possess to perform the duties and meet the responsibilities of a given position. Because qualification standards are pertinent to the recruitment process, they will be discussed in connection with that topic. It should be remembered, however, that the disagreements about use of position classification and job design techniques have implications for all the actors in the political system. The people and groups who benefit from the system as it exists (the middle class, professionals, public employee unions) are often protective of the classification system, whereas those who have difficulty gaining access (the poor, minorities, women) recognize the biases and problems of the system and work for adaptation to accommodate their needs. The general public and political leaders are concerned with effective service and often evaluate the classification and job design process in terms of its technical neutrality; thus they are likely to favor it as a means of insuring against political influence and abuse.

FACTOR COMPARISON

The factor comparison/point evaluation system is a quantitative method for classifying positions. It is common in the private sector and is now being used by the Office of Personnel Management on a limited basis, with attempts to extend it throughout the civil service system. Some state and local units are also beginning to employ the method.[5]

The first step in factor comparison is the same as in traditional position classification. Thus it is necessary to inventory the positions and put them in occupational groupings. Factor comparison/point evaluation then is done to establish the relationship of positions within classes. Job factors, also called benchmarks, are decided upon for the jurisdiction, and all positions are evaluated in terms of those factors. Any number of factors can be used, but there are usually five to seven general categories, with each of these then being broken down into more specific factors. The general factors are characteristics all jobs have in common in varying degrees.

The Civil Service Commission uses nine general factors: (1) knowledge required by the job, (2) supervisory controls, (3) guidelines, (4) complexity, (5) scope and effect, (6) personal contacts, (7) purpose of contacts, (8) physical demands, and (9) work environment. Within each of these factors more precise benchmarks are identified. Those for supervisory control, for example, might include the number of people supervised, the type of supervision, and whether subordinates are spot-checked or under constant supervision. Within each position, each benchmark is assigned a point value. The total of the point values for each position is then used to establish the relationship of positions in the various occupational groupings and to determine which class within a given occupation grouping the position belongs. The same procedure can then be used to rank classes of positions relative to one another using the same major job factors.

Factor comparison/point evaluation is favored by many personnel specialists because it makes classification specific and the relationship among positions easily understandable. Additionally, as duties and responsibilities change, it is simple and quick to change the classification by adding or subtracting point values. Many people think that quantitative techniques eliminate subjective judgments from the classification process. In reality the subjective factor is still there but at a different point in the process. Subjective judgment affects the point value assigned each of the benchmarks. A check on the subjective element is provided by having a variety of raters. Thus the Office of Personnel Management has used its experts, experienced managers, and representatives of employee organizations to factor-rank positions and has found relative consistency in point ratings.[6]

In the federal service, responsibility for classification is shared by the Office of Personnel Management and the operating agencies. OPM develops overall classification standards and methodology. It then authorizes agencies to classify positions with the exception that GS 16, 17, and 18 positions are classified by OPM. OPM provides technical assistance to the agencies in their classification functions. In rare cases it audits classifications before they become effective.

Agency personnel should be intimately involved in the classification process, since they are most familiar with the actual work being performed. The major responsibility for classification is normally delegated to the agency in the federal service for that reason. In state and local governments the pattern is varied, but most states have some centralized staff who classify positions in agencies using a merit system.

Although the argument for agency responsibility is strong, an agency's actions also need to be audited. Unless a central agency has the authority to review and adjust classifications, many abuses develop. The most frequent is overclassification. If the employee currently in the position is depended upon for the job description, duties and responsibilities may be exaggerated. In many instances, however, employees underestimate or overlook factors. Of more concern is the supervisor's tendency to inflate the position. Rigid compensation schedules sometimes lock a subordinate into a certain salary level for a long time, and the supervisor finds reclassification of the position the only way to increase the employee's pay. Or the desire of supervisors to make their own positions seem more important may cause them to upgrade the classification of subordinate positions.[7]

Overclassification of positions also results from a tendency of classifiers to look at the most complex duty of the position as the basis for classifying it. Often the frequency of performance of that duty or the proportion of time it takes is given little consideration, and positions are classified more highly than is justifiable.[8] The factor comparison/point evaluation approach reduces the overclassification of positions but does not eliminate it entirely.

Regardless of the reasons for overclassification, the problem requires some form of remedial action. Centralized personnel agencies such as civil service commissions, personnel boards, or personnel directors usually monitor the classification process. In most cases, the central agency may review any position at any time, but most audits are done in response to agency or employee request. However, most personnel systems utilize some form of periodic review.[9] The standard mode of operation is to review each agency's classification plan at regular intervals, but some systems are beginning to review occupation groups across all agencies rather than make plan-by-plan reviews. The idea is that a reviewer's standards of evaluation will be more uniform if applied simultaneously to similar positions across the board. It is true that occupational similarities should be a basis for classification. However, there may be a tendency to exaggerate the importance of an occupation in any particular agency as well. Thus the problem is not easily resolved, but there is no question that constant review is necessary as long as positions are the basis of ranking.

Monitoring position classification places personnel administrators in a difficult spot. The internal political considerations of agency behavior and the concerns of the individual employee make downgrading a classification particularly problematic.[10] Monitors who attempt to lower a classification are seen as indifferent to the welfare of the individual and as a threat to the agency manager's ability to control his or her operation. Moreover, the employee union or association is likely to get involved as well. Given the alignment of opposition to downgrading classifications, it is no surprise that classification auditors tread lightly. It is a wonder they act at all.

A number of approaches have been developed to make the monitoring process more palatable. One is to permit the employee to retain the salary he or she received before the position was downgraded. Another is to audit the classification before it takes effect, but such audits are often cursory and inaccurate. It has also been suggested that reduction in classification be made effective only after the position becomes vacant and that until then the job could be redesigned to make it more consistent with the standing classification. All these alternatives may lessen employee resistance, but they will not necessarily soften agency opposition. Thus some form of discipline of offending agencies seems to be necessary to resolve the problem.[11] The nature of such discipline is not easy to imagine but could involve loss of positions or the like, taking into consideration how such action would affect the capacity of the agency to conduct its affairs.

Position classification has been attacked from other perspectives as well. The most popular charge at present is that the system has outlived its usefulness. Although it provided a way of treating people equitably and eliminating spoils in an era of relatively uncomplicated activities, position classification is not always relevant to current needs. Critics suggest that because activities are so highly specialized, the classification system works against competition or merit in many instances.[12] Thus it fails to serve one of its purposes—the development of effective examinations and recruitment policies—because position descriptions are so narrow that they effectively limit available applicants.

Another criticism derived from the concern with the effects of specialization is that classification is irrelevant to the type of organization the public service will need in the future. According to this view, task-oriented work groups will replace the hierarchical organizations on which position classification is based.[13] The idea here is that since people are being hired for their expertise and ability to develop ideas and new solutions to problems, it is expected that the work situation will become more democratic and project-oriented with people working in a collegial rather than a hierarchical relationship. In such cases, position classification has little meaning.

Rank-in-Person

The second method of classification is the rank-in-person system. It uses the abilities, credentials, and experience of the individual as the basis for making various personnel decisions, particularly the setting of compensation. Personnel decisions in this approach are much more subjective than the rank-in-job system. Moreover, subordinates find it difficult to accept another as "better" when they cannot see the whole picture. Consequently, supervisors experience more anxiety in making their decisions. The problems that develop when one person seems to move up the ranks too quickly may give pause to most personnel administrators considering the use of this system. Because position classification is easier to implement, it is more popular and likely to remain so regardless of its limitations.

A survey of states and counties found that rank-in-person systems are most likely to be used for professional personnel.[14] Professionals are accustomed to being evaluated on the basis of their experience, education, and other credentials and thus fit more easily into such a system. Nonetheless, ranking people still becomes highly political as bases for evaluation are developed.

Short of adoption of the rank-in-person concept, many people suggest some method of combining the two. In reality the rank-in-person approach frequently comes into play. Indeed, it is almost impossible to conceive of a position classification system in which the incumbent does not influence the classification process. Each employee brings different capabilities to the position, and each may expand or contract the scope of duties or responsibilities. A highly capable person who can assume responsibility is likely to perform a wider range of activities than one who looks to others for answers and does only as instructed. The result is that positions are often reclassified because of the incumbent's abilities. Thus the individual does affect rank, even where the position classification system is used.

As society becomes more highly specialized and professionally oriented and as educational quality continues to improve, there will be pressure to recognize individual contribution. In many types of activity the collegial style of organization will become more prevalent. People who spend long periods in relatively independent study are more comfortable in positions of equality with colleagues than in positions based on hierarchical arrangements. In such collegial systems recognition of personal qualifications is more appropriate than the requirements of a given position description. To meet such changes, more attention must be focused on the person. This need is particularly great in higher-level management positions but obtains at all levels.

Current concern for meaningful employment situations and individual liberty will continue to have an impact, but position classification is likely to retain its hold on most public personnel activities. Most bureaucracies are still organized according to the traditional hierarchy, and position classification is a natural complement to that form of organization. Personnel administrators are not likely to exchange such

a convenient instrument for one that makes decisions more difficult and is likely to arouse greater conflict among employees. For
these reasons position classification should be made as effective as
possible.

Position classification plans are particularly prone to obsolescence.
It is difficult to keep the position descriptions and classifications current.
Positions often change drastically without the supervisor or incumbent
even recognizing it. Consequently, there is a need for constant review and
revision, especially in these days of rapidly accelerating change in
knowledge and technology.

Summary

The work of an organization has to be organized if it is to accomplish
its goals. It can be organized according to the specific duties to be performed—the rank-in-job approach. Jobs are arranged in a hierarchy
according to how they relate to one another. The work can also be
organized on the basis of the individual doing the work—rank-in-person.
This concept focuses on the individual employee's qualities. The employee carries the same rank regardless of specific duties performed.

Position management attempts to apply the findings of behavioral
science through job design techniques which aim to make work more
interesting and challenging. The important concern in managing positions is to utilize those approaches which maximize organizational
performance.

NOTES

1. Civil Service Assembly, *Position Classification in the Public Service*
   (Chicago: Civil Service Assembly, 1941, reprinted in 1965 by the Public Personnel Association, successor of the Civil Service Assembly).
   Chapter 2 provides an excellent discussion of historical development.
   This book is the most comprehensive available on the concept of position classification.
2. See chapter 8 in this book for a discussion of the Hawthorne studies.
3. Much of this discussion is based on Donald E. Hoag and Robert J.
   Trudel, *How to Prepare a Sound Pay Plan* (Chicago: International Personnel Management Association, 1976), ch. 2 and app. 1.
4. Jay M. Shafritz, *Public Personnel Management: The Heritage of Civil
   Service Reform* (New York: Praeger, 1975), ch. 4.
5. For a discussion of the U.S. Civil Service Commission's movement
   toward factor ranking, see Lawrence L. Epperson, "The Dynamics of
   Factor Comparison/Point Evaluation," *Public Personnel Management*,
   4 (January/February 1975), 38–48; for state and local jurisdiction
   developments, see Gary Craver, "Survey of Job Evaluation Practices in

State and County Governments," *Public Personnel Management*, 6 (March/April 1977), 121–131.

6. Epperson, "Dynamics of Factor Comparison," p. 38. Philip M. Oliver, "Modernizing a State Job Evaluation and Pay Plan," *Public Personnel Management*, 5 (May/June 1976), 168–173, examines adaptation of the Civil Service System's approach to the state of Indiana.

7. For an excellent discussion of this problem, see Bernard H. Baum, "Getting Caught in the Middle on Classification Decisions," in Robert T. Golembiewski and Michael Cohen, eds., *People in Public Service: A Reader in Public Personnel Administration*, 2nd ed. (Itasca, IL: Peacock, 1976), pp. 107–116; and Frank J. Thompson, "Classification as Politics," in ibid., pp. 515–529, especially pp. 525–527.

8. See Merrill J. Collett, "Re-thinking Position Classification and Management," *Public Personnel Review*, 32 (July 1971), 171–176, at 174.

9. Carl F. Lutz, "Efficient Maintenance of the Classification Plan," *Public Personnel Management*, 2 (July/August 1973), 232–241.

10. For an excellent examination of the issue, see Gilbert A. Schulkind, "Monitoring Position Classification: Practical Problems and Possible Solutions," *Public Personnel Management*, 4 (January/February 1976), 32–37.

11. Schulkind, ibid., elaborates on all these suggestions.

12. For instance, E. S. Savas and Sigmund C. Ginsburg, "The Civil Service: A Meritless System?" *The Public Interest*, 32 (Summer 1973), 79–85, at 73.

13. Ibid.; Jay F. Atwood, "Position Synthesis: A Behavioral Approach to Position Classification," *Public Personnel Review*, 32 (April 1971), 77–81, at 79–81; and Frederick C. Mosher, "The Public Service in the Temporary Society," *Public Administration Review*, 31 (January/February 1971), 47–62, at 57–59.

14. Craver, "Survey of Job Evaluation Practices," p. 123.

SUGGESTED READINGS

Craver, Gary. "Survey of Job Evaluation Practices in State and County Government." *Public Personnel Management*, 6 (March/April 1977), 121–131.

Epperson, Lawrence L. "The Dynamics of Factor Comparison/Point Evaluation." *Public Personnel Management*, 4 (January/February 1975), 38–48.

Jensen, Ollie A. "An Analysis of Confusions and Misconceptions Surrounding Job Analysis, Job Evaluation, Position Classification, Employee Selection, and Content Validity." *Public Personnel Management*, 7 (July/August 1978), 258–271.

Shafritz, Jay M. *Position Classification: A Behavioral Analysis for the Public Service*. New York: Praeger, 1973.

Suskind, Harold, ed. *Job Evaluation and Pay Administration in the Public Sector*. Chicago: International Personnel Management Association, 1977.

U.S. Civil Service Commission. *Job Analysis for Improved Job-related Selection*. Washington, D.C.: Government Printing Office, 1975.

Auditing Classifications

Helen Fixit was looking forward to her new job as a classification review specialist with the Office of Personnel Management. She began the job with review of classifications in Internal Revenue Service district offices. She was pleased to see the general uniformity in classifications, although she did find a few exceptions. One office, however, the Wayne office, was a major exception. It was a relatively small office of fifteen employees. All the employees worked well together, and it was the most productive district office she encountered. The problem, however, was that every position was greatly overclassified.

If you were Helen:

1. What courses of action would be available?
2. What would be potential consequences of each alternative?
3. What would your recommendation be?

Chapter 6

Compensation

Compensation of public employees is a sensitive issue. The pay that public servants receive must be adequate to attract, retain, and motivate competent personnel, and it must also be fair and equitable. Further, the taxpayers must perceive it to be reasonable. To accomplish all these objectives is no easy matter, and compensation systems often come under attack for failing in such an endeavor.

Forms of Compensation

Compensation includes direct pay for the work done as well as other kinds of monetary considerations such as fringe benefits and other perquisites of employment. Sometimes people use the term to mean only wages and salaries, ignoring the other benefits.

WAGES AND SALARIES

Wages and salaries represent the pay rates for each of the job classifications in the classification plan. Pay is determined by the nature of the particular position and by the performance of the incumbent of the position. In government the earnings of employees performing similar duties in other organizations and collective bargaining agreements must also be taken into account.

Generally public pay policy is set by the legislative body. It establishes the criteria to be used in determining compensation and outlines the methods used for setting compensation levels. Occasionally state constitutions or city charters stipulate pay policy and even salaries. Such systems are being changed, however, given the difficulty of adapting to changing economic realities. Where pay is set by charter or constitution, it is usually for elected officials and not the civil service employees.

Once the general compensation policy is set, there are three major methods for actually developing a compensation system. The legislative body may set pay for public employees; the responsibility may be delegated to the executive branch; or collective bargaining may be the mechanism used.

Legislative Determination.   United States legislative bodies have had a tradition of guarding the taxpayer's interest by maintaining control over the level of pay for public employees, with the result that compensation adjustments frequently become political issues. To impress the voters at home, the legislators may use public employees as scapegoats by being parsimonious in giving raises; or in cases in which public employees make up a large bloc of voters (as federal employees do), the tendency is to legislate significant raises just before elections. Both situations lead to inequity for the employee and for the public service as a whole. As a result, public jurisdictions, including the national government, have found a method of placing most responsibility for salary adjustments elsewhere.

Taxpayers have an obvious interest in public compensation in that they do not want tax money squandered. Attitudes of taxpayers towards government employees often suggest that taxpayers do not believe they are getting their money's worth. However, if they understand the plans, they are not likely to be as hostile. In recent years freedom-of-information and open-access ("sunshine") legislation has made public employee salaries matters of public information, enabling taxpayers to know how their money is being spent.

Besides the political problems legislative bodies experience in setting public pay, there are other difficulties. First, for large governmental jurisdictions it is impractical to use the legislative method. The legislative body normally does not have the time or expertise to make detailed pay decisions. Small local governments, however, commonly set compensation by council action. State governments occasionally use such a method for some employees, but changes have been taking place because of the large size of the work force.

Second, legislative bodies normally have trouble treating people equitably when they have the major responsibility for setting pay. This problem is exemplified by the experience with the spoils system through-out much of the history of public personnel management in the United States. Thus people doing the same work may be paid vastly different salaries depending upon such factors as how the legislative body perceives the individual employee or the employee's department. Such a system leads to political intrigue and does not contribute to high morale or productivity among employees. Legislative bodies often like to intervene in pay concerns because it is one way they can deal directly with the cost of government. They can gain political currency by demonstrating to their constituents that they keep a close watch over public employee salaries.

Executive Branch Determination.   Because of these difficulties many legislative bodies have delegated the responsibility for setting pay to the executive branch or to some independent agency. Of course, the legislature retains overall authority to set pay, but it gives someone else the job of doing most of the work. Congress, for example, delegated to the executive branch much of the responsibility for determining what pay should be through the Salary Reform Act of 1962, the Postal Revenue and Federal Salary Act of 1967, and the Federal Pay Comparability Act of 1970. These acts were aimed at improving the salaries of white-collar personnel and making adjustments in congressional, judicial, and executive salaries less politically sensitive. For blue-collar workers pay has been based on prevailing wages in the region since the 1860s, when Congress provided that navy-yard workers receive pay comparable to skilled craftsmen in the private sector. Since then blue-collar employees in other agencies have been accorded the same coverage. Legislation recently proposed by President Carter would also require that white-collar pay scales be adjusted according to the prevailing rates in the region rather than use one national standard for all similar positions.

The Postal Revenue and Federal Salary Act of 1967 established the Commission on Executive, Legislative, and Judicial Salaries, whose task is to make recommendations for quadrennial salary adjustments for judges, members of Congress, cabinet members, and other high-level executive appointees as well as the president. Based on data from comparability studies, the commission's recommendations are presented to the president, who then makes recommendations on adjustments. Unless Congress changes those recommendations within thirty days, they become effective.

White-collar workers in the General Schedule (GS) are covered by the Federal Comparability Act of 1970. The president selects someone to advise him on adjustments in GS salaries—currently the director of the Office of Personnel Management and the director of the Office of Management and Budget (OMB) have that responsibility. They work with the Federal Employees Pay Council and the Advisory Committee on Federal Pay, made up of three nongovernment personnel. The Pay Council is a five-member body selected from federal government employee organizations. After reviewing statistical data on pay for comparable positions in the private sector and advice from the council, the director of the Office of Personnel Management and director of OMB recommend pay changes to the president. The Advisory Committee also makes recommendations to the president. The president's recommendations go into effect on October 1 of the given year. No action is taken by Congress on this annual evaluation and adjustment of white-collar pay unless the president chooses to delay or to change the plan because of concerns for the general welfare. In such a situation either house of Congress has thirty days to object.

Essentially, Congress has given the responsibility for setting pay to the executive branch, although it still retains some control over the process. It makes for more automatic pay increases without Congress having to worry about the political pressures usually associated with public employee compensation questions.

State and local levels have also moved to put the compensation responsibilities more on the executive or managerial staff. Thus in some states, such as Michigan, the responsibility has been delegated to the executive in much the same manner as at the national level. Municipalities are doing the same, normally delegating the responsibility to the city manager or the personnel department. Typically the management staff makes recommendations for changes to the council, which then passes it as an ordinance.

Negotiated Pay.   The third process by which pay is set is collective bargaining. The private sector, of course, has long used collective bargaining for setting compensation. Because public jurisdictions generally prohibit bargaining on compensation as such, the process is not used much in public organizations. However, states such as Alaska, California, and Missouri, as well as many cities, do bargain on wages and salaries, thus providing more bargaining rights than the national government extends to its employees. Even in cases where salaries and wages are not bargainable, employee organizations do affect those issues; they often illegally strike or take other actions to press their demands for pay increases.

OTHER FORMS OF COMPENSATION

Compensation takes forms other than direct cash payment. In many instances, employees receive meals, lodging, or other allowances. These amenities should be considered compensation, although they are often difficult to measure. In the federal government, benefits now represent more than 30 percent of total personnel costs. While fringe benefits tend to be less generous at the state and local levels, they are significant and have been blamed for some of the financial problems of jurisdictions such as New York City. Common to most jurisdictions are paid vacations, insurance programs, holidays, sick pay, and retirement programs paid for by the employing jurisdiction. In special circumstances the employer may pay hazardous duty or hardship allowances to those serving under unusual conditions. In such cases, the public jurisdiction spends a lot of money for employee benefits, and it is considered part of the personnel costs. Overtime costs are also part of the compensation costs for public personnel.

Costs of public personnel retirement systems have been the subject of much discussion in recent years. The idea behind pension plans is to provide for a reasonable standard of living for retired employees. As pension plans have evolved, the employer and employee usually both contribute to the retirement fund. In some cases, as in the state of Massachusetts, the government unit does not invest its share; rather it pays its share to the employee after retirement from tax money. Most plans, however, involve the government putting money into a fund as the employee works. Upon retirement, income from the fund is used to pay the retirement annuity.[1]

The problem being faced by many public jurisdictions is that the amount invested in the fund is not adequate to pay the annuities, and promises of such payment are considered contractual obligations on the part of government jurisdictions. As a result, many jurisdictions are finding that they have to increase taxes to pay their retirement benefits. In some cases, as much as 21 percent of the tax dollar and 70 percent of personnel costs are for retirement benefits.[2] Often the jurisdictions agree to this form of deferred compensation without considering how the expenses will be met at a later date. New York City's financial woes of the mid 1970s have been attributed in part to such shortsightedness.

At the national level much of the criticism has centered on the way in which pensions are adjusted. As the cost of living rises, annuities are increased accordingly. The annuity is automatically increased if the cost of living rises by at least 3 percent for a three-month period and is increased by the highest percent increase plus 1 percent. These increases are often attacked as being inflationary and leading to excessive retirement pay. State and local governments usually adjust benefits along similar lines, although they may not be automatically applied.[3]

"Double dipping" is another aspect of public personnel functions often criticized as costly to the taxpayer. Double dipping refers to employees who retire and draw benefits and then take another job, thus receiving a salary as well as retirement benefits. It is common for military personnel to retire and then take a civilian government position, thus drawing both a pension and salary from the national government. Congress makes noises about changing the system occasionally, but political realities make action difficult. Employees may also retire from one governmental jurisdiction and then take a job with another, thus drawing pension from one and salary from another. One way of dealing with such a situation might be to require that pensions not be drawn until a given age if the person earns money from another job. Policies encouraging early retirement are likely to undergo much scrutiny as a result of these concerns.

Other costs to governments which appear to be rising at alarming rates are workmen's compensation claims in which the employee is paid for work-related illness or injury. Between 1968 and 1973 in California, for example, costs for such compensation jumped 154 percent for local governments.[4] While some reasons for increased costs are legitimate, there is also much concern that programs are not properly monitored and that fraud and abuse are rampant. Such agencies as the United States Postal Service have begun cracking down. They have uncovered instances in which people collected for injuries which supposedly incapacitated them but then were found doing heavy lifting and the like.[5] Similarly, many jurisdictions find that some of their employees take disability retirement shortly before reaching mandatory retirement age. The fact that such jurisdictions pay higher benefits for disability retirement leads some people to suspect that something is wrong. The employees are not always at fault; rather the system often encourages such abuses.[6] Whatever the causes, such problems increase the taxpayer's expense, and efforts to monitor the system more effectively are needed.

Generally the public tends to react negatively to the costs involved in employing public servants. Given the problems outlined here, this attitude is not surprising. Nonetheless, if services are to be provided, employees must be paid adequately. The challenge to government is to insure that both the employee and the taxpayer are given fair consideration. There is little doubt both groups will continue to take much interest in the compensation issue.

Criteria Used in Setting Pay

Several factors affect the decision on what pay to attach to given jobs. The duties and responsibilities of the positions are primary considerations. Comparability pay and collective bargaining also affect the decisions on pay. Overshadowing all these concerns is the amount of revenue the jurisdiction can devote to personnel costs.

THE JOB

Duties and responsibilities are used to establish the place of a position in the position classification plan. Based on the evaluation of the relative importance of the position, it is fitted into a compensation plan. Comparing jobs is a difficult task, although, as noted in chapter 5, more sophisticated, quantitative techniques for differentiating among jobs are constantly being developed. These techniques also assist in placing positions properly in the compensation plan.

COMPARABILITY PAY

The prevailing wage, or comparability pay, principle has become prominent since passage of the Salary Reform Act of 1962 and Federal Pay Comparability Act of 1970. The 1962 act declares that federal white-collar workers will be paid salaries comparable to what private industry pays similar workers. Prior to this time white-collar workers were subject to the beneficence of Congress for salary adjustment. State and local governments have found it necessary to use similar approaches to retain good employees.

To establish comparability it is necessary for the government jurisdiction to survey prevailing rates of pay. The Bureau of Labor Statistics conducts such surveys on a continuing basis, and they are used by most jurisdictions. However, the bureau does not always cover categories which are useful to public employees. As noted in earlier chapters, some public positions have no counterparts in the private sector. Additionally, as David Lewin points out, very small numbers of executive and managerial positions are surveyed in most comparability pay studies.[7] Since a large part of public service is white collar, it is often difficult to make comparisons on the basis of the information collected.

Although comparability in itself is ordinarily recognized as legitimate, there are many difficulties associated with its implementation.[8] For instance, at the national level, whereas each agency has final responsibility for adjusting rates of the blue-collar workers in line with the requirements of the Coordinated Federal Wage System[9] and local wage boards, a national scale is applied to white-collar positions. Because cost-of-living and other factors make the same scale inequitable from one part of the country to another, President Carter's compensation reform proposals call for putting white-collar employees on a pay system related to local variations.[10] As it is now, the national standard causes some federal employees to be ahead of the prevailing wage in low-wage areas and to lag behind in those regions where wages are high. If, however, the labor market is defined on a regional basis, difficulties may arise from the fact that professional and managerial positions usually require talents which call for competition on a national rather than regional scale.[11]

In recent years much criticism has been leveled at the comparability principle. A main concern is that many federal government workers appear to be overpaid in comparison with their counterparts in the private sector. Such is particularly true with blue-collar and lower-level clerical employees. On the other hand, people in high management levels in the federal service tend to make less than they could earn in the private sector.[12] Another complaint has been that only wages and salaries have been used in calculating comparability. Because fringe benefits tend to be better in the federal government than elsewhere, excluding them from the calculation puts federal employees in an advantageous position when total compensation is considered. A key feature of President Carter's pay reform proposal is the recommendation that total compensation comparability be used as the standard for setting pay.

In addition to excluding fringe benefits, the federal comparability program also excludes state and local employees from the survey of wages and salaries. Because these employees usually lag behind both federal and private-sector employees, federal employees once again benefit by not being compared with lower-paid colleagues. Carter's reform proposals would also correct this shortcoming of the system.

Others charge that comparability pay leads to a never-ending upward spiral of wages, with governments raising pay to compete with the private sector. The private sector then adjusts its compensation upward, and the process goes on. In the national government, top-level managers have ceilings placed on their salaries; thus their pay cannot continue to rise indefinitely. The ceilings have political appeal, but they have the potential effect of making high-level positions unattractive to outstanding candidates.

The automatic adjustments associated with comparability compensation have many advantages for public employees and for those making the pay decisions. Public employees are no longer so subject to the mercy of election-year politics as they used to be. Furthermore, Congress can avoid direct responsibility for raises in pay, and workers can receive fair salaries without a great deal of political outcry. Of additional interest to Congress is that recommendations of the Commission on Legislative, Executive, and Judicial Salaries apply to members of Congress as well as to presidents and judges. Congress can avoid the embarrassment of raising its own salary, although some members customarily introduce resolutions eliminating congressional pay increases from the president's recommendations. During the fall of 1979, for example, funding for several agencies was held up while Congress argued over excluding itself from the pay-raise recommendations. With an eye to elections in 1980, many members of Congress were reluctant to vote in favor of pay increases for themselves. They were especially wary given the prevalence of taxpayer revolt sentiment across the country.

Regardless of the problems which exist, it is unlikely that comparability will be eliminated as a method of determining pay levels. The idea that people receive "equal pay for equal work" makes comparability a very attractive concept. The increasing unionization of public employees lends further support to the principle, because unions usually base their demands on some form of comparability with others.

COLLECTIVE BARGAINING

Through collective bargaining, employees themselves can bring pressure to bear on the setting of wages. Union representatives bring demands from their constituents to the negotiating session, and management reacts. Negotiation continues until agreement is reached or both sides conclude that agreement is impossible. If such an impasse occurs, strikes may be called or other methods of resolving disputes may be employed. Although pay is not bargainable at the national level, many state and local jurisdictions do bargain over the issue.

The Compensation Plan

After considering the criteria for deciding the level of pay for given positions, jurisdictions draw up a compensation plan. At the national level the GS ratings make up the compensation plan. The plan is used to maintain equity among positions across government agencies and to determine what tax revenues are going to be needed. Compensation schedules can also inform employees about their prospects regarding pay and provide an orderly method for rewarding performance.

Compensation schedules set out pay which is assigned to jobs grouped into categories on the basis of the criteria outlined above. The schedule may assign one rate to a given grade. Thus city councils in small cities often pay all fire fighters or all street laborers the same wage. Such a system is called a single-rate compensation plan.

More common in larger jurisdictions is a multi-rate pay plan in which people in the same job classification may be paid different wages or salaries. Normally the jurisdiction establishes various ranges of pay with a number of steps in each range. Positions are assigned to particular salary ranges according to the scope of responsibilities, duties, qualification requirements, working conditions, and, of course, to the concept of the prevailing wage. An employee in a given range may move through a number of steps before reaching the top of the range. Part of a typical

Table 6—1   Multi-rate Salary Plan (nonintegrated)

Salary Range	Steps (weekly salary in dollars)				
	1	2	3	4	5
1	100	105	110	115	120
2	125	130	135	140	145
3	150	155	160	165	170

plan stated in weekly salary might be as shown in Table 6–1. This example is known as a nonintegrated pay plan in that there is no overlap from one range to another. An integrated compensation plan would have such overlap and might be as shown in Table 6–2. Thus someone in range 1, step 5, would earn more than an employee in range 2, step 1, 2, or 3. The steps may be stated in hourly, weekly, monthly, or annual salary, depending upon the system and the jurisdiction. Commonly, blue-collar wages are stated in hours or weekly rates, whereas managerial pay is stated in monthly or annual pay.

The assignment of jobs to a given range and step depends on the job description, experience, seniority, and service of the incumbent. Although employees are ordinarily supposed to receive step increases on these bases, frequently no discrimination is made between those who merit increases and those who do not. As a result, seniority usually becomes the sole determining factor. For an employee to change ranges, the job has to be reclassified, or all jobs of the same description must be changed in compensation rate.

Beyond the regular compensation schedule, many jurisdictions have longevity pay plans that permit people with many years of service who have reached the top step in the appropriate range to receive additional increases. Longevity pay plans are based on the belief that employees become more valuable to the organization with time and that good employees will leave unless they have the possibility of earning more. Frequently there will be five-, ten-, or fifteen-year periods of waiting

Table 6—2   Multi-rate Salary Plan (integrated)

Salary Range	Steps (weekly salary in dollars)						
	1	2	3	4	5	6	7
1	100	110	120	130	140	150	160
2	110	120	130	140	150	160	170
3	120	130	140	150	160	170	180

before employees become eligible for the longevity steps. Those who reach the top step in their pay range often feel frustrated in having to wait so long for the longevity step, but many state and local jurisdictions use the approach.

Traditionally, compensation plans have been developed in accordance with the aforementioned criteria. However, as with almost everything else in our society, they have been considered less than sacred in recent years. The legitimacy of putting all employees on a scale with the same number of steps may be questioned, for instance. David Norrgard suggests that it is actually inequitable to treat skilled laborers and professional employees in the same range-step type of scale.[13] His argument is that blue-collar workers are ordinarily expected to be able to use their skills from the time they are hired, whereas professional employees usually are expected to take a while to orient themselves and become valuable to the organization over a period of time. As a result, he argues, skilled labor should start at a relatively high rate of pay and have only a few steps in the pay range, whereas the professional scale should have a wider range with more steps in it. In this manner the skilled employees are rewarded in direct relation to their contribution to the organization, whereas the professional employees receive compensation in accordance with their increasing worth.

Another question about compensation plans regards how effectively they adjust to merit. Most public jurisdictions suggest that employees progress through the steps in their pay ranges on the basis of merit; so pay raises are often called merit increases. All too often, however, performance ratings are not done carefully, and employees move up the steps automatically. In fact, the employees usually expect it, and the superviser seldom disappoints them. As a result, step increases are usually seniority increases.

If compensation plans are to be fair, they must be evaluated and updated constantly. They can be justified if the employees are paid according to their worth and comparably with their counterparts in the private sector. For the plan to incorporate these considerations, effective measures of merit must be established, and supervisors must be trained to evaluate people impartially. It is almost impossible to avoid using seniority as a factor in compensation decisions, but if it is combined with other considerations, such as employee growth, it is legitimate. Giving raises only on the basis of seniority should be avoided, however. It has the potential of perpetuating the employment of those who are not competent and incurs the resentment of those who are.

Compensation plans should be subject to continuous revision as well. Lodging responsibility for study and recommendations regarding compensation adjustment in an independent commission seems to be an effective means of permitting reasonable adjustments that are somewhat free of extraneous political pressures. Legislative bodies have enough to do in establishing general policy without becoming involved in the details of setting pay. As a corollary, there should be adjustments to reflect cost-of-living fluctuations. When the cost of living increases, public employees should not be asked to provide their services at a reduction in real earnings.

All the decisions regarding compensation of public employees must obviously be made within the confines of the financial resources of the jurisdiction. Taxpayer revolts and public disinclination to pay more are putting a strain on budgets. At the same time, public employees are becoming more militant in their demands. The result is likely to be a long period of evaluation and possibly confrontation in our political system.

Summary

Compensating public employees, like other personnel activities, is subject to numerous pressures from those affected by pay decisions. Employees need certain levels of pay to maintain their economic well-being, but they also view pay in an egotistic light. They need to feel they are being treated fairly relative to others. Management and taxpayers also have interests in equitable compensation, since there are limits to the tax resources available. To make the most of those resources, the personnel system needs to construct a compensation system which encourages optimum performance from its employees.

To provide for orderly pay of employees, the public sector has to set criteria for differentiating among positions and develop the tools for measuring the criteria. A plan based on examination of the standards used for differentiating among positions must then be worked out so that compensation decisions can be made on the basis of informed judgment.

NOTES

1. See Tax Foundation, *Employee Pension Systems in State and Local Government* (New York: Tax Foundation, 1976) for explanation of various approaches.
2. An excellent discussion of the problem can be found in William N. Thompson, "Public Pension Plans: The Need for Scrutiny and Control," *Public Personnel Management*, 6, no. 4 (July/August 1977), 203–224.
3. For detailed accounts of various state and local approaches to retirement benefits, see Robert Tilove, *Public Employee Pension Funds* (New York: Columbia University Press, 1976).

4. As reported in "California Study Shows Big Increases in Employee Compensation: Project Underway to Cut Claims Costs," *Intergovernmental Personnel Notes*, November/December, 1977, p. 12.
5. *Newsweek*, February 27, 1978, pp. 64, 69.
6. "California Study Shows Big Increase in Employee Compensation."
7. David Lewin, "The Prevailing Wage Principle and Public Wage Decisions," *Public Personnel Management*, 3, no. 6 (November/December 1974), 473–485.
8. The problems and questions are raised succinctly and with much insight by Elmer B. Staats, "Weighing Comparability in Federal Pay," *Tax Foundation's Tax Review*, 34, no. 1 (January 1973), 1–4.
9. William J. Lange, "The Federal Wage Board System of the United States," *Public Personnel Review*, 32 (October 1971), 238–245, notes some of the problems resulting from lack of common standards in the past.
10. For information on the reform proposal, see Office of Personnel Management, "Background Paper on Federal Employees' Compensation Reform," unpublished paper, June 1979; and Alan K. Campbell, "Federal Employee Compensation: Why We Need Reform Now," *National Journal*, 40 (October 6, 1979), 1666–1667.
11. See Lewin, "The Prevailing Wage Principle," p. 476.
12. Among studies indicating such are Walter Fogel and David Lewin, "Wage Determination in the Public Sector," *Industrial and Labor Relations Review*, 27 (1974), 410–431; and Tax Foundation, *Recent Federal Personnel Cost Trends* (New York: Tax Foundation, 1974).
13. See David L. Norrgard, "The Public Pay Plan: Some New Approaches," *Public Personnel Review*, 32 (April 1971), 91–95.

SUGGESTED READINGS

Council of State Governments. *Fringe Benefits in State Government Employment*. Lexington, KY: Council of State Governments, 1975.

Fredlund, Robert R. "Criteria for Selecting a Wage System." *Public Personnel Management*, 5 (September/October 1976), 323–327.

"Public Employee Pensions in Times of Fiscal Distress." *Harvard Law Review*, 90 (March 1977), 992–1017

Stelluto, George L. "Federal Pay Comparability." *Monthly Labor Review*, 102 (June 1979), 18–28.

Suskind, Harold, ed. *Job Evaluation and Pay Administration in the Public Sector*. Chicago: International Personnel Management Association, 1977.

Thompson, William N. "Public Pension Plans: The Need for Scrutiny and Control." *Public Personnel Management*, 6 (July/August 1977), 203–224.

Warner, Kenneth O., and J. J. Donovan, eds. *Practical Guidelines to Public Pay Administration*. 2 vols. Chicago: Public Personnel Association, 1963 and 1965.

CASE 6.1

Equity in Pay

Harry Forbes, a budget analyst with Mine City, was elated that a friend from college was coming to work in the same capacity as he at Mine City. The budget director had been impressed with Harry's contributions to the organization and had wanted to employ another product of the same college department. Harry's friend, Joy Strider, had taken a year longer to complete her degree because she could not take a full course load. Now, however, she was finished and looking forward to starting her new job.

When Joy got to the city, she stayed with Harry and his wife while finding a place to live. They talked about how nice it was going to be working in the same office in the same jobs. Harry offered to help her adjust to the particular expectations of the budget office, and Joy was pleased to be able to look to him for assistance.

Joy told Harry that she had had three job offers and had decided to take one of the others because the salary was significantly higher. When the Mine City budget director learned that, however, he matched the offer of the other city. The $17,500 salary was very attractive, especially since Mine City was her first choice on all other counts.

Harry became pensive. He was surprised at Joy's salary since he had started at $15,000 and was now making $16,000.

1. What should Harry do?
2. Is there any justification for the difference in pay?
3. What would you have done in Joy's case if you were (a) the budget director, (b) the personnel director?

CASE 6.2

Compensation and Declining Resources

Silver City had been very fortunate in always having more tax money than it required to operate. However, the past five years have been troublesome. The majority industry in town phased out its operations, and many other smaller enterprises suffered. The result has been a dwindling tax base and a decline in population as young people moved away to find opportunity elsewhere.

Because the city had always been financially well off, employees enjoyed relatively good salaries. There was no formal compensation plan, but department heads would recommend pay adjustments and then justify the recommendation to the city council.

Silver City now has to find a way of making decisions on pay increases with recognition that money is very limited. The employees are beginning to get anxious. In the past they did not have to worry much about compensation. Now they are becoming aware of how much each one makes, and conflicts are developing.

The city council hires you as a consultant to deal with its compensation problems. What recommendations would you make and why?

Chapter 7

Employing
Quality Personnel

If the public-sector organization is to operate effectively, it must have the ability to identify, attract, and employ competent personnel. To do so requires a great deal of planning and an understanding of a great many legal restrictions imposed through legislation or judicial decisions. It also requires information concerning the needs of the organization and the labor market.

Human Resource Planning

Human resource planning, often called manpower planning, determines what kinds of employees will be needed in what numbers and how the labor market may be able to supply them. It also develops the skills of employees once they are in the organization. Obviously, a first step is identifying the kinds of skills needed. Such a task may appear relatively straightforward, but sudden shifts in the mood of the public can make planning for long-term needs a difficult matter at best. In California, for example, state and local agencies had for many years been operating under an assumption of continued growth in financial resources. As a result, a wide range of programs and services were developed. Then came the tax revolt and the passage of Proposition 13 in 1978. Resources were suddenly drastically reduced. While many activities, particularly school and municipal programs, were temporarily bailed out by the state government, many other services had to be reduced or eliminated. The immediate effects were not severe, but a real crunch may come when the state no longer has a surplus to distribute among local governments.

The effects of this situation on personnel planning are immense. People in recreation management and library services are hit particularly hard by the reduction in resources. Dealing with them poses many problems for personnel managers. One simple solution, when faced with dwindling financial resources, is to lay off people. Humane considerations, however, lead most managers to look for other solutions. Sometimes natural attrition of workers takes care of the problem, but not in situations where the reduction has to be sudden. Another option is to try to place people in other positions in the agency. The personnel office spends much time in trying to arrange such reassignment. The trouble is that the skills of the recreation worker or the librarian may not be useable in many other units of the jurisdiction. If layoffs are used, personnel managers must determine which employees are to be laid off and what reinstatement rights they have. Employee unions may also limit the flexibility of the organization to accommodate the change. Negotiated agreements may spell out what can or cannot be done. Some unions in California succeeded in preventing staff reductions after Proposition 13 was passed. As the California experience suggests, human resource planning is more complex than it appears.

Because personnel costs are the major expense of public service, it is imperative that government plan well for human resources. Within the public sector per se, human resource planning has not been a high priority. The labor market has been seen as having a ready supply of needed skills in most cases, and, until recently, reductions in the work force have not been very common. The increasing emphasis on cut-back management, however, has made planning in this area extremely important.

The public agency must know not only what skills it needs but also whether they are available in the labor force. If they are not, planning will also entail the development of those skills. If the skills are in high demand, training programs and the like may produce good employees who then move on to another organization. Thus human resource planning must make an effort to develop means for retaining employees as well.

The general employment picture must also be taken into account. Current unemployment rates are relatively high, and many people are looking for jobs. This means that most employers have a surplus of qualified applicants, although some occupational fields may differ. Many economic and labor forecasters are predicting a change in the 1980s and 1990s, when a shortage of labor is predicted.[1] At the same time, the Age Discrimination in Employment Act (ADEA) of 1967, is likely to reduce promotional opportunities as older workers stay on the job.[2] Thus there may be frustrations ahead for employees and personnel planners alike. Cyert argues that mandatory retirement helps personnel planning and that the extension of the retirement age and perhaps eventual elimination of mandatory retirement greatly complicate the human resource planner's task. Mandatory retirement is opposed by others, however, on the grounds that it is inhumane to tell people they are no longer useful. Additionally, the services of many talented people are lost through such policies.

Numerous government policies affect human resource planning by public agencies, but probably the most significant has been the federal government's Comprehensive Employment Training Act (CETA) of 1973, which subsidizes public service employment (PSE). PSE actually developed out of the Economic Opportunity Act of 1964, one of the Johnson administration's War on Poverty programs, which funded various training programs for the unemployed, minorities, and the handicapped.[3] The purpose of PSE/CETA programs has been to help individuals learn marketable skills and to reduce or possibly eliminate the unemployment problem—especially among minorities and the hard-core unemployed. At the end of a transition period the host organization is supposed to absorb the individual into its work force and assume the responsibility for paying the employee. Thus the individual gains, and the organization receives "free" help as an incentive to train the unskilled. Another aspect of the programs is vocational training in educational institutions, but it is not so directly related to the planning for personnel activities.

While CETA began with lofty ideals, it has experienced virtual disaster in much of its efforts. Often the objective of placing people on the payrolls of the host agencies or jurisdictions never materialized. In many cities CETA jobs were used as substitutes for regular payroll employees, and cities became dependent upon these funded positions. CETA officials at the national level have not maintained effective monitoring and have not recognized that curing social problems cannot be accomplished through jobs alone. As a result, human resource planners are left not knowing whether CETA would enforce its ideal guidelines.[4] Their planning efforts are further beset by constant fluctuation in policy and in the amounts of money available for the program.

The ultimate objective of human resources management is the staffing of the organization. Staffing requires procedures for recruiting, examining, selecting, and promoting people so that the work of the agency gets done. The rest of the chapter deals with those issues.

Recruitment

Recruitment is the process whereby an employer seeks qualified applicants for vacant or potentially vacant positions. In times of high unemployment, such as the late 1970s, attracting a large pool of qualified applicants poses little problem. In most occupational categories, employers are flooded with applications and frequently have few or no positions for which the applicants can be considered. Government has not always been blessed with such a wealth of applicants. During the 1950s and early 1960s governments had to actively pursue potential employees. In those and earlier times, public employment had less appeal than the private sector because government salaries were low and benefits few. The situation has since changed, as public-sector salaries have become competitive and fringe benefits have surpassed those of many private-sector firms. Comparability-pay legislation and collective bargaining have been responsible for the dramatic changes in public employee fortunes.

Public opinion polls still indicate that public service employment is considered attractive by a fairly small portion of the general public. In a 1979 Harris poll among young people, for example, only 9 percent said they would choose government employment, while 34 percent would seek employment in private business.[5] The findings represented a worsening of the government's position from the 1960s, when similar polls indicated a 13 percent interest in government employment and only 19 percent interest in the business sector. Despite the polls, however, public employers normally have more applicants than they need and will probably continue to have a surplus so long as unemployment remains relatively high.

The problem posed by recruitment now centers on whether government can attract the most competent and innovative personnel. The Harris poll cited above also found that government employment is of least interest to those people who have a high regard for creativity. Thus those who apply for public service jobs may not be the best candidates. A more serious consideration has developed in response to the Ethics in Government Act of 1978, which bans the postgovernment employment of public servants in areas that were part of their official responsibilities. As a result, government may not be able to attract highly qualified people because they would not be allowed to practice their professions in the private sector after leaving the public service. Intended to eliminate the problem of employees using their government contacts as ways of getting private-sector jobs and to avoid preferential treatment in return for later employment, the act may have been written so strictly that it creates new problems.

Also affecting the recruiting process is antidiscriminatory legislation at all levels of government. The Equal Employment Opportunity Act of 1972 extended the provisions of Title VII of the Civil Rights Act of 1964 to all employers of fifteen or more employees. Other legislation and grants incorporate specific nondiscrimination provisions as well. One intent of the Equal Employment Opportunity Act is to give all groups access to jobs in the public bureaucracy and a voice in the decisions and activities of the government.[6]

As a result of these measures, public employers have found it necessary to take positive affirmative action to recruit members of target groups, especially females, minorities, and the handicapped. While employers have traditionally advertised in management and professional journals, the general media, and internal mechanisms, they must now make good-faith efforts to reach the target groups. The practice of recruiting applicants from among the relatives, friends, and associates of labor union members is also affected by affirmative action requirements because it does little to open up the process. Target groups can be reached by contacting special organizations such as women's groups or minority and handicapped organizations and by advertising in their newsletters and bulletins. They may also be recruited through colleges and universities with large concentrations of the target groups.

Affirmative action has led to the establishment of goals, that is, the number of target-group individuals the agency will attempt to employ, and of timetables, the length of time it will take to accomplish the goals. Goals and timetables have generated a great deal of controversy, as people debate the distinction between goals and quotas. Generally, a quota is not considered legitimate, as it suggests that a specified number of target-group members will be employed regardless of qualifications. Goals are more vague and indicate that the employer will make every attempt to find and hire the suggested number of *qualified* target-group people. Many skeptics suggest that goals are really quotas by another name.[7]

The issue of whether quotas are permissible has been avoided by the courts to a great extent, but two recent Supreme Court decisions have provided some insight. In the *Bakke*[8] case involving a white medical-school applicant's challenge of preferential treatment for minority applicants, the Court ordered his admission, at the same time saying race could be considered in the admission process. How it was to be used was not made clear, but a quota system was not permitted. In *Kaiser Aluminum Co. v. Weber*,[9] the Court did hold that quotas were lawful means for a company to voluntarily correct underrepresentation of target groups in its work force. Public-sector cases may be argued on constitutional issues of equal protection; private corporations are not governed by these constitutional provisions. The *Weber* case was argued pursuant to Title VII of the 1964 Civil Rights Act. Although not specifically settling the issue for the public sector, the *Weber* case certainly provided impetus for affirmative action efforts.

In recruiting employees, the government has to evaluate its needs so that the necessary skills and educational requirements can be identified. The process helps identify a relevant pool of applicants by specifying the qualification requirements for any given position. Determining the appropriate levels of skill, experience, or education and training necessary for successful performance is a difficult task. There is often a tendency to overstate the credentials needed to fill a position. This tendency is being curtailed by affirmative action policies which require that qualifications be relevant to the job being performed.

The desire to have the best available employee often motivates employers to exaggerate requirements. In some cases, professional groups may insist that only people with their skills be permitted to perform certain functions, and thus employers may need to recruit for skills beyond what is really necessary. The conflict between M.D.'s and paramedical people or nurses regarding certain medical services, especially in places where M.D.'s are in short supply, is but one example. The special degree or training required becomes a way of insuring a need for the professional. Certainly professional organizations have as their primary objective the improvement of their professional service, but the line between improvement and self-protection is often unclear, and their efforts sometimes exacerbate the credentialism problem. Employee organization requirements may also lead to imposition of certain skill requirements. Unions, in particular, may require apprenticeship and other standards, thus restricting management's discretion.

Credentialism has also been used as a way of undermining efforts to implement affirmative action. By requiring qualifications which are not commonly found among target-group members, the employer effectively excludes those groups. Academic requirements, for example, may exclude those who have not had access to educational opportunity. Height and weight standards, common for police and firefighters in the past, may discriminate against females or some minority groups. Qualification requirements must be relevant to the job being performed to satisfy equal employment opportunity guidelines. Court cases and Equal Employment Opportunity Commission decisions continue to stress the relevance issue.

In some cases, restructuring of jobs can help employers satisfy the requirements of equal employment opportunity. By separating relatively low-skill tasks from positions which also require a high level of skill, two different types of positions can be created, one of which would be open to relatively nonskilled persons. Caution has to be exercised to insure against creating dead-end positions, however, or new kinds of personnel problems may arise. Equal employment opportunity is also fostered through hiring of people with potential but not acquired skills. They can then be trained to fit the needs of the employer. This approach has been used by many public employers to improve their affirmative action records.

The recruitment process, if successful, results in a number of applicants who meet the minimum standards for a position. The next step is to select which applicant to hire. Selection is based on an assessment of the candidates' qualifications. In many jurisdictions an examination is used to further narrow the field of applicants.

Examinations

Examinations are the mainstays of public-sector selection processes. The exam may be either assembled or unassembled. The unassembled exam normally consists of evaluation of an applicant's background, experience, and references. The information comes from the application and other documentation required in the application process along with follow-ups on recommendations and with former employers. These exams are most useful for managerial and professional positions, but many small jurisdictions without extensive resources use the procedure for most of their positions.

The assembled exam is more commonly employed, particularly at the state and national levels and in large local jurisdictions. Assembled exams are usually written examinations but may also involve oral interviews or problem-solving situations. In some cases, assessment-center procedures are used in which applicants are placed in a highly structured situation and engage in some form of simulation exercise.[10] Assembled exams may also require some type of performance test such as taking shorthand or running a computer program. Combinations of any of these types of exam are used by many jurisdictions. The written exam is commonly used as a preliminary screening device, and then others may be used as appropriate.

The need for assuring that exams test the appropriate skills leads to a concern with their validity. A problem often develops with regard to the relevance of general knowledge or aptitude exams, although they are very common forms of exams. There are three main types of validity —content, criterion, and construct.

Content validity means that an exam measures factors directly related to the duties and responsibilities of the position in question. In other words, does the exam measure skills or abilities which are contained in the position description or actual work itself? Content validity is particularly useful in positions calling for a definable and measurable skill. Typing tests would be easy to verify in terms of content validity for secretarial work.

Criterion validity refers to whether an exam is a good predictor of performance on the job. Thus employees may be selected and then a year later a comparison made between their scores on the entrance exam and on performance evaluations or other performance criteria. This is known as predictive validation. Concurrent validity is another type of criterion validation and involves giving an exam to those already in the positions. If the exam is valid, those who score well on it should be successful employees whose performance is rated high by their supervisors and vice versa.

Construct validity is more difficult to achieve because it applies to tests that measure more elusive qualities, such as ability and flexibility. Construct validation is useful for managerial, decision-making positions where precise job content is difficult to establish.

The validity of examinations has become a major issue in the wake of equal employment opportunity. To insure that the personnel system is not discriminatory, employers need to make sure that their examination procedures are valid. If examinations are found to have adverse impact on minorities and females, they may be invalidated by the courts. Adverse impact means that members of the groups have a lesser chance of being selected than others. In federal guidelines, adverse impact is assumed if the selection rate for a given protected group is less than 80 percent of the rate of the group with the greatest selection success. This selection rate is widely used, but the Supreme Court has demonstrated flexibility, indicating that the overall employment record and the particular context of the employer's actions will be taken into consideration in deciding on cases.[11] While examinations will continue to have to meet the relevance criterion, it does seem that the total personnel system of the employer is being given more consideration.

Selection

Examinations are used by personnel offices to determine which applicants will be certified to the unit doing the hiring. Certification means that the employing unit may choose from among the candidates listed as eligible by the personnel office. In the federal government, and in thirteen states, the rule of three is usually used, meaning that selection can be made from among the top three applicants.[12] Other jurisdictions use some variation in the number certified as eligible.

The purpose of certifying more than one name is to give the manager doing the hiring some flexibility in the process. Because of the fallibility of exams, few people want to rely on them exclusively. Moreover, some people may do well on assembled exams but may not fit into the organization satisfactorily. The manager has the opportunity to make these judgments, while the decision rules also limit that discretion to top candidates.

The rule of three or other such rules may be unrealistic given that the time elapsed between administration of the exam and certification is usually long. Top candidates often have other job offers, and the agency may be forced to go down the list to find one willing to accept the position. Scores are often separated by very small differences, and differentiating among candidates on the basis of fractions of points is questionable, especially in jurisdictions where exams are not regularly validated and updated. One solution is to group examinees by natural breaking points in the scores and then select from those above the relevant breaking point. Such suggestions have not been given much weight in the public sector.

Complicating the rule of three is the fact that veteran's preference has been institutionalized in the public service. Veterans have always been an important force in the political system, and they have been effective in influencing legislation. Members of Congress and state legislatures usually see veteran's preference policies as an easy way to gain political support from an influential group, a way that seemingly costs the taxpayer nothing. Of course, if the process results in less efficient and less effective public service, the costs are there but are not easily seen.

In the federal service, veteran's preference gives a bonus of five points to all veterans and a ten-point bonus to disabled veterans who pass the general competitive exam. In some jurisdictions veterans get absolute preference; that is, they go to the top of the list if they make the minimum passing score. At the national level preference traditionally had been limited to those who served during a period of war or other national emergency, but in 1966 it was extended to all veterans, regardless of time of service. The preference given veterans may interfere with the appointing official's ability to select the best candidate, because frequently the top scorers are pushed aside by veterans who receive the bonus points. In most instances, they probably perform ably, but there is always the chance that more capable people are being denied opportunity. The absolute preference system used at some state and local levels and at the entry level in the federal service for disabled veterans represents the most extreme problem. Sometimes spouses and children of veterans are given the same preferences as the veterans themselves. Thus the inequity of the policy is increased.

In recent years veteran's preference laws have been under strong attack, but change has not been forthcoming. President Carter attempted to reduce the preference extended veterans and to limit the time during which they could claim the preferential treatment. As the reform legislation moved through Congress, however, the well-organized veteran's lobby successfully killed the proposed changes. The legislation did provide additional benefits to veterans with service-connected disabilities of 30 percent or more. Among the new benefits are appointment without competitive examination and retention rights when the work force is reduced.[13] Challenges at the state level have concentrated on suits in the courts, but that avenue now seems effectively blocked. Helen Feeney challenged the Massachusetts absolute preference law, which put veterans who passed the exam ahead of everyone else. She had taken the civil service promotion exams three times while employed for twelve years with the state. Each time veterans were put ahead of her because of the absolute preference system. By a seven-to-two decision, the court upheld the state statute, noting that the law did not discriminate on the basis of sex, even though veterans are almost universally male.[14] Thus any efforts to change such provisions will have to be directed to legislative bodies. The implications for public service go beyond quality; such preferential treatment will remain an obstacle to females and thus to the affirmative action process.

The veteran's preference system is based on humane considerations for the most part, but it has gone beyond its intent of helping those who sacrificed for the security of the country during wartime. Most people do not object to veterans being given special treatment as they return home, but many do question whether veterans should be given a permanent preference over others. A frequently suggested alternative would give veterans preference for a year or two after discharge from the armed services. Even this system, however, ignores the fact that many civilians also sacrifice during wartime. Additionally, it does not necessarily differentiate between those who fight in wars and those who hold noncombat positions in the service. When the fact that women have been particularly victimized by veteran's preference policies is considered, the policies become even less justifiable to many. Establishing a readjustment policy fair to all is difficult.[15]

Selection procedures usually provide for temporary or emergency appointments when competitive selection would be impossible. Ordinarily such appointments expire within a specified period of time. The time is provided so that examinations and other procedures can be prepared. If the position itself is a temporary one, competitive exams may not be required by personnel rules. Abuse in using temporary appointments often occurs. Employers may use the temporary appointment to retain people who might not qualify for a permanent position. Some employers reappoint "temporary" employees on a continuous basis, renewing appointments each time they expire. They thus become permanent employees for all intents and purposes. Most jurisdictions disallow such practices, although the city of Chicago was a notable exception, especially during the administration of Mayor Daley. Another possible abuse of temporary appointments is that employees can be intimidated under threat of not renewing the appointment.

Selection may be made from within the agency, thus excluding from consideration those outside. Frequently examinations open only to those within the organization will be given. Promotion is the common method of filling positions from within and will be discussed below. Selection from within is often favored by employee organizations as a way of assuring employees opportunity for advancement. Management normally favors outside recruitment to bring in new ideas, but collective bargaining has tended to increase the practice of selection from within. The future is likely to see greater influence by employees in the process.

Promotion

Selection and promotion policies are often the products of bureaucratic self-protection. The selection process, whether internal or external, tends to weed out those who may challenge the organization's values and goals.[16] Promotion in particular can serve the agency's self-interest since it can be conferred only on those who have shown the "proper" respect for agency policy and values.[17] Employees welcome internal promotion because it excludes competition from the outside. Thus employees tend to favor seniority as a basis for promotion. Management often goes along because it thereby avoids conflict and because the criterion of seniority is easily measured. Furthermore, because evaluations are not involved, all can understand the basis for the promotion, and questions are not likely to arise as they are in competitive situations.

Selection and promotion policies that serve the interests of the power structure within the organization do not necessarily produce the most effective service to the public. In fact, they may work to the detriment of the public to the extent that like-minded bureaucrats are not apt to raise questions about the agency's activities or bring its problems out in the open. Rather protection of the status quo or accretion of greater power may be the aim. By the time employees work their way up through the ranks, they are usually socialized to agency norms or else eased out of the agency. Selection is most likely to produce innovative and responsive public agencies when the process is open and competitive. In addition, political interests of those outside the system require openness if these groups are to gain representation.

Except for seniority, the criteria for promotion are difficult to establish. Managers frequently promote an employee who has demonstrated good or outstanding performance in a given job. Supervisory responsibilities, however, normally require different kinds of skills from those needed to do the work supervised. Thus employees may be, and often are, promoted to positions they are not qualified to fill. Agencies in the public sector have been attempting to resolve this problem by using assessment centers and other devices to evaluate the managerial potential of employees. Training programs for supervisors have also become common. Or employees may be promoted on a trial basis with return to the former position without prejudice if the promotion does not work out well. Dual track systems that reward people for their technical proficiency without advancing them in the authority hierarchy are yet other ways of dealing with the problem.

Summary

Most experts agree that merit should be the basis for selection, promotion, and other personnel decisions, but frequently those who advocate this position most strongly also suggest that it is impossible to implement. The problem comes in establishing criteria of merit. Supervisors argue that criteria cannot be agreed upon and that their own flexibility will be greatly reduced if they have to create precise standards about merit. The result is that employees often feel insecure about what the criteria are. While some criteria, seniority for example, are objective and easily measured, they do not necessarily relate to quality of performance. The recent changes in federal personnel management that stress performance may bring about some changes in the criteria and methods used for selection and promotion.

NOTES

1. Among them, Richard M. Cyert, "Extending the Retirement Age," *Invited Essay*, Beta Gamma Sigma, March 1979, pp. 1–6. He also notes others' projections.

2. Ibid.
3. See James A. Craft, "New Directions for Public Service Employment in Manpower Programming," *Public Personnel Management*, 5 (January/February 1976), 60–66.
4. Ibid., 60–61. A particularly harsh indictment of CETA on this and other grounds can be found in Juan Cameron, "How CETA Came to Be a Four-letter Word," *Fortune*, April 9, 1979, pp. 112–120.
5. According to a Louis Harris poll, as reported in the *Lubbock Avalanche-Journal*, February 20, 1979.
6. See David H. Rosenbloom, "Forms of Bureaucratic Representation in the Federal Service," *Midwest Review of Public Administration*, September, pp. 159–177; David H. Rosenbloom and Douglas Kinnard, "Bureaucratic Representation and Bureaucrats' Behavior: An Exploratory Analysis," *Midwest Review of Public Administration*, March 1977, pp. 35–42; and Frank J. Thompson, "Minority Groups in Public Bureaucracies: Are Passive and Active Representation Linked?" *Administration and Society*, 8 (August 1976), 201–226.
7. For a cogent discussion of both sides of the argument, see Lucy Sells, ed., *Toward Affirmative Action* (San Francisco: Jossey Bass, 1974). Nathan Glazer, *Affirmative Discrimination: Ethnic Inequality and Public Policy* (New York: Basic Books, 1975) provides the arguments against affirmative action policies.
8. *Bakke* v. *Regents of the University of California*, 438 U.S. 265 (1978).
9. *Kaiser Aluminum Co.* v. *Weber*, 99 S.Ct. 2721 (1979).
10. For an excellent analysis of what assessment centers are and the abuses associated with them, see Joyce D. Ross, "A Current Review of Public-sector Assessment Centers: Cause for Concern," *Public Personnel Management*, 8 (January/February 1979), 41–46.
11. See Dee Ann Hortsman, "New Judicial Standards for Adverse Impact: Their Meaning for Personnel Practices," *Public Personnel Management*, 7 (November/December 1978), 347–353, for an in-depth analysis of the Court's position. This whole issue is devoted to affirmative action concerns.
12. U.S. Civil Service Commission, *State Provisions for Initial Job Appointments* (Washington, D.C.: USCSC, Bureau of Intergovernmental Personnel Programs, August 1978).
13. For a brief description, see U.S. Civil Service Commission, *Introducing the Civil Service Reform Act* (Washington, D.C.: USCSC, November, 1978), p. 10.
14. *Massachusetts* v. *Feeney*, 47 LW 4651 (1979).
15. For a more detailed analysis of the pros and cons, see O. Glenn Stahl, *Public Personnel Administration*, 7th ed. (New York: Harper & Row, 1976), pp. 153–159.
16. See Charles Perrow, *Organizational Analysis: A Sociological View* (Belmont, CA: Brooks/Cole, 1970), pp. 52–54; and Anthony Downs, *Inside Bureaucracy* (Boston: Little, Brown, 1967), pp. 228–231.
17. Robert T. Golembiewski, *Behavior and Organization: O & M and the*

Small Group (Chicago: Rand McNally, 1962), pp. 186–190; and Downs, *Inside Bureaucracy*, deal with this issue.

SUGGESTED READINGS

Bowman, James S., and David L. Norman, Jr. "Attitudes towards the Public Service: A Survey of University Students." *Public Personnel Management*, 4 (March/April 1975), 113–121.

Burack, Elmer H. "Human Resource Planning and Labor Market Information—Need for Change Now." *Public Personnel Management*, 7 (September/October 1978), 279–286.

Craft, James A. "New Directions for Public Service Employment in Manpower Programming." *Public Personnel Management*, 5 (January/February 1976), 60–66.

Donovan, J. J., ed. *Recruitment and Selection in Public Service.* Chicago: International Personnel Management Association, 1968.

Finkle, Arthur L. "Averted Collision: EEA and the Merit System." *State and Local Government Review*, 9 (September 1977), 85–87.

Magnum, Garth L., and David Snedeker. *Manpower Planning for Local Labor Markets.* Salt Lake City: Olympus, 1974.

McGregor, Eugene B., Jr. "Problems of Public Personnel Administration and Manpower: Bridging the Gap." *Public Administration Review*, 32 (November/December 1972), 889–899.

National Manpower Council. *Government and Manpower.* New York: Columbia University Press, 1964.

Sells, Lucy, ed. *Toward Affirmative Action.* San Francisco: Jossey-Bass, 1974.

Wright, Grace H., ed. *Public Sector Employment Selection: A Manual for the Personnel Generalist.* Chicago: International Personnel Management Association, 1974.

CASE 7.1

Hiring a Budget Director

The city of Plains Heaven was in the process of recruiting and hiring a budget director. All the proper procedures for recruiting and receiving applications were followed, and some very good applicants were found. The person coordinating the process for the city manager was the personnel director, Mr. Sharpe. Sharpe reviewed all the candidates and recommended to the manager that Ms. Tightley be offered the job. Tightley is currently employed by the city of Cornfield as their budget director and has had experience in several cities beginning with a very small one and progressing through cities of increasing size.

Letters of recommendation on Tightley were good, and her background experience was perfectly suited to Plains Heaven's needs. The city manager agreed with Sharpe's recommendation and proceeded to set up an interview with the city council, as it had to make the final decision on department heads.

Sharpe then called Tightley and arranged for the interview to take place next week. He indicated that she was his and the manager's choice and that the city council would accept their recommendation but liked to meet candidates before formalizing the decision.

The next day Sharpe had lunch with some visiting personnel directors, including Ms. Sail from Sunset, a city in which Tightley had once worked, and Mr. Cobb, who was from Cornfield. Sharpe mentioned privately to Sail that Plains Heaven was interested in Tightley. Sail commented that she had heard that Tightley had left some of her positions under less than pleasant circumstances. During the general conversation around the lunch table, Cobb mentioned that he had had a big personnel problem in the budget office ever since they hired their current budget director. Also none of the other departments got along with the director. Cobb did not know of Tightley's interest in the job in Plains Heaven.

Imagine you are Mr. Sharpe.

1. What do you do now? What are your alternatives and how would you handle each one?
2. What are the implications of the various alternatives?
3. If you had been Sharpe from the beginning, what would you have done differently?

Naming the Personnel Director

Cool Grove is a city with 1,200 employees and a personnel office with a staff of 25, four of whom are professional-level employees. The personnel director is retiring, and the city manager needs to replace him. The city council has decreed that selection is to be made from within whenever possible. All three assistants to the personnel director have expressed a desire to be considered. The city manager has asked his assistant, Karen Poole, to evaluate the candidates and make a recommendation.

Bill S. Low has been an assistant director for seventeen years, and knows the personnel function through and through. The last two directors have relied heavily upon him for details regarding decisions they have made. Bill never failed to provide thorough information. While Bill is very good at detail, he is not much of an idea person and tends to resist change. He feels comfortable doing things the way they have been done in the past. His relationship with the rest of the office is correct, although few people feel close to him.

Jenny Mar has been an assistant for six years and has been the trouble-shooter for the office. Whenever personnel problems develop in other departments of the city, she is sent in and seems to be able to resolve the difficulty with a minimum of disruption to the department. She is well liked by the other department heads and works well with them. Within the personnel office, however, she is resented by much of the staff because she tends to use her good rapport with other departments and the city manager's office to insulate herself from effective control by the personnel office director, and his policy. She seems to get away with more independence than others in the office.

Carter Hoyle is the third assistant. His major responsibility is policy development. He has been an assistant for four years and has been effective in getting major changes in personnel policy adopted by the council. He is politically astute and works well with members of the council. The city manager appreciates his ability in working with the council but has been concerned a few times at the lack of preparation Hoyle has shown in some of his presentations. Hoyle tends to focus on policy innovation without considering how it will affect day-to-day personnel operations. As a result, policy changes have on occasion disrupted the ongoing activities of the department.

1. Whom should Poole recommend to the city manager?
2. Why would the others be rejected?
3. What factors would weigh most heavily in the decisions?
4. Are there any alternatives?

Chapter 8

Performance of
Public Employees

The ultimate test of the public service and its personnel system is the performance of the employees. In recent years performance and its improvement have been of particular concern to public managers and citizens. Shrinking resources, inflation, and collective bargaining demands all contribute to a need for top performance by public employees. This chapter examines the role of supervisors, motivation techniques, productivity, performance evaluation, discipline, and training and development, all of which are concerned with assuring optimum performance.

The Supervisor

Supervisors are generally considered to be key links in the overall performance of employees. While some evidence exists to suggest that supervision contributes only a small part to productivity of the organization, it is still important in establishing the smooth operation of the organization so that work can be accomplished.[1] Supervisors have a number of tasks related to the performance of those under them. They must see that the job gets done, keep work areas safe, encourage teamwork and cooperation, assist in developing employee skills, and maintain records.[2] Because employees and work situations vary from agency to agency, approaches must vary as well. The supervisors themselves need training in their supervisory tasks if organizations are to avoid the pitfalls of the Peter Principle, which states that "In a hierarchy, every employee tends to rise to his level of incompetence."[3] To perform well as a supervisor calls for many kinds of skills.

The supervisor's job requires dealing with a wide variety of needs and types of employees. Hughes and Flowers, using a theory developed by Clare Graves, suggest six types of personal value systems of employees which are important to the work situation and the role of the supervisor: (1) tribalistic; (2) egocentric; (3) conformist; (4) manipulative; (5) sociocentric; and (6) existential.[4] Each requires a different approach by the supervisor if employees are to do their work well. It should be noted that this is only one of many typologies of employees.[5]

The tribalistic person enjoys work in a situation where the supervisor spells out what to do and how to do it. The tribalistic worker is motivated by a friendly atmosphere and a good job which brings in enough money to pay the bills. The supervisor has to be fairly detailed in dealing with such an employee and must make sure that he or she feels comfortable and wanted.

The egocentric employee is motivated primarily by money and the material goods it buys. This type of employee does not like work, and only works to gain economic rewards. Such a person will not be motivated through involvement in decision making or the like; instead, this type needs rather authoritarian supervision to be kept on track.

The conformist believes in hard work as long as rewards are forthcoming. With such employees the supervisor must be sure policy or rules and regulations are clearly established and followed. These employees are motivated by rewards for a good job and are suspicious of supervisors who do not apply the rules in an impartial manner.

The manipulative employee feels personal responsibility for success. These employees like to have an open organization in which they can engage in a variety of activities and assume responsibility for their own jobs. Thus a supervisor who can provide leadership yet delegate authority is effective in motivating them. These employees need the opportunity to advance and find satisfaction in recognition of their abilities and the status that money and position can bring.

The sociocentric person wants meaningful work that benefits society. These employees need the friendship and sense of accomplishment which comes from working with good colleagues toward a common goal. Supervisors need to befriend such people and to create a congenial work situation. Promoting social good, not making money, is the important motivator.

Finally, employees who fit the existential value system focus on goals but want to do their work in their own way. Thus supervisors who allow maximum freedom in accomplishing the job are especially appreciated. The job must be one which accomplishes goals considered important by the employee for that employee to be motivated. Money motivates these employees to the extent that it purchases freedom.

These different value systems underscore the need for different approaches to subordinates. No two employees are going to be exactly alike, and supervisors must use varied techniques to motivate performance from different people. Some of the resources needed for motivating employees are available to the supervisor, but others are outside his or her scope. Certainly the creation of a friendly, open, and authority-sharing work situation is largely a function of the supervisor. However, the monetary rewards, advancement, and opportunity for controlling the work situation are only partially determined by supervisors. Upper management usually has final say in these matters.

The approach used by the supervisor will depend upon the supervisor's knowledge of the employees and their needs. It will also depend upon the technology available and the authority the supervisor has to make changes. Additionally, employee unions and organizations increasingly affect the ability of management to utilize performance improvement techniques. Thus the role of the labor organization determines, in part, what will be done in the agency.

Approaches to Motivation

Traditional theorists approached issues of motivation and morale on the assumption that the human being is primarily rational and is motivated by economic considerations. Furthermore, traditional theory based its techniques on the belief that people disliked work and had to be induced to work through economic rewards that would permit them to satisfy their material needs. According to this view, the way to attract employees is to offer them good pay, and the way to increase productivity is to raise salaries. In the industrial sector, where productivity was usually more easily measured, emphasis on material incentives led to the use of piece-rate forms of compensation in which the employee could earn more by producing more. Gradually, theorists learned that money would motivate employees to a certain point, but then it lost value as an incentive.[6]

With the recognition that the appeal of monetary incentives had its limits, attention turned to the physical environment of the workers. The Scientific Management school was at the forefront of the trend. Actually the physical environment and monetary incentives were closely linked in that morale would be improved by pleasant surroundings, thus leading to greater production, which in turn would lead to greater pay. Ironically, the concern with surroundings was responsible for the discovery of the importance of the human element in organizational behavior. The well-known Hawthorne studies at Western Electric were directed at finding the optimum physical conditions under which assembly-line workers could produce. Experiments in changing illumination levels and other aspects of the work environment led to the discovery that the psychological factors were more important than physical conditions in determining levels of productivity.[7]

The human relations approach to management, focusing on the social nature of mankind, grew out of the Hawthorne studies. Creating a work situation in which employees feel that management cares about them is supposed to lead to greater productivity. Fostering of interpersonal relationships and group dynamics became the fad of the immediate post–World War II era. Students of organization emphasized the informal groups and norms in organizations and frequently ignored the formal structure.[8] Most studies in the human relations areas concentrated on the way the requirements of the formal structure created unnatural specialization and led to the development of informal groups to overcome the tediousness of work. Little attention was given to the need for reevaluating the work process itself; managers were supposed to become the friends of the worker. Such approaches led to charges that employees were being manipulated by human relations programs, and workers often saw through managers whose interest was still that of increasing productivity—only now it was through psychological rather than monetary means. Although the human relations approach certainly helped to humanize the work situation, it still focused on the individual as a part of the machinery of the organization.

One student of management, Chester I. Barnard, saw very early that the requirements of the individual and the organization had to be matched in some way.[9] Still, his focus was on motivating the worker by effective management techniques and leadership qualities. For some time, leadership traits and styles were seen as the major concerns for gaining cooperation of employees. Particularly important to students of organization was the style of leadership employed. Generally it was concluded that the democratic style is most effective over the long range, authoritarian leadership may be effective over the short range, and laissez-faire leadership seems to be ineffective.[10] Barnard combined research on leadership with the reactions of employees to the leader and was an early advocate of considering the personality of workers and manager as well as the psychological factors involved in worker reactions to commands and directives. It was a short step to the studies concentrating on the relationship between human personality and organizations.

The organizational humanists, typified by Chris Argyris, tried to go beyond the manipulative approaches of human relations and to identify the needs of individuals that affect their roles as members of organizations.[11] In essence, Argyris claimed that organizations require individual activities that conflict with the needs of the mature human personality. Instead of fostering independence and creativity, organizations require submissive and dependent workers who will do as they are told; the incongruity between personality and organization needs becomes greater the lower one is in the hierarchy. Argyris called for adaptation in organizations to promote greater responsibility for their members. In recent years, as will be discusssed shortly, many others have built on his approach, and exciting programs have been introduced to capitalize on the abilities of workers long neglected by traditional approaches.

Although many did not choose to appreciate it, Argyris was not saying that all people reacted in the same way. All he was arguing was that the needs of the mature personality were inconsistent with the needs of organizations modeled on traditional principles. Robert Presthus, among others, had pointed out that personalities differed in their adjustments to the needs of complex organizations.[12] Once the ground was broken, however, a whole new approach to maximizing the potential of individuals was unleashed. People were no longer viewed as disliking work per se; rather the way work was organized was the culprit. People could be motivated to produce if they were permitted to develop themselves in the work situation. Behavioral scientists have been busy ever since in devising new approaches to human self-actualization. Some of their approaches are summarized in the next section of this chapter.

The work of Presthus and others has led to the recognition that different types of personalities are found in different levels of organizations. Those at the highest levels of management are usually less concerned with material rewards and the need to feel wanted by the organization than they are with recognition, prestige, credentials, or accumulation of the symbols of success. The relationship of their success inside the organization to success or recognition in society may be much more of a driving force than for those in the middle and lower levels of bureaucracy.[13]

The behavioral approach stresses that human beings enjoy and need work as much as recreation; therefore, ways should be found to permit employees to use their capacities to their fullest in the work situation.[14] The key to effective organization became what Douglas McGregor called the Theory Y form of organization, stressing people's independence, creative ability, intelligence, and willingness to perform what they view as useful tasks. The realization that people do not hate work, are capable of making intelligent judgments, and are motivated to achieve objectives that they have a part in determining has led to advocacy of democratic, or participative, administration by many.[15]

Behavioral scientists base their analysis on the belief that individuals have a hierarchy of needs—physiological, safety, social, ego, and self-actualization, in that order.[16] As each need is met, it ceases to be a motivator, and the next higher one takes its place. Frederick Herzberg suggested that most organizations do not actually build on these needs as motivators; rather they tend to focus on "hygiene" factors—physical surroundings, status, and the like—which all members of an organization expect anyway.[17] Basing his analysis on the hierarchy of human needs, Herzberg advocated that organizations use positive growth factors as motivators because motivation comes only from within the individual. People are motivated by their own achievement, recognition, increased responsibility, and the like.[18]

Motivating employees through behavioral science approaches has involved a variety of techniques, some specifically motivational in intent and others more generally concerned with humanizing the organization. Perhaps the most general and most widely accepted behavioral prescription is that employees will be more committed and more productive if they have the opportunity to participate in the organization's decisions, particularly those involving the work situation itself. The call for democracy in the work situation is common but not easily implemented, particularly in the public sphere.

The meaning of employee participation in the decision-making process is often vague. The human relations approach frequently suggested participative processes, but most seemed to be cosmetic attempts to convince employees that they were important. Managers often resist real employee participation because they are not trained in behavioral techniques and are unsure about their proper roles in the new approaches. As a result, the programs often become manipulative, and employees become confused and alienated.[19] Certainly employee participation in job decisions is appropriate in many instances, particularly problem-solving situations relevant to a task-oriented work group. Many argue that it is inappropriate to assembly-line work, but some experiments have produced impressive evidence to support participation by these workers as well.[20]

Employee participation is also used in management-by-objectives (MBO) techniques. MBO involves agreement on objectives by the members of the organization. Decision making may be on the unit level or, in smaller organizations, may encompass the organization as a whole. Studies by Robert Ford and others indicate that employees set higher goals for themselves than management would set, but more importantly, the employees have a stake in meeting the goals and are motivated to prove themselves.[21] MBO has been used chiefly in the private sector, but it has had some application in public agencies. However, there are constraints on its use in the public sector, such as the unpredictability of annual budget allocations, the high rate of turnover of top political executives, and changing priorities. Moreover, political realities may bring about new program goals and emphases.[22] Regardless of the problems, there is a possibility of the limited use of MBO in the public sector.

Job enrichment is another motivational technique suggested by many behavioral scientists. Job boredom seems to be a major problem in all sectors and levels of society but particularly for lower-level employees.[23] By making the job interesting, management can obtain greater commitment and motivation from the employee. Employees who have control over and responsibility for their work, who see the results of their efforts, and who have diversified duties are likely to identify with the job and take pride in doing it well. They are also likely to be more productive than those who perform a highly specialized task with no clear idea about the end product.[24] Although most behavioral students of public administration recognize the advantages of job enrichment, they are usually imprecise in outlining methods of implementing it. Managers often find the principle difficult to apply, but as with participatory administration, the reasons for resistance are usually lack of understanding of the technique and unfounded fears of loss of status or role. As the Ford study indicates, those who have used the approach usually like it. Combined with an assessment of the individual's needs and capabilities, job enrichment offers a great deal of promise for motivating employees. In addition, it opens up communication, improves understanding, and increases respect among employees and supervisors.[25] Obviously, there are limits to how far job enrichment can go, but that fact should not be used to rationalize doing nothing.

On the fringes of motivation theory are a number of experimental movements known as T-group, sensitivity training, or encounter sessions. These are all part of a larger movement known variously as organization development, organization change, or organization renewal. The focus in much of the literature is on adapting the organization to the changing environment and, particularly relevant to our considerations, to the changing needs of people within the organization.[26] The idea of organization development is to break down barriers to effective communication. The hope is that through self-awareness and awareness of others and organization needs, all the individuals in the organization will become more trusting of one another, more committed to organization goals, and more self-directed and responsible in attempting to solve organizational problems.[27] In general, the approach is based on the assumption that people will change their attitudes and behavior for the better if there is an open problem-solving atmosphere.

Such a program endeavors to help employees realize their full capacities. Many agencies use organization development techniques, but there are often limitations to its use in the public sector. Of primary concern are the political forces under which public agencies operate. Explaining the value of encounter sessions to a legislator who gets a complaint from a disgruntled employee is not easy. Justifying such use of tax money to a legislative body or the general public is not relished by most public administrators; therefore they are not always eager to adopt such programs.[28] Because of the "bad image" of many early organization development programs, there is greater emphasis now on training seminars and in-house training programs in which people are asked to evaluate their organizations in open sessions where personality factors are minimized. Still there are problems, particularly where the programs consist of short training sessions without follow-up programs to continue the process.

Behavior modification, another approach which is enjoying some attention in the public sector, attempts to motivate employees through the use of rewards and punishments.[29] These may be "positive reinforcers, negative reinforcers, and/or punishers."[30] In fact, the approach uses many of the traditional modes of getting people to perform better. Thus money, bonuses, promotion, and the like are promised for improved productivity. Similarly, docking pay or assigning the employee to less desirable duties are used to penalize poor performance. Feedback to the employee on performance is an essential element of such a system. To use behavior modification techniques, the organization must develop specific performance measures and then develop clear strategies to stimulate desired behavior.

One federal agency experiment with behavior modification resulted in a dramatic 92 percent and 78 percent performance improvement in different units.[31] While improvement in performance is likely to be applauded, there are also many problems with the behavior modification approach. Many people associate behavior modification with operant conditioning, symbolized by the Skinner Box. Such views lead to automatic opposition. Unions and employee organizations are likely to object that the approach is manipulative. Such objections carry much weight in our society, where openness and honesty are supposed to characterize people's dealings with one another. People do not like to feel that they are being managed deviously. It should be pointed out that many of the techniques of behavior modification are well-accepted practices in dealing with employees. Attaching the label "behavior modification" to them and fitting them into a structured system may arouse opposition.

Behavioral approaches to motivating employees have produced a number of techniques. Unfortunately, many achieve the status of fads, and the experiments have often led to failure and the heightening of problems. There has been no paucity of analysis of the reasons for failure. The most common complaint of critics is that managers are not trained in behavioral techniques and think that they can implement various organization development aproaches after attending a short training session. More often than not, the results are disastrous for employees as well as for supervisors.[32] Even though the supervisors may believe in the program, their attitudes about employees may be the same as they always were, and employees do not know how to react to being told to be open and frank while the supervisors ignore them or penalize them for it. Additionally, Harry Levinson believes that the sharing of power, implicit in organization development approaches, runs counter to the manager's role expectations and personality.[33]

Another common criticism of the behavioral approaches is that they are viewed as panaceas for all organization problems and that particular techniques are adopted because of their faddishness rather than because they fit the problems of the organization.[34] To avoid such inappropriate uses of behavioral techniques, it is necessary to assess the problems of the organization, the personnel, and management. Only then can an appropriate technique be determined. Were agencies to follow such procedures, argue some critics, behavioral approaches would be effective.[35]

There are no easy answers to the questions of how to motivate employees. Basically, however, managers should recognize that they are dealing with people who have diverse needs, who consider work a natural part of their lives, who react differently to the same situation, and who can be motivated only from within. External motivation may produce some short-term improvements but over the long run will probably create negative reactions. The more effective approach is to provide an environment in which people can develop themselves to their fullest capacities.[36] Approaches to motivating employees must consider the organization and the level of the individual within it. What motivates the top-level manager is not likely to motivate the worker whose job calls for little thought and much repetitive action. Similarly, the value systems discussed earlier affect the receptivity of individual workers to various motivational techniques.

Productivity Improvement

A major aspect of performance improvement is productivity improvement. Concern with productivity and productivity improvements has almost become a fad, although the specific elements of given programs have long been around in different form.[37] Productivity refers to the "efficiency with which resources are consumed in the effective delivery of service."[38] Thus productivity concerns both the quality and quantity of output produced for any given input of resources, but it also concerns the effectiveness of the output. Whether the service or product is needed or of value has become increasingly important, especially in the public sector. Public managers are under ever-mounting pressures to increase the productivity of their organizations as taxpayers demand increased services and decreased taxes. At the same time, employee collective-bargaining organizations are skeptical of most productivity improvement efforts.

As with performance generally, productivity is a function of the technology utilized, the work force, and management. Each of these elements of the public service can contribute to or obstruct productivity. Perhaps the simplest method of improving productivity is to improve the technology available to the work force. For example, containerized trash collection or computerized record keeping can increase the amount or quality of work, while maintaining or even decreasing the resources required. There are, however, limits to the amount of improvement technology can produce.

Improved management can also contribute to productivity increases, as was the case in the state of Washington.[39] The state created an advisory council made up of representatives of business, state government, state employees, higher education, and citizens' groups. The council identified areas in which problems existed and improvements could be made. Acting on its findings, the council took steps to establish clear lines of authority and responsibility; to improve communication among employees, management, and agencies; to strengthen employee suggestion programs; and to improve the collective bargaining process. Along with technological improvements, these changes enabled the state to increase the productivity of its public service agencies.

Employees, and especially employee unions, are often suspicious of productivity improvement programs that are unilaterally imposed by management. In fact, such programs are often viewed as a throwback to the piece-rate days preceding unionization in the private sector, or as an effort to either reduce service or increase the workload of employees.[40] In the face of employee opposition, the programs are almost certainly doomed to failure, as the employees are the ones who will have to increase effort if success is to be achieved.

Employee participation appears to be a major factor in the success of improvement plans.[41] In addition, employees seem to respond best to those programs where their job security and job satisfaction are protected.[42] As was noted in the discussion of motivation, employees are most likely to be committed to programs in which they have had a say.

Commitment is usually translated into increased effort and thus productivity. To address the issue of job security and satisfaction, employers can institute retraining or reassignment programs or reduce employment only through attrition.

Motivation, participative management, job redesign and enrichment, and behavioral techniques such as organization development and MBO, all discussed earlier, are methods for improving productivity. However, most productivity improvement efforts spell out specific goals and the particular actions which will be utilized to achieve them. Management often institutes new work rules which are supposed to improve productivity. In Harrisburg, Pennsylvania, and Kansas City, Missouri, such work rules detailing how certain activities should be done and how long they should take led to resistance by employees, and the programs failed.[43] As was suggested above, employees resent unilateral attempts at increasing their productivity, and in these cases they either ignored or tried to sabotage the efforts.

A way in which employees participate in productivity improvement programs is through collective bargaining in what is known as productivity bargaining. This approach is becoming increasingly common due to mounting pressure from taxpayers for greater productivity from public employees.[44] Productivity bargaining is one way in which management obtains a promise for increased productivity in return for concessions (especially pay increases) by the local government.[45] Management hopes thereby to hedge against the inflationary effects of wage increases and continue providing services in a time of dwindling financial resources.[46]

Productivity bargaining, as defined by Chester A. Newland, is "the negotiation and implementation of formal collective bargaining agreements which stipulate changes in work rules and practices with the objective of achieving increased productivity and reciprocal worker gains."[47] As the process is implemented, employees change to more efficient work practices in return for a share of the organization's savings produced by the increased productivity. In theory, everyone benefits: management eliminates inefficiency, employees receive pay increases or other benefits, and the public enjoys improved quality and quantity of public services. The promises seem too good to be true. Actual experience tends to uncover problem areas.

Discussion of difficulties in productivity bargaining is plentiful in the literature on the public sector. Some of the problems are generic to productivity standards, while others apply directly to the bargaining process. The major criticism and issues raised revolve around problems in measuring productivity, management's giving up its prerogatives to manage, and the idea that the public is being asked to pay more to get employees to perform the jobs they are hired to do in the first place. The discussion above has already dealt with the management prerogative issue, so the following examines the other concerns.

Productivity measurements pose a problem in the public sector. A common theme in the literature on productivity is that public services do not lend themselves to quantification. Because government is service oriented and not product oriented, measures of productivity tend to appraise activities or outputs rather than results or outcomes.[48] Supporters of productivity improvement and productivity bargaining, however, note that measures for many programs are readily available and the problems in less tangible areas can be overcome if work is done on developing indicators of productivity.[49] Lineberry and Welch, for example, have developed numerous indicators for public services which can be used as a starting point for measuring productivity.[50] It should be apparent that various public services can be quantified in part but that some aspects of the services are less susceptible to measurement.

In evaluating a fire department and its productivity, for example, some of the factors which might be measured would be:

The number of fire department employees per capita.
The per capita expense for the department.
The number of fire calls.
The number of fires extinguished.
The value of property damaged by fires.
The fire insurance rates in the city.
The fire prevention program; its audience, presentations, and demonstrations on fire safety.
The response time of the department to fire calls.
The number of cases solved when fires of suspicious origins occurred.
The reaction of citizens to the service provided.

Some of these items are activities and do not necessarily tell much about the qualitative aspects of the service. The items can be used for making some qualitative judgments, though, by making comparisons with similar cities. The point is that there are some indicators now available, and with continued effort to develop more sophisticated measures, productivity measurement and improvement can be accomplished. The difficulties of measuring service functions should not be ignored, but they should not stand in the way of efforts to improve measurement.

Care is necessary to insure that quantitative factors which ignore quality do not become the only considerations in measuring productivity. The potential exists that productivity bargaining can affect the priorities of employees in performing their duties and possibly work to

the disadvantage of general service to the public. The following example illustrates some of the possible dysfunctional effects of overemphasizing specific measurable activities.

Productivity bargaining normally produces agreements specifying that employees will receive certain benefits (pay increases, reduction in working hours, more vacation, etc.) for a given demonstrated increase in productivity. Because productivity measures are not yet very sophisticated, there is a tendency to use certain fairly easily measured activities as indicators of productivity. Paul D. Staudohar examined a productivity bargaining agreement that the city of Orange, California, worked out with its unionized police force.[51] The city and union agreed to use four easily quantifiable aspects of police activity for indicators of productivity. The police were to earn pay increases based on reductions in the incidence of rape, burglary, robbery, and auto theft. Subsequently the incidence of burglary and rape decreased, while robbery and auto theft actually increased. The decrease in burglary and rape was large enough, however, to offset the other, and the police received the maximum pay increase provided for by the agreement.

While the results reported by Staudohar provided encouragement in one way—reduction in certain crime—there are also potentially dysfunctional aspects.[52] One difficulty is that police officers not only fight crime but also provide numerous services to the public. Even within the crime-fighting function, there are many crimes other than the four singled out in the Orange experiment. Nonetheless, the agreement rewarded officers only for improved performance in those areas.

It seems only natural that overall performance would be sacrificed to produce a good record on the items cited in the bargaining agreement. As Peter Blau has demonstrated in examining performance evaluation, using particular parts of employee performance as criteria for increased pay or promotion leads employees to focus on developing a good record on those criteria which count in their favor.[53] Since productivity measures are simply alternative means for measuring performance, the same effects can be expected with productivity bargaining.

Regardless of the service provided, efforts should be made to minimize such distortion in performance. One approach is to include provisions in agreements to insure that the overall level of productivity does not decrease as specific indicators show improvement. If overall quality of service declines, it hardly seems appropriate to reward employees for improvement in certain aspects of their performance. Such provisions will depend, of course, upon management's ability to measure all aspects of productivity.

A new approach, "total performance measurement," is now being utilized to cope with some of the pitfalls of productivity improvement programs.[54] This approach uses productivity data along with other information to evaluate overall performance and improve productivity. Employees, clientele, and citizens are surveyed to determine whether the organization is perceived as being productive and whether its service is effective and useful. Data on productivity is also evaluated. Feedback to employees and managers is a central focus of total performance measurement. Such feedback permits everyone to understand what needs change and encourages participation in making changes. This approach differs from others primarily in terms of the systematic way in which data are collected and utilized. Otherwise, it uses techniques already contained in other approaches.

Performance Evaluation

Evaluating employee performance is an essential part of the personnel process and is particularly important in this period of concern with productivity. Performance evaluations serve several purposes in the organization. They aid in identifying problem areas and in improving the ability of employees to perform their duties. They also help employees understand how they relate to the organization as a whole and where they stand in the perception of management. Such knowledge normally creates a situation in which employees can be relatively free from anxiety. In addition, performance evaluations assist personnel officers in making decisions about training needs, promotion, discipline, and pay increases, to mention just a few.

While many uses are made of evaluation data, there are also many problems associated with the process. Performance evaluation should have as its primary function the maintaining, correcting, or improving of performance; thus the emphasis should be on the positive uses. Unfortunately, most performance rating systems in the public service fall far short of their aim. More often than not, they are haphazard and lead to deterioration in the employee-supervisor relationship.[55]

The responsibility for performance evaluation rests with the supervisor or manager, but recent trends have stressed the need for employee participation in the process. Today the tendency is to have the employee either rate himself or at least discuss the evaluation with the supervisor. In many instances, supervisor and employee determine what the performance criteria should be, and evaluation is made relative to attainment of the given objectives.

The greatest problem is that supervisors frequently keep subordinates in the dark about what is expected of them and what the criteria for evaluation are. For employees to feel secure, they need to know what

standards they are expected to meet. Thus a key in the evaluation process is setting up clear, identifiable standards against which employees can measure their performance. Because of ignorance of evaluation techniques and because of difficulties in being honest with employees about their performance, some supervisors prefer to evaluate in terms of vague criteria, thus leaving themselves more flexibility in dealing with employees. Such an approach can get the supervisor into difficulty as there is little specific data on which to base personnel decisions. With increasing pressures from employee organizations, the law, and the courts to have performance evaluation and other personnel functions based on valid job-related criteria, supervisors need to regularize the process and provide protection for the organization and employee both.[56]

The trend in recent years has been toward the use of formal evaluation procedures. Previously employees were left to feel that performance was adequate if no negative personnel actions were taken against them. There was always the possibility that employees would be told after a number of years, however, that their performance was unsatisfactory. Thus the supervisor could easily be capricious in releasing employees. However, increasing concerns with individual rights and dignity in our society have helped to change such unfair practices, although there are still many problems and much resistance to the establishment of legitimate performance criteria. In a survey of sixty large cities, 20 percent of the fifty respondents indicated that no formal performance evaluations were used, and the types of systems used by many of the others suggest that performance is not the central focus of much of the evaluation process.[57] If the record of major cities is such, it is unlikely that many smaller cities have very highly developed systems.

Performance ratings can take various forms, such as measurement of output or the use of examinations. More common are numerical ratings on various characteristics such as punctuality, attitude, and ability to work with others. Additionally, narrative or essay evaluations are fairly common. Each of these approaches has numerous variations, and each has negative and positive features. For example, output measurement may be effective in evaluating performance where an identifiable product is made, but it is inappropriate in situations where service or policy is the output. Examinations are useful in measuring potential or capacity, but they may be ineffectual in judging actual performance.

The rating of employees on various qualities and narrative evaluations can be effective if they are carefully constructed and properly used.[58] The check-off, or objective evaluation, assigns employees a score on such qualities as promptness, courtesy, writing ability, and initiative. The narrative approach permits the supervisors to describe the good and bad points of the subordinates. In some narrative evaluations, specific items must be discussed. These evaluations are not very popular because they

are difficult to compare, and there is little control over what qualities are evaluated. Rating people on specific qualities is easier and provides for greater comparability, but there are problems here as well. Frequently the qualities that are appraised relate more to personal traits than to relevant performance factors. While personality factors may be very important in some jobs, such is not the case for all or even most positions.

Several methods of evaluation incorporate elements of both the rating and the narrative approaches. The critical-incident type of evaluation has the supervisor record specific behaviors of the employee which are indicative of good or bad performance. This method highlights performance-related activities and thus conforms to one of the major criteria necessary for effective evaluation. However, it tends to focus on behavior extremes and, as such, may ignore the overall, less visible aspects of performance which might tell more about the employee's role in the organization. The employee who does well consistently but seldom does anything spectacular may be at a disadvantage.

The narrative approach has many variations as well. It may require the supervisor to write an overall evaluation of the employee's performance, or it may require explanation of the employee's most significant contribution to the organization and most serious weakness. Or it may call for a description of specific factors such as quality of work, ability to get along with others, innovation, potential for growth, and the like. As noted above, these approaches usually do not lend themselves well to comparing employees, but they do provide flexibility and an opportunity for supervisors to stress individual contributions and provide a broader perspective on performance. A drawback is that supervisors vary in their ability to identify strengths and weaknesses and then write about them. The employee then benefits or suffers according to the skills of the supervisor.

Forced-choice evaluation is another form which is used. In this method the supervisor may be required to choose a certain percentage of employees who are deserving of recognition for meritorious performance. Such an approach is often used in merit pay decisions where perhaps one-half, one-third, or one-fourth of a supervisor's subordinates may be singled out for merit pay increases. It usually forces the supervisor to develop specific criteria by which the decisions are made. It is not, however, an easy process to administer and can create morale problems.

In recent years, group and peer appraisal have been used in many organizations. Peer appraisal may use any of the forms suggested above but frequently requires numerical rating on specific characteristics. It often also entails a simple listing of those individuals who should be considered good and poor workers. This method can provide illuminat-

ing perspectives on employee performance. However, it may produce inflated evaluations.

In the self-appraisal system employees examine their own performance relative to specified criteria. In most instances, they then discuss their evaluation with the supervisor. Employees tend to judge themselves relatively harshly and do not always see themselves in relation to the total organization; thus the evaluations can be distorted. Nonetheless, used in combination with other techniques, they can provide useful examination of employee activities.

Performance evaluations have the potential of distorting the importance of particular activities in the organization. For instance, if output is the major criterion on which employees are evaluated, it is not surprising that employers neglect other concerns, such as coordination of effort or quality of output. The likelihood is that employees will focus on the activities that gain them favorable evaluations.[59] Thus agencies must be careful not to emphasize some criteria at the expense of others.

Often supervisors are ill-trained in effective evaluation techniques and find it difficult to confront employees. As a result, employees may all be rated approximately the same or all very highly, especially when ratings are important to other personnel decisions. In addition, there are usually no effective checks on the prejudices of the supervisor.

Perhaps the greatest problem with performance ratings is that they tend to be done hurriedly and on a periodic basis. When the deadline for evaluations approaches, the supervisor does them quickly—often remembering only the exceptional or most recent occurrences. The result is a distorted view of the employee. The process should be an ongoing one in which the supervisor discusses the good and bad aspects of performance as they occur so that the employee can make adjustments as needed. Waiting until the end of the year, or until the end of five years, to tell an employee that he or she has not lived up to expectations is grossly unfair.

Perhaps there is no part of personnel administration that produces as much anxiety as performance evaluation.[60] The major cause of anxiety is simply a poor evaluation process. Subordinates usually react negatively to evaluations because they do not understand them and because the supervisor is not frank in explaining the criteria on which the assessment is based. Most important is a relationship of trust between supervisor and subordinate. Where the supervisor constantly tries to be secretive, the subordinates become very insecure. Employees and management should work together to see to it that all understand the evaluation system, and the supervisor should communicate with subordinates on a continuing basis regarding performance, counseling and encouraging them to improve when necessary. Effort should be made to insure that automatic disciplinary action does not follow each evaluation. At the same time, records on the employee's performance should be kept. If an employee does not correct inadequate performance over a reasonable period of time, disciplinary action is in order. Similarly, when the employee feels unfairly judged, a review process should be available. Most importantly, evaluations should have as their goal the improvement of performance, and punishment should be a last resort.

At the national government level, performance of public employees has long been an issue, and a major aim of President Carter's reform efforts has been to improve that performance. Before 1978 all government agencies were required to use a standard rating form, but the Civil Service Reform Act permitted agencies to begin developing their own approaches. The process began in January 1979 and was to be fully operational by 1981. The Office of Personnel Management (OPM) intends the new evaluation systems to be used for personnel decisions regarding training, rewards, assignments, promotions, and disciplinary actions. The guidelines of OPM require that employees participate in development of the systems, that performance standards be decided upon and made known to employees, that employees be assisted in improvement of deficient performance, and that necessary action be taken if they do not take advantage of the opportunity to improve performance. As the agencies develop their systems, it is likely that variety similar to that at the state and local levels will be apparent.

In recent years, performance evaluations have served to protect employees from capricious action by superiors. A record of periodic evaluations makes it difficult for the supervisor to suddenly dismiss an employee who is out of favor. In the days when employees were not regularly evaluated, they could be told after a number of years of service that they did not meet the (often unspecified) standards of the agency. Now employees should know whether their performance is acceptable and, if not, why not. With an appeals process the employee has more chance of fairness in personnel decisions. Of course, supervisors may argue that employees are difficult to get rid of; but if they evaluate their subordinates honestly, they can weed out those who do not do a good job and refuse to improve. The key is in having competent and well-trained supervisors in the first place.

Discipline

Disciplining employees is a task most supervisors would rather avoid. If the organization has effective personnel policies in general, discipline should be needed only on rare occasions. Because of the spotlight in which the public service must operate, however, public employers often judge their employees by higher standards of conduct than are found in the private sector.[61]

Public reaction may work against an agency that is lax in monitoring and disciplining its employees or one that uses discipline illegitimately to punish employees for differing with policies or exposing agency problems. Unfortunately, despite the protection employees are supposedly given, it is all too easy for them to be dismissed or badgered until they resign because they embarrass their agencies or disagree with administration policy. The case of Ernest Fitzgerald, fired for giving embarrassing information to Congress—and later reinstated by the courts—is one example. Just holding different views was enough to cause "forced" resignations for some civil servants in the Nixon administration.[62] Because of concern over such pressure, the Civil Service Reform Act of 1978 contains protections for "whistle blowers." Reprisals against whistle blowers are prohibited, and an independent special counsel, appointed by the president for a five-year term, has the power to investigate such reprisals and bring disciplinary charges against those who institute them.

As for legitimate disciplinary action, employees who are chosen and dealt with under effective personnel policies can be expected to practice self-discipline for the most part. For those few cases where self-discipline is inadequate, there should be a policy that is fair and speedy. Delayed actions are ineffectual; unjust actions create discontent and lower morale.

An effective discipline policy is one that is clearly stated, clearly understood by the employees, and uniformly applied. Thus management needs to develop procedures for letting the employees know what is wrong with their conduct. Additionally, procedures for investigating misconduct should be established. Opportunity for employee appeal to an impartial party is needed to protect the employee's interests. Whatever discipline is imposed must also fit the situation for which it is used.

The most commonly used forms of discipline are reprimands, suspension (with or without pay), demotion or other reassignment, and removal. Others used to a lesser degree include loss of salary increases, of seniority rights, or of overtime work, or noting of demerits on the employee personnel record. These latter forms of discipline were once used extensively but are now considered demeaning and not particularly productive.

Reprimands, both oral and written, should be enough to correct most problems, particularly if there is good communication and mutual respect between employee and supervisor. The purpose of the reprimand should be to correct employee actions and not to embarrass or humiliate the person. The training and personality of the supervisor are important to making this type of disciplinary action effective. A fumbling and inconsiderate use of reprimands can cause irreparable harm to employee-supervisor relations.

Suspension, demotion, and reassignment are more severe types of discipline. They should be used with care and only if reprimands are ineffective. Suspension often leaves the employee with a loss of pay and may only kindle hostility. Demotion and reassignment are appropriate only where the employee has demonstrated a lack of ability in a particular position. The change of job should be made on the basis of more effectively utilizing the employee's capabilities. Using it as a disciplinary action is humiliating to the employees and only makes them more resistant to the idea of reassignment and demotion, even though it may be best for the worker and the organization. Reassignment may result in the palming off of incompetent employees on other units of the organization and thus the weakening of the public service. Consequently, careful consideration should be given to the employee's potential for fulfilling the needs of the new position and to the welfare of the organization as a whole.

Removal is the most extreme penalty and should be used only when other methods fail. It should not have to be resorted to very often, but there are always some instances when it is necessary. Dismissal policies should be clearly stated and impartially applied. The rights of the employee to know the basis for removal should be scrupulously honored, and review should be available if the employee feels mistreated.

Disciplinary policies need to recognize the employee's right to have his or her case reviewed. They also must disallow capricious and partial action on the part of the supervisor. Too much procedural detail, however, may lead to inflexibility for the manager, and care must be taken to balance the rights of the employee against the right of the people to effective public service. Generally, disciplinary policies, like performance evaluation, should strive to improve the way employees do their job.

Employee Training and Development

Some personnel programs have as their objective the development of skills and capabilities of the employees in the organization. The history of training in the public service has not been a good one. Policy makers (especially members of Congress) long considered employee training a waste of the taxpayer's money. It was believed that the public services could obtain trained personnel through effective selection processes. No thought was given to technological changes and the absolescence of many employees' skills. In recent years, happily, there has been a change; and since passage of the Government Employees Training Act of 1958, training has become a major focus of many government agencies. The Office of Personnel Management is a leader in training program development.

There are several reasons for the increasing number of training programs. First, people recognize the importance of providing workers with the opportunity to improve themselves through specific training and development programs. Second, there has been increasing pressure from various minority groups for their legal rights in the employment process. Often these groups have found government positions unattainable because they lacked the opportunity to gain the necessary skills. Many of the new training programs attempt to remedy the situation by providing training on the job.

A third reason is that government often requires skills not readily available in the labor market. Finally, the changing technology and increasing scope of governmental activity brings about new demands for training programs. There is no question that government has recognized the need for the programs; the question now is how it goes about the process and with what effect.[63]

In instituting a training program, the personnel agency and operating department should both be involved. Frequently the personnel agency can supply the advice and experts for the programs, but the operating agency must evaluate the training needs and actually implement the programs. Thus the process involves determination of training needs, how they can be met, and what form the program assumes.

The most elementary training program is a new-employee orientation program, which can have a significant impact on behavior and productivity.[64] Traditionally agencies spent a short time introducing the employee around and explaining the rules, regulations, and benefits of the job. Now the orientation process tends to be stretched out over a longer period—depending on the job, of course—and employees are encouraged to discuss problems in adjusting and in learning their duties. The result is that employees become more productive more quickly.

On-the-job training is another approach. An individual without the needed skills is hired and learns the job from another employee. Often the person serves an apprenticeship. Such training may also be used to help employees move up in their organizations by learning new skills. All employees should be able to grow in their positions, but not all agencies have specific programs to encourage such growth.

Lately it has been common to encourage individual employee development through a variety of programs in and outside the organization. The main beneficiaries of such programs are frequently supervisors and managers, but many other employees have benefited as well. These programs involve workshops and institutes, professional conferences, university and college programs, and sabbaticals. The national government has sponsored such programs for a long time and has permitted state and local government employees to participate. Since passage of the Intergovernmental Personnel Act of 1970, programs have multiplied, and cooperative arrangements have expanded significantly.

Not surprisingly, the national government has been a leader in many types of training programs. The Office of Personnel Management sponsors a variety of programs and has training centers in each of its regions. Although the regional centers are primarily for middle- and upper-level federal officials, state and local personnel may be accepted on a space-available basis.[65] In addition, the Executive Seminar Centers at Kings Point, New York; Berkeley, California; Oak Ridge, Tennessee; and elsewhere provide opportunities for intensive programs for management personnel. The Federal Executive Institute at Charlottesville, Virginia, provides small, intensive courses for high-level administrators and shows OPM's commitment to excellence in the public service.

State and local governments have been slow to follow the national government's lead in developing training programs. However, most states have instituted some specialized programs in areas such as law enforcement, fire fighting, water and sanitation, and tax assessment training. Others, such as California, have developed general programs with regional training centers for all types of public employees. The Intergovernmental Personnel Act has provided funds for a large number of training programs as well, so great strides are now being made on the state and local levels.

A traditionally neglected method of providing for individual employee growth is rotation or transfer from unit to unit, or among agencies. Employees have often looked upon this sort of mobility as a negative personnel process, believing it to be a way of getting rid of undesirables rather than an opportunity for advancement and growth.[66] Employee mobility is now receiving increasing attention. Within the federal government the president established the Executive Assignment System by executive order in 1967; under the reform act it became the Senior Executive Service. The system provides a list of "eligibles" from the top three grades of the federal service. These persons are to be called upon for filling top-level positions and may be given a variety of assignments. In addition, OPM has agreements with other merit systems (TVA, etc.) permitting transfer of employees without loss of protection and benefits. The objectives of these programs are primarily to help agencies find and hire the best available personnel and to protect employee rights, but they also have the effect of increasing the employee's perspective and value to the organization.

More directly related to training, and stimulated by the Intergovernmental Personnel Act, is the IPA Mobility Program, in which people from all levels of government and academic institutions take temporary assignments in government (mostly federal) agencies.[67] There is a great deal of flexibility in the program, and learning experiences can be tailored to the needs of the participants. The participating agencies and institutions benefit from the differing perspectives of their temporary assignees as well. State and local agencies may use the program as one way of developing contacts with federal agencies from whom they may later seek grants.

Private foundations and institutions are also providing funds and programs that encourage training of public officials. The Brookings Institution is one of the most prestigious of those concentrating on management development. Another private effort is the nonprofit Scholarship and Education Defense Fund for Racial Equality, which offers training programs for newly elected and appointed black officials.[68] Of course, universities and colleges (public and private) have been sponsoring programs, conferences, and institutes for many years.

A type of training aimed at new and prospective employees is the internship. Many institutions of higher education require public internships as a part of graduate, and sometimes undergraduate, public administration programs. Other disciplines are also providing opportunities for relevant internships. Students gain experience in practical application of what they learn in the classroom. The internship would not be possible without the willingness of local, state, and federal agencies to budget money for them. Certainly they benefit along with the student, but government recognition that such programs offer opportunity for improved preparation of prospective employees is essential to the success of the programs. The Presidential Management Internship Program, administered by OPM at the national level, is another example of an effort to provide opportunity for new graduates to gain experience in government. Each year 250 MPA graduates (or those with similar degrees) are selected to spend two years with a federal agency with the expectation that successful interns will become permanent federal employees. Texas and Montana are two states which are emulating this national government program. Kansas City, Phoenix, and the Metropolitan Dade County government are examples of local efforts which have been under way for many years.

Training is costly, and the costs lead to controversy over whether training should be undertaken. Fortunately, government leaders have recognized that in terms of stagnation and discontent, the long-term costs of recruiting without training programs far outrun the training costs. As a result, efforts to improve the public service through employee development are growing all the time, although recent spending constraints produced by tax revolts are curbing such programs. The trends in training emphasis seem to be shifting from personal development to organization development, but the majority of programs still focus on improving the skills and effectiveness of the individual.

Personnel specialists are increasingly recognizing that they need a comprehensive approach to the training process. They must evaluate needs and then work toward attaining the objectives. More and more attention is focused on internal or "in-house" training efforts so that the program can be tailored to the particular characteristics and needs of the agency involved. Trainers find that the results are better as the process relates more specifically to the organization.[69]

Training is particularly important in our modern society as expertise and technical know-how rapidly become obsolete. Employees, through their unions, as well as the public and management, demand training opportunities so that public service can be provided at optimum effectiveness. Government managers must recognize the value of such programs. As training programs are instituted, it should be remembered that the most successful are those that motivate employees to learn and to recognize their own capabilities. Then, of course, the opportunity to utilize those capabilities must exist.

Summary

This chapter has reviewed the performance of public servants and the methods by which optimum performance can be insured. There is little question that taxpayers will continue to pressure governments to get the most out of their tax monies. As those pressures mount, governments need to find ways of insuring high levels of performance from employees. The options outlined above will provide methods for doing so. Certainly no one method will prove best for all governmental entities. Rather combinations and adaptations of approaches will provide the best alternative for any one organization.

NOTES

1. For examination of how important supervision is, see George C. Homans, "Effort, Supervision, and Productivity," in Robert T. Golembiewski and Michael Cohen, eds., *People in Public Service* (Itasca, IL: Peacock, 1976), pp 248–259, originally published in Robert Dulim, ed., *Leadership and Productivity* (San Francisco: Chandler, 1965), pp. 51–67.
2. For detailed examination of these and other tasks, see International City

Manager's Association, *Effective Supervisory Practices* (Washington, D.C.: ICMA, 1978).

3. For an entertaining look at problems of promotion in organizations and how to deal with them, see Lawrence J. Peter, *The Peter Prescription* (New York: William Morrow, 1972).

4. Charles L. Hughes and Vincent S. Flowers, "Shaping Strategies to Disparate Value Systems," *Personnel*, 50 (March/April 1973), 8–23.

5. Other typologies are developed by Chris Argyris, *Integrating the Individual and the Organization* (New York: Wiley, 1964); Robert Presthus, *The Organizational Society*, rev. ed. (New York: St. Martin's Press, 1978); Anthony Downs, *Inside Bureaucracy* (Boston: Little, Brown, 1967); and Amitai Etzioni, *A Comparative Analysis of Complex Organizations*, rev. ed. (New York: The Free Press, 1975).

6. William Foote Whyte et al., *Money and Motivation* (New York: Harper & Row, 1955) is one of the major works on this issue. It presents an analysis of the strong and weak points of monetary incentives in a series of case studies.

7. The Hawthorne studies have been widely reported in public administration literature, so they will not be detailed here. For excellent analyses, readers may wish to check J.A.C. Brown, *The Social Psychology of Industry* (Baltimore: Penguin, 1962); or George C. Homans, "The Western Electric Researches," in Schuyler Dean Hoslett, ed., *Human Factors in Management*, rev. ed. (New York: Harper & Row, 1951). A new perspective on the studies is offered by H.M. Parsons, "What Happened at Hawthorne?," *Science*, 183 (March 8, 1974), 922–932.

8. One of the leaders in informal organizational research is Peter Blau, who has two major works in the area: *The Dynamics of Bureaucracy: A Study of Interpersonal Relationships in Two Government Agencies*, 2nd ed. (Chicago: University of Chicago Press, 1963); and with Marshall W. Mayer, *Bureaucracy in Modern Society*, 2nd ed. (New York: Random House, 1971).

9. Chester I. Barnard, *The Functions of the Executive* (Cambridge, MA: Harvard University Press, 1968, originally published in 1938).

10. The evidence is mixed. In an early study delineating the three styles, Ronald Lippitt and Ralph White, "An Experimental Study of Leadership and Group Life," in T.M. Newcomb and E.L. Hartley, eds., *Readings in Social Psychology* (New York: Holt, Rinehart & Winston, 1947) reached the conclusions noted; but Robert T. Golembiewski, "Three Styles of Leadership and Their Uses," *Personnel*, 38 (July/August 1961), 35–42, concludes that no one style is more valid. Still others seem to validate the conclusions of Lippitt and Hartley, e.g., Rensis Likert, *The Human Organization: Its Management and Value* (New York: McGraw-Hill, 1967).

11. Argyris has written several books and articles on the issue, but the most exhaustive is *Integrating the Individual and the Organization*.

12. Robert Presthus, *The Organizational Society*.

13. Anthony Downs, *Inside Bureaucracy*, pp. 81–91 and ch. 9, has some

interesting observations on this issue; and see Peter Rand, "Collecting Merit Badges: The White House Fellows," *Washington Monthly*, 6 (June 1974), 47–56, for an excellent evaluation of the motives and pressures for achievement.

14. Perhaps the seminal work on this issue is Douglas McGregor, *The Human Side of Enterprise* (New York: McGraw-Hill, 1960).

15. Among the earliest were Warren G. Bennis and Philip E. Slater, *The Temporary Society* (New York: Harper & Row, 1968).

16. Based on Abraham Maslow, *Motivation and Personality* (New York: Harper & Row, 1954).

17. Frederick Herzberg, *Work and the Nature of Man* (Cleveland: World Publishing, 1966), especially ch. 3.

18. Ibid., chs. 6–9, explain his theory. Also see Herzberg, "One More Time: How Do You Motivate Employees?," *Harvard Business Review*, 46 (January/February 1968), 53–57.

19. The literature regarding problems is awe inspiring. Some recent materials: Harry Levinson, "Asinine Attitudes towards Motivation," *Harvard Business Review*, 51 (January/February 1973), 70–76; David Sirota and Alan D. Wolfson, "Pragmatic Approaches to People Problems," *Harvard Business Review*, 51 (January/February 1973), 120–128; and Daniel Zwerdling, "Beyond Boredom—A Look at What's New on the Assembly Line," *Washington Monthly*, 5 (July/August 1973), 80–91. Some excellent articles on the effect of participatory administration for the public sector are found in "Symposium on Alienation, Decentralization, and Participation," *Public Administration Review*, 29 (January/February 1969), 3–63.

20. Zwerdling, "Beyond Boredom."

21. Robert N. Ford, *Motivation through the Work Itself* (New York: American Management Association, 1969) cites many examples at AT&T, for instance.

22. Rodney H. Brady, "MBO Goes to Work in the Public Sector," *Harvard Business Review*, 51 (March/April 1973), 65–74, gives an excellent discussion of these problems.

23. See *Work in America*, Report of a Special Task Force to the Secretary of Health, Education, and Welfare (Cambridge MA: MIT Press, 1973) for a discussion of worker dissatisfaction and boredom.

24. Robert N. Ford, "Job Enrichment Lessons from AT&T," *Harvard Business Review*, 51 (January/February 1973), 96–106, outlines some very interesting examples. Also see Zwerdling, "Beyond Boredom."

25. Charles Albano, "Try It You'll Like it," *Public Personnel Management*, 2 (September/October 1973), 336–341; and Vincent W. Kafka, "A Motivation System That Works Both Ways," *Personnel*, 49 (July/August 1972), 61–66, provide interesting evidence for, and analysis of, the two issues.

26. There is a vast array of literature on the issue, including Likert, *The Human Organization*; Warren G. Bennis, *Changing Organizations* (New York: McGraw-Hill, 1966); Bennis and Slater, *The Temporary Society*;

Robert B. Blake and Jane S. Mouton, *The Managerial Grid: Key Observations for Achieving Production through People* (Houston: Gulf, 1964); Saul W. Gellerman, *Management by Motivation* (New York: American Management Association, 1968); Gordon L. Lippitt, *Organization Renewal: Achieving Vitality in a Changing World* (New York: Appleton, 1969).

27. For one of the most precise statements of organization development objectives, see Robert T. Golembiewski, "Organization Development in Public Agencies: Perspectives on Theory and Practice," *Public Administration Review*, 29 (July/August 1969), 367–377, especially 368.

28. Ibid., 368–376, notes other constraints for public agencies.

29. For a detailed explanation of the approach and an example of its use, see Craig E. Schneier, Robert Pernick, and David E. Bryant, Jr., "Improving Performance in the Public Sector through Behavior Modification and Positive Reinforcement," *Public Personnel Management*, 8 (March/April 1979), 101–110.

30. Ibid., 103.

31. Ibid., 103.

32. Levinson, "Asinine Attitudes," 70–76.

33. Ibid., 72–73. The sentiment is echoed by Chris Argyris, "The CEO's Behavior: Key to Organizational Development," *Harvard Business Review*, 51 (March/April 1973), 55–64.

34. Sirota and Wolfson, "Pragmatic Approaches."

35. Ibid.; Kafka, "A Motivation System"; Albano, "Try It"; and Samuel J. Bernstein and Leon Reinharth, "Management, The Public Organization, and Productivity," *Public Personnel Management*, 2 (July/August 1973), 261–266.

36. Thomas C. Clary, "Motivation through Positive Stroking," *Public Personnel Management*, 2 (March/April 1973), 113–117; and Herzberg, "One More Time."

37. See Robert W. Galloway, "Productivity and the Personnel Agent," *IPMA News*, March 1978, pp. 8–11, for an analysis of it as a fad.

38. As defined by Nancy S. Hayward, "The Productivity Challenge," *Public Administration Review*, 36 (September/October 1976), 544–550. Also see Committee for Economic Development, *Improving Productivity in State and Local Government* (New York: CED, 1976).

39. As reported by Hayward, "The Productivity Challenge."

40. See John A. McCart, "Public Employee Department AFL-CIO," *Civil Service Journal*, 19 (January/March 1979), 37–38.

41. Alan J. Whitney, "National Association of Government Employees," *Civil Service Journal*, 19 (January/March 1979), 43–44; and Kenneth T. Blaylock, "The American Federation of Government Employees," 39–41 of the same journal.

42. For discussion of these issues, see National Commission on Productivity and Work Quality, *So, Mr. Mayor, You Want to Improve Productivity . . .* (Washington, D.C.: Government Printing Office, 1974), pp. 26–29; and Jerome M. Rosow, "Now Is the Time for Productivity Bar-

gaining," *Harvard Business Review*, 50 (January/February 1972), 78–89.

43. As reported in "City Workers Hike Productivity," *Search*, 7 (Winter 1977), 1–3.

44. See Blaylock, "The American Federation of Government Employees." Even managers and employees in the public sector believe their organizations are not well managed or productive, as reported in *The Municipal Reporter* published by the New Mexico Municipal League, vol. 78 (July 1978), p. 7.

45. This discussion on productivity bargaining is based largely on N. Joseph Cayer, "Is Productivity Bargaining All You Ever Wanted It to Be?" *IPMA News*, March 1977, pp. 6–7.

46. Rosow, "Now Is the Time"; and Sam Zagoria, "Productivity Gains a Spot at the Bargaining Table," *Nations Cities*, 11 (July 1973), 16–18.

47. Chester A. Newland, "Personnel Concerns in Government Productivity Improvement," *Public Administration Review*, 32 (November/December 1972), 807–815, at 808. Raymond D. Horton, "Productivity and Productivity Bargaining in Government: A Critical Analysis," *Public Administration Review*, 36 (July/August 1976), 407–414, at 409–410, takes issue with the definition on the basis that it offers few guidelines for implementation.

48. A good starting point for anyone interested in these issues is Chester A. Newland, ed., "Symposium on Productivity in Government," *Public Administration Review*, 32 (November/December 1972), 739–850.

49. One of the bluntest statements to this effect is in Edward K. Hamilton's presentation to the National Conference on Productivity in Policing, Washington, D.C., April 14–16, 1975, reprinted in part in *Public Productivity Review*, 1 (September 1975), p. 54. Similarly, Rosow, "Now Is the Time," and Zagoria, "Productivity Gains a Spot" play down the problems.

50. Robert L. Lineberry and Robert E. Welch, Jr., "Who Gets What: Measuring the Distribution of Urban Services," *Social Science Quarterly*, 54 (March 1974), 700–712.

51. Paul D. Staudohar, "An Experiment in Increasing Productivity of Police Service Employees," *Public Administration Review*, 35 (September/October 1975), 518–522.

52. There may be more than one disturbing aspect, as suggested in a letter by Dorothy Guyot, "What Productivity? What Bargaining?," *Public Administration Review*, 36 (May/June 1976), 340–343.

53. Blau, *The Dynamics of Bureaucracy*, especially ch. 3.

54. National Center for Productivity and Quality of Working Life, *Total Performance Measurement: Some Pointers for Action* (Washington, D.C.: Government Printing Office, 1978).

55. For two excellent critiques from differing perspectives, see Douglas McGregor, "An Uneasy Look at Performance Appraisal," *Harvard Business Review*, 35 (May/June 1957), 89–94; and Douglas S. Sherwin, "The Job of Job Evaluation," *Harvard Business Review*, 35 (May/June 1957), 63–71.

56. A good review of some of the legal aspects can be found in William H.

Holley and Hubert S. Field, "Performance Appraisal and the Law," *Labor Law Journal*, July 1975, pp. 423–430.

57. See the report of Kenneth J. Lacho, G. Kent Stearns, and Maurice F. Villere, "A Study of Appraisal Systems of Major Cities in the United States," *Public Personnel Management*, 8 (March/April 1979), 111–125.

58. Margaret A. Howell and Sidney H. Newman, "Narrative and Check-off Evaluations of Employee Performance," *Public Personnel Review*, 32 (July 1971), 148–150, present a comparison of the validity of the two techniques and conclude that each is approximately as valid as the other.

59. Blau, *The Dynamics of Bureaucracy*, ch. 3, provides an excellent demonstration of the possible dysfunctional effects of performance evaluation.

60. This result need not be the case, as noted by Thomas H. Stone, "An Examination of Six Prevalent Assumptions concerning Performance Appraisals," *Public Personnel Management*, 2 (November/December 1973), 404–414.

61. See W.D. Heisel and Richard M. Gladstone, "Off-the-job Conduct as a Disciplinary Problem," *Public Personnel Review*, 29 (January 1968), 23–28, for an excellent review of the issue.

62. The Fitzgerald case is discussed by Edward Weisband and Thomas M. Frank, *Resignation in Protest* (New York: Penguin, 1975), p. 131. The book examines numerous instances in which pressure was applied to "disloyal" employees. Leon E. Panetta and Peter Gall, *Bring Us Together* (Philadelphia: Lippincott, 1971), tell the story of Panetta being "forced" to resign for diverging views. Charles Markham, "A Democratic Vassal in King Richard's Civil Service," *Washington Monthly*, 5/6 (July/August 1973), 49–56, explains how a lower-level civil servant also faces problems for differing political views.

63. A recent example of concern with training is in Kenneth T. Byers, ed., *Employee Training and Development in the Public Service* (Chicago: Public Personnel Association, 1970).

64. See Earl R. Gomersall and M. Scott Myers, "Breakthrough in On-the-Job Training," *Harvard Business Review*, 44 (July/August 1966), 62–72, for a good analysis of how the orientation process affects performance.

65. See John J. Scholzen, "Southwest Intergovernmental Training Center," *Civil Service Journal*, 14 (July/September 1973), 30–36, for a discussion of the program.

66. A notable exception is described by Herbert Kaufman, *The Forest Ranger* (Baltimore: Johns Hopkins Press, 1967), pp. 175–199, in which he notes that employees learned to accept transfer as a growth possibility and utilized it to their advantage and the advantage of the organization.

67. For a brief analysis of the impact of the mobility program, see Joseph M. Robertson, "Talent Sharing for Better Government Performance," *ASPA News and Views*, 23 (October 1973), 7–9.

68. See Barry A. Passett, *Leadership Development for the Public Service* (Houston: Gulf, 1971), p. 57.

69. See Yoram Zeira, "Is External Management Training Effective for Or-

ganizational Change?," *Public Personnel Management*, 2 (November/ December 1973), 400–407; Irvine Marsters, Jr., "Training for Results at BPA," *Public Service Training in Maine* (University of Maine, Orono, Bureau of Public Administration, August 1973), p. 1; and Richard V. Telthorst, "Change in Emphasis in BPA Training," *Public Service Training in Maine* (University of Maine, Orono, Bureau of Public Administration, January 1974), p. 1. H. Kent Baker and Ronald H. Gorman, "Evaluating the Effectiveness of Management Development Programs," *Public Personnel Management*, 7 (July/August 1978), 249– 257, provides analysis of costs and benefits of such programs.

SUGGESTED READINGS

Balk, Walter, L., ed. "Symposium on Productivity in Government." *Public Administration Review*, 38 (January/February 1978), 1–50.

Byers, Kenneth R., ed. *Employee Training and Development in the Public Service*. Chicago: Public Personnel Association, 1970.

Committee for Economic Development. *Improving Productivity in State and Local Government*. New York: CED, 1976.

Frank, Thomas M. *Resignation in Protest*. New York: Penguin, 1975.

Hayward, Nancy S. "The Productivity Challenge." *Public Administration Review*, 36 (September/October 1976), 544–550.

International City Management Association. *Effective Supervisory Practices*. Washington, D.C.: ICMA, 1978.

Newland, Chester A., ed. "Symposium on Productivity in Government." *Public Administration Review*, 32 (November/December 1972).

Panetta, Leon E., and Peter Gall. *Bring Us Together*. Philadelphia: Lippincott, 1971.

Rosow, Jerome M. "Now Is the Time for Productivity Bargaining." *Harvard Business Review*, 50 (January/February 1972), 78–89.

Weinstein, Deena. *Bureaucratic Opposition: Challenging Abuses at the Workplace*. Elmsford, N.Y.: Pergamon Press, 1979.

CASE 8.1

Discipline Policy

Phil Jones, a social welfare counselor, talked with a number of his co-workers about the lack of congeniality among people in the office, and they decided to organize an informal get-together for Friday afternoons. It was seemingly successful: most of the office workers began to stop by the local coffee house for a relaxing hour or two before going home. Darlene Green, the office supervisor, did not participate and felt that Jones was becoming so popular with office personnel that they looked to him for advice and guidance rather than to her. She decided something had to be done.

One Friday Jones had to be out of the office working with clients during the afternoon and stopped by the coffee house a few minutes earlier than usual. Green happened to drive by at that time on her way back to the office from a professional conference.

A week later Jones made an error in deciding on a case review by Green, who did not notice the mistake and was remonstrated by her superior for the problem it created.

Green called Jones and said his work had not been up to standards lately. She said she was recommending that he be suspended for a week. Jones wanted to know what was wrong with his work, to which Green said he had been interfering with the ability of the staff to perform effectively by making them less responsive to her authority. She also said he was guilty of quitting work early to party and was making mistakes in his work.

1. What was good about Green's approach?
2. What was bad about Green's approach?
3. Does Green's approach follow good discipline policy?
4. Was Green's action justified?

CASE 8.2

Moving About

Jim Abbott was nervous as he approached his department head, Norma Karl. He had been in the department for three years and had moved quickly up the ladder until he was now Karl's assistant. As in every other state government department for which he had worked, his supervisors liked him and thought he performed in a superior manner. In each of those other departments, just as he seemed to have mastered almost every aspect of its activities, he had asked for a transfer to another department. He had transferred four times in the past seven years. Now he was asking Karl to recommend him for a transfer to yet another department. Karl was about to retire and was planning to recommend that Abbott be given her job. Abbott was told of such plans by Karl.

---

1. If you were Karl, how would you react to Abbott's request?
2. If you wrote an evaluation letter on Abbott, what would you say?
3. What advice might you offer Abbott?

CASE 8.3

The Internship

Carrie Dent looked forward to her first day as an intern with the state auditor's office. As an MPA student, she was well aware of the importance of gaining experience in her chosen occupational field. Her interview with Ted Merrill, the intern coordinator for the auditor's office, had gone well, and they were enthusiastic about having her there.

Carrie spent the first day completing forms for personnel and meeting other people in the office. Everyone appeared to be pleasant and eager to help her.

During the first three weeks Carrie was assigned various chores such as running errands, copying documents, and obtaining reports from other agencies. Feeling that it was a part of getting adjusted to the new situation, she did not think much about the kind of tasks she performed.

However, after another three weeks she felt that she was doing nothing but busy-work and called Professor Meek, her internship advisor, to say that she wished to resign from her internship. She explained that she was bored and never had anything challenging to do. It was as though she were in the way, and the office did not know what to do with her. The management staff, all male, excluded her from their activities, and she spent most of her time with the clerical staff in the office.

---

1. If you were Meek, what would you say to Carrie?
2. Is there any course of action which could salvage the internship for Carrie?
3. If you were an advisor to the auditor's office, what suggestions would you have for its internship program?

Chapter 9

Rights and Duties of Public Employees

Greater attention is focused on the off-the-job conduct of public employees than on the behavior of employees in the private sector. In its eagerness to insure a high quality public service, government often restricts the rights of those providing the service. Balancing the need for an impartial, fair, and high quality public service with the protection of the individual rights of employees creates intense controversies and difficulties for public personnel systems. Of course, such problems are particularly likely to occur in a democratic system, where individual rights are many and highly prized.

Restrictions on public employees' private lives have stemmed from the doctrine of privilege as applied to public employment. The courts have long held that privileges and gratuities are not subject to the same protection as rights. Thus if it is determined that something is a privilege, no one has a right to it, and such protections as due process may not apply in the same way as they would if a right were involved. Over the years the courts have held that government employment is a privilege extended to those employed and that if people want the privilege, they have to abide by the conditions imposed on it. Recently the courts have been modifying their stand on the subject. They seem to be insisting that even though individuals lack the right to gratuities, they have a right to fair treatment in the dissemination of those gratuities once government decides they are to be available. For example, the courts have decided that no one has a right to education, but once it is provided, governments have obligations to be fair in making it available. Thus the distinction between rights and privileges is a hazy one, but it has been an important justification for denying public employees certain types of freedom of activity.[1]

General Employee Conduct

Administrators in the public sector are usually forced to demand a higher standard of behavior of their employees than is true in the private sector.[2] Public employees are watched by the taxpayers and media, and any misstep is likely to result in some kind of public pressure for remedy. Private-sector employers can be more understanding of their employees because they are less dependent upon the good will of the public and face fewer consequences from the misbehavior of their employees. Support of the public, and especially of the elected political leaders, is critical to public agency existence. Any behavior which has the potential of jeopardizing such support is likely to result in action by the agency. Sensitivity to public attitudes and the possibility that politicians may use any indiscretion as a basis for political gain leads many public employees to take the expedient route of restricting employee rights or imposing discipline. While the same reactions may exist in the private sector, it is not subject to the same kind of pressure from the political environment.

Police officers frequently come under scrutiny from the community and are often dismissed for their indiscretions. The case of police officers in Amarillo, Texas, during 1977 and 1978 provides an example. Some citizens reported that an unmarried male and female officer were living together. With no more evidence than that both their cars were in one officer's driveway at early morning hours, the department dismissed them both. The dismissals were upheld by the review board. Regardless of how one feels about the case or issues involved, the officers were fined for behavior which is rather common, even in Amarillo. Employees in the private sector would seldom be disciplined for the same behavior. Another fairly common issue is the smoking of marijuana. While still illegal in most places, its use has become widespread. Public employees who admit to its use, however, are likely to be disciplined. The community clearly disapproves of its public servants acting in a way that deviates from its standards. It seems that public employees are expected to be models of good behavior.

In recent years the matter of life style has become a major concern in public employment. The June 1977 referendum in Dade County, Florida, epitomizes the hysteria which surrounds the issue of gays in the public work force. After the county commission passed an ordinance prohibiting discrimination in housing and employment against homosexuals, celebrity Anita Bryant organized a highly emotional campaign to force a referendum to repeal the ordinance. The campaign was based largely on fears that gays would be given legitimacy and freedom to recruit children into homosexuality and on biblical quotations supposedly condemning homosexuality. That 45 percent of the voters (a percentage almost unheard of in referenda elections) turned out to overwhelmingly repeal the ordinance illustrates the community's unwillingness to recognize the legitimacy of gays' claims to rights such as freedom from discrimination. Similar actions were taken in other communities across the country, among them Wichita, Kansas, and Minneapolis, Minnesota. However, gays have been successful in some places, notably the state of California where, in 1978, voters rejected Proposition 6 which would have prohibited gays from being employed as teachers in the public schools. Cities with large gay populations, such as San Francisco and now Los Angeles, have been passing various ordinances to protect rights of gays, including the right to employment opportunity. They are also actively recruiting gays for their police forces.

As gays continue to press for protection in hope of winning the kind of recognition given other civil rights organizations, the controversy over the issue is not likely to abate. It will probably be a long time before gays are generally accepted in public employment. They have few political allies. Little by little, however, they are making progress. At the national level, being homosexual cannot be used as a reason for denying employment. However, agencies such as the Department of Justice and the FBI have been hesitant to follow the guidelines of the Office of Personnel Management on this issue. Similarly, many sensitive government positions are not open to gays. As time passes, however, it is likely that gays will be treated as others and that personnel policies regarding them will be based on factors relevant to ability and not on their being gay.

Loyalty and Security

There is probably no aspect of public personnel administration that has been more directly affected by forces in the political environment than the area of loyalty and security. At times, officials and the public alike have reacted out of hysteria in restricting activities of public employees. Loyalty and security are two separate concepts that are often perceived as one. Loyalty refers to the support of the employee for the system. A loyalty risk is one who would be likely to consciously subvert the political system. A security risk is someone who, without malicious intent, might divulge information or act in a way detrimental to the system. Thus someone can be a security risk without being disloyal or may be a security risk in one position but not in another.

Loyalty and freedom are competing objectives that have created numerous problems for the political system. President Washington demanded loyalty to the new federal system from his public servants, and Lincoln required loyalty to the Union. Specific tests of loyalty did not become formalized until 1939, when the Hatch Act (section 9A) prohibited employees from being members of organizations advocating overthrow of the government. Every period of crisis in our history, however, has produced some policies to insure loyalty of public servants. After World War II the anti-Communist frenzy led to a variety of loyalty and security programs in the public service, and a number of studies of employee loyalty were conducted. For the most part, the issue attracts much less attention today, but there are still programs to protect against disloyalty. All employees of the federal government are subject to investigation of their backgrounds to determine suitability for the public service, although for workers in nonsensitive positions the investigation may be conducted after placement. Those appointed to sensitive positions are investigated before appointment and are subject to more in-depth investigations. At the state and local levels, the tendency has been to require employees to sign loyalty oaths as a condition of employment, but the courts have invalidated many as being too vague and unenforceable. A recent Supreme Court decision did uphold the Massachusetts loyalty oath, however, so loyalty oaths are still useable.[3]

Although it may seem reasonable that those disloyal to the system should not be employed by the government and that security risks not be employed in sensitive positions, there is little agreement on what constitutes a loyalty or security risk. Consequently, loyalty and security programs have been subject to much abuse. Many of them virtually ignore the individual rights of employees, partly because of the privilege doctrine discussed earlier.[4] Employees who are dismissed for questions of loyalty or security ordinarily can have a hearing to answer the charges.[5]

The most insidious invasion of individual rights occurs among those applying for positions. A person may be denied a position on the basis of background information acquired during the investigation. Whether the information is accurate may never be determined because the unsuccessful applicants are rarely apprised of why they are unsuccessful. Thus people may be denied jobs in the public service based on information they have no chance to see or challenge.

Loyalty and security programs may also be pursued overzealously, and people may be denied job opportunities not because they are disloyal or are security risks, but because they are nonconformists. Thus people are presently rejected because their sexual orientation differs from that of the majority of the population or because they associate with "radicals." Prospective employees' expressions of opinions or espousal of a cause may lead to their being labeled "unstable" or "strong willed" and thus security risks. Loyalty and security programs that deny employment to those with differing approaches and ideas not only violate individual rights, but also tend to produce stagnation in public agencies. Until society is unafraid of diverging points of view, loyalty and security issues will continue to present problems.

Political Activity Restrictions

Interest in loyalty and security programs has waned somewhat, but concern about restrictions on the political activity of public employees has become a major contemporary issue. Such restrictions date from the English canon law tradition that certain offices or activities are inconsistent with one another.[6] Conflict-of-interest satutes, orders, and rulings, and legislation or constitutional provisions prohibiting holding certain public offices concurrently, have been the major methods of embodying this canon law tradition into practice. The belief that politically active public servants cannot provide service free from prejudice led to the prohibition of certain political activities as well. In a democratic society, there is a conflict between the rights of public employees as individuals and the right of the public to impartial service. So far in the United States, priority has been given to the public right to service, and limits have been placed on the rights of public employees as a legitimate cost for political neutrality of the public bureaucracy.

Political activity of national government employees is restricted by the 1939 Hatch Act. In 1940 the act was amended to restrict the political activities of state and local government employees whose salaries are paid in part or in full by federal funds. The Federal Election Campaign Act Amendments of 1974 repealed many of the restrictions on state and local government employees, although the state and local governments have their own restrictions. Prior to the passage of the Hatch Act the Civil Service Commission developed a body of rules and regulations pursuant to a 1907 executive order of President Theodore Roosevelt barring activity in "political management or in political campaigns" for those covered by civil service.[7] In implementing its rules and regulations, the commission decided some three thousand cases involving political-activity restrictions prior to 1940. It is generally believed that Congress intended the Hatch Act to incorporate these decisions as established precedent for interpreting the political-activity prohibitions of the act. Thus Congress would effectively deny the commission the authority to interpret the legislation differently. There is some disagreement about congressional intent, but the effect has been to hamper the flexibility of the Office of Personnel Management in dealing with the issue.[8]

Regardless of the intent of Congress, the Office of Personnel Management now administers the Hatch Act and has determined that, among other specific provisions, the act prohibits:

1. Serving as a delegate or alternate to a political party convention or as a member of a political committee.
2. Soliciting or handling political contributions.
3. Serving as an officer or organizer of a political club.
4. Leading or organizing political meetings or rallies or making partisan speeches to them.
5. Soliciting votes or engaging in other partisan election activity.
6. Being a candidate for partisan political office.[9]

The rationale for such restrictions is that they will help protect public employees from being coerced into working for particular candidates or parties, that they will protect beneficiaries of public services from such coercion, and that they will prevent public officials from using public monies and positions to further their own political careers. A more immediate political reason for the passage of the Hatch Acts was a fear that the New Deal bureaucracy could be mobilized as a vast political machine in support of the administration. A similar concern among many legislators that the party in power might be able to take political advantage of politically active career servants is a major factor in the reluctance of Congress to liberalize the restrictions.[10] At any rate, the Hatch Acts were passed as a response to overindulgence in spoils politics, and they retain a lot of support among those who fear that unfettered spoils would return if public servants could engage in politics. Nonetheless, there is strong support in Congress for reform or repeal of the Hatch Act, and President Carter has promised to back repeal. Unions on the federal level are giving elimination of these restrictions top priority. As a result, liberalization of the act is a distinct possibility.

The controversy over Hatch Act restrictions concerns the constitutional right to freedom of expression, assembly, and petition. Because these rights are limited by the act, many public employees argue that they are doomed to second-class citizenship.[11] In recent years a number of assaults on the Hatch Act and similar state legislation have surfaced in the courts. For a while it seemed as though the courts would invalidate many of the restrictions—as some lower courts did—but the Supreme Court, by a six-to-three decision, upheld the constitutionality of the Hatch Act and a similar state act.[12] With the Supreme Court denying their arguments, public employees will have to focus on Congress as a means of removing restrictions on their political activity.

Whether or not restriction of political activity is a legitimate means of insuring a nonprejudiced public service is debatable. Many contend that the only effect is to constrict legitimate rights of public employees while denying the public the opportunity to hear opinions on controversial issues from those who have the greatest amount of information.[13] Others suggest that the restrictions discourage many qualified people from accepting government positions and thus hurt the overall quality of the public service.[14] It does seem that the United States has gained sufficient political maturity to be able to accord its public servants greater freedom in political affairs. The days of unmitigated spoils are over, and public employees should be able to participate in political activity as long as it does not impair their ability to perform their duties. Those who have little or no direct impact on policy decisions certainly should not be restricted to any great degree.[15] Perhaps the United States could follow the lead of the British, who permit almost complete freedom in political activity. There is little doubt that public employees will continue to press for reform.

Additionally, the growth of collective bargaining has numerous implications for political activity. On the one hand, unions could exert a great deal of pressure in the political realm if permitted to engage in partisan political activities. As a result, employee organization activity in directly partisan politics is usually restricted. Nonetheless, unions do support their friends through endorsements and campaigns. On the other hand, collective bargaining undermines one of the justifications for prohibiting political activity in that it tends to reduce the likelihood that employees could be coerced or intimidated into engaging in political activities desired by the supervisor. Because unions provide workers leverage with management, employees have greater independence from managers. Thus they have union support in resisting attempts by management to coerce them into political activity.

Other Restrictions

In recent years, there has been a return to some general restrictions imposed on public employees after a period in which such restrictions have been relaxed. While the Supreme Court seems willing to permit restrictions on various aspects of the employee's personal life, it does seem to insist upon procedural regularities in the imposition of such limitations.[16] The Court also seems to be clear in not wanting to inter-ject itself into state and local personnel policies without compelling reasons to do so. As a result, many jurisdictions are reinstituting residency requirements, limitations on freedom of expression, and regulations con-cerning appearance.[17]

Residency requirements stipulate that employees live within the jurisdiction. They are imposed by public employers for three major reasons:

1. Employees needed in emergencies should be readily available.
2. Employees should identify with the community.
3. The tax money spent to pay the employee should remain in the jurisdiction.

As to the first reason, while emergency response is a reasonable expecta-tion, living in the jurisdiction does not necessarily ensure ready avail-ability, especially in large cities. The second argument is built on the idea that people who live in a city are likely to identify with it, take pride in it, and thus feel more committed to their work for that city.

The third argument, which has become increasingly important, justi-fies residency requirements on financial grounds. Since the property tax is the major source of revenue for local governments, they often feel the employees should contribute to that tax base. Central cities in particular are losing middle-income taxpayers while costs of services go up. Keeping their own employees in the city helps to offset the problem. There may also be concern about racial balance on the part of some central cities. Affluent white employees fleeing to the suburbs have left large minority populations behind. Perhaps this trend is reversing itself as transportation time and fuel costs appear to be generating a return to the city.

Grooming and appearance are also the subject of regulation and have been held valid in certain instances by the Supreme Court. Rules governing hair length of police officers, for example, are considered by the Court to be proper methods of encouraging esprit de corps and good discipline.[18]

Another sort of restriction is that placed on "moonlighting." Prohibit-ing the taking of a second job, especially when combined with the low salaries in many jurisdictions, may create unnecessary hardships. The question once again comes down to the legitimacy of such restrictions. They should be evaluated in terms of whether they are justified and should be abandoned if they are not. Usually an employee's ability to perform a full-time job will be affected by holding yet another. If such is the case, the jurisdiction should be concerned. If there is no conflict, however, prohibition of such activity does not seem justified.

Ethics and Public Employees

Interest in the ethical behavior of public employees appears to fluctuate greatly from time to time.[19] Watergate and other scandals involving national leaders and some state and local governments have made ethics in the public service one of the central issues of our time.[20]

One of the reasons ethical considerations are so important in public administration is that its employees are entrusted with a great deal of discretion to decide on numerous issues which have the potential to benefit or hurt differing parties. This discretion also puts public servants under pressure to act in ways which benefit parties affected by the agency. Public employees often find themselves on the spot, and it is up to them to decide what is right and what is wrong.

Ethical behavior is influenced by both internal individual factors and external controls. The internal controls involve the degree to which individuals perceive themselves as responsible for their actions.[21] Theoretically, employees who are chosen correctly and who embrace democratic and professional values will control their own conduct because of their dedication to the public, their professional group standards, and peer pressure.[22] The need for individual responsibility has led many to suggest that ethics become a formal part of public service education curricula. The idea is that the personal and professional integrity of the employee will assure ethical public employees.

Unfortunately, the pressures faced by public servants are too complex and contradicting to allow easy formulation of right or wrong responses. It is difficult to decide when a conflict between personal values and official duties warrants resignation or protest. Nor is it easy to determine whether action such as the leaking or withholding of information are valid.[23] In other words, internal controls are not enough.

Because the internal controls are inadequate, external controls are necessary. External controls, as James Bowman notes, can be grouped into three categories: individual acts of leaderships, codes of conduct, and legislation.[24] Individual leadership requires a superior who serves as a model of behavior for subordinates. If the supervisor has lax standards of behavior, the subordinates can hardly be expected to maintain high standards in their performance. Managers set the tone for the organization as a whole.

Officials commonly use codes of conduct to regulate behavior, but there are differences of opinion as to their effectiveness. President Johnson issued an executive order "Prescribing Standards of Ethical Conduct for Government Officers and Employees,"[25] but no mention of it was made during all of the Watergate proceedings, suggesting that it was not taken very seriously by public employees or by the elected political leadership. Codes of conduct provide guidelines for behavior but are often so general as to have little meaning. Without enforcement efforts the codes are of little value—and enforcement is rarely pursued.

The Johnson executive order was specific in many of its provisions. The order prohibited such practices as the acceptance of gifts and the use of federal property or confidential official information for private gain. It even required employees to pay their debts. Furthermore, employees were forbidden to accept outside employment that would create, or even appear to create, a conflict of interest. What constitutes the appearance of a conflict of interest poses a problem; what seems like a conflict of interest to some people may not appear to be one to others. Accepting lunches or gifts from people one normally deals with might influence one's decisions or actions even if the individual insists otherwise. Even though the individual may resist any temptation, others may not be convinced of it. Therefore, the temptation must be avoided.[26]

Codes of ethics have become as widespread in state and local governments as they have in various federal agencies. One of the problems is deciding which employees the codes are to cover. Legislators are likely to require codes for others but exempt themselves. It is also difficult to adopt a single code that is applicable to elected political leaders, bureaucrats, and judicial employees alike.

Because of the difficulties with codes of ethics, other methods of prohibiting certain practices are increasingly used. Codes of ethics are sometimes embodied in other legislation, but specific legal prohibitions on various practices are more common. Most states have passed legislation on ethical behavior of public employees in recent years, and the Ethics in Government Act of 1978 cited specific prohibitions for federal employees. It also mandated the Office of Personnel Management to spell out specific rules and regulations implementing the act[27] and established an Office of Government Ethics within OPM. The law requires financial disclosure by those at and above the GS 16 level and provides that for two years after leaving government service ex-federal employees may not accept jobs with private-sector firms with whom their agencies dealt. Additionally, employees are restricted from representing others before their former government employer agency or influencing that agency. Many officials are concerned lest these restrictions on post-governemnt employment deter competent people from seeking public-sector jobs. The broadness of the statute has caused employees to petition Congress to change the law.[28]

The difficulties with the federal law point up the problems in attempting to insure the integrity of public employees. The question is how far government should go in controlling employee behavior. Certainly government should be able to expect employees not to use their positions for their personal gain. But can the public expect its public servants to exhibit a standard of behavior significantly higher than what is condoned in the private sector?

Grievance Procedures and Appeals

When employees feel that they have been wronged, they need a fair and speedy system for examining and resolving the complaint. Increasingly, with collective bargaining, a grievance procedure is negotiated in the bargaining agreement. Provision is made for an outside neutral party to decide on the complaint. Normally each party is committed to accepting the decision of the neutral party. Such a system is usually referred to as grievance arbitration.

In the absence of a negotiated grievance procedure, many employers have developed grievance procedures of their own. A chief reason for the development of such systems is the recognition that courts usually insist upon procedural regularities in dealing with discipline or in processing employee complaints. As Philip Martin notes, however, the Supreme Court has not offered much real protection to the employee and seems to be reinstituting the privilege doctrine for public employees.[29] Others argue that nonunionized employers develop grievance procedures to give employees one less reason to unionize; at the same time, the procedures provide a good mechanism for dealing with employee complaints.[30]

Basically, a grievance procedure spells out the situation in which employees may seek redress of a grievance, provides steps for processing the grievance, specifies time limits in which action is to be taken on the complaint, and provides for a final decision. In most systems, informal resolution of the problem is encouraged. Thus communication between the supervisor and subordinate is utilized to solve problems. The subordinate is supposed to work the problem out with the immediate supervisor. If the problem remains unresolved, various alternatives may be available.

Ronald L. Miller found in his survey of 1,000 public and private employers that there are five basic models of grievance procedure systems for nonunion employees.[31] The models are differentiated primarily on the basis of whether external review is available and on who makes the final decisions. The first model provides for grievances on any issue and allows for several review steps within the organization. The chief administrator of the organization makes the final decision on the grievance; thus employees have no access to outside neutral review. The second model is a variation of the first except that after the internal review a neutral party is used in an advisory capacity. The advice of the neutral party may go to the chief administrators or possibly to an outside arbitrator depending on the issues involved.

The third model permits grievances only on a certain number of issues. Sometimes issues such as suspension or dismissal cases are given a single internal review, while other issues are appealed through several internal steps. Then the case goes to a neutral third party and finally the chief administrator; again management is the final judge. The fourth model has cases go through an internal review process to a third neutral party and then to arbitration, thus paralleling most negotiated grievance procedures. The last model permits internal review, after which cases go directly to a governing board such as a civil service commission or to the chief executive officer.

The first model in which virtually anything can be a grievance and management judges itself was found to be the most common. Such a finding supports Epstein's contention that grievance procedures in nonunion organizations provide little support for the employee. Instead, employees are likely to be suspicious of the system; and even if the employee's complaint is upheld, morale in the organization is damaged as management adjudges one of its own to be deficient in supervision.[32] On the other hand, where a neutral third party is involved, supervisors feel threatened. As a result, it is not easy to choose between the credibility given the system by employees and the need of management's supervisors for the support of the organization.

The Civil Service Reform Act of 1978 streamlined the grievance and appeals process of the national government for those not covered by negotiated grievance procedures. In agencies without negotiated procedures, employees may appeal adverse actions (removals, suspensions, reductions in grade or pay) to the Merit Systems Protection Board. Where an organized bargaining unit exists, the union may seek arbitration instead. When adverse action is proposed, the employee is entitled to:

1. Thirty days written notice of the proposed action.
2. Representation by an attorney or other representative.

3. A reasonable period of time in which to prepare an oral and written response.
4. A written decision stating reasons for the decision.

The decision can then be appealed to the Merit Systems Protection Board (MSPB), which reviews it. If the board decides against the agency, the agency may be required to pay the fee of the employee's attorney.

In cases of alleged discrimination, the appeal of agency action may go to the Equal Employment Opportunity Commission (EEOC). If the case involves issues over which the MSPB has jurisdiction, but also includes discrimination complaints, the case will be decided by MSPB and reviewed by EEOC.

At the state and local level the procedures vary greatly but, as was noted earlier, may be categorized into several major types. As collective bargaining continues to grow in the public sector, negotiated grievance procedures are likely to predominate even more than at present. Employees probably feel more secure with the negotiated procedure because their representatives had a part in establishing it.

Employees can usually appeal to the courts if they are dissatisfied with the results of the normal appeals process. In cases where grievance arbitration is used, however, courts rarely intervene. Even when court review is possible, it is rarely a realistic alternative because of the crowded court dockets and high costs of court relief. Nonetheless, courts are stepping into such cases and are insisting that due process be followed in personnel matters.[33]

Fair and effective appeals processes work to the advantage of both employees and the public service. If the cases are handled expeditiously and justly, employees will not linger in uncertainty, and the agency can avoid waste of time and money as well as protect employee morale. If evaluation and discipline policies are fair and effective in the first place, employees will not need to use the appeals process. Problems often develop because supervisors are unskilled in conducting performance evaluations and in communicating with subordinates. If the object of adverse actions is to improve performance, preventive action would seem to be a better alternative. Preventive action would include continuous performance evaluation and open communication with employees.

Management often perceives grievance procedures as something available to employees to buck the will of management. Joseph Shane, however, suggests that the procedures have a number of positive effects as well.[34] One of the most important has been the recognition that supervisory training is a significant need in many organizations. In addition, grievance procedures may help bring about solid collective bargaining procedures, correct dysfunctional agency practices, develop equitable methods of dealing with employees, insure accountability, and lead to further evaluation and modification of the grievance mechanism itself. Without a doubt, the increasing militancy of public employees will put more pressure on the grievance procedure, and the public service must be ready to accommodate itself to these pressures.

Summary

Employees obviously have certain duties and responsibilities as members of the public service. Government also has an obligation to protect the rights of employees. Balancing employee rights with the expectations of supervisors and the public is a difficult task. There is no way it can be avoided, however, as employees increasingly insist on their rights and the public clamors for more effective and responsive government.

NOTES

1. For a complete explanation of the privilege doctrine and its implications, see Kenneth Culp Davis, *Administrative Law Text*, 3rd ed. (St. Paul: West, 1972), pp. 175–189.
2. W.D. Heisel and Richard M. Gladstone, "Off-the-Job Conduct as a Disciplinary Problem," *Public Personnel Review*, 28 (January 1968), 23–28, present an interesting study of the issue. For an excellent case study, see Peter Schuck, "The Curious Case of the Indicted Meat Inspectors," *Harper's*, September 1972, pp. 81–88.
3. *Cole v. Richardson*, 403 U.S. 917 (1972).
4. See the Supreme Court decisions in *Bailey v. Richardson*, 341 U.S. 918 (1951), and *Greene v. McElroy*, 360 U.S. 474 (1959), for divergent holdings on the issue.
5. Of course, during periods of hysteria such as the 1950s, hearings may not be available, and even if they are, they can become abuses in themselves. For a variety of perspectives, see Hans J. Morgenthau, "The Impact of the Loyalty and Security Measures on the State Department," *Bulletin of the Atomic Scientists*, 11 (April 1955), 134–140; Bar of the City of New York, *Report of the Special Committee on the Federal Loyalty Security Program* (New York: Dodd, Mead, 1956); and Earl Latham, *The Communist Controversy in Washington: From the New Deal to McCarthy* (Cambridge, MA: Harvard University Press, 1966).

6. Otto Kirchheimer, "The Historical and Comparative Background of the Hatch Act," *Public Policy*, 2 (1941), 341–373, presents an outstanding analysis of the history and philosophy behind restrictions on political activity. Another good source is H. Eliot Kaplan, "Political Neutrality of the Public Service," *Public Personnel Review*, 1 (1940), 10–23.

7. Executive Order 642, June 3, 1907.

8. Henry Rose, "A Critical Look at the Hatch Act," *Harvard Law Review*, 75 (January 1962), 510–526, reviews the congressional debate and intent as well as differing opinions.

9. As outlined by United States Civil Service Commission Pamphlet no. 20, *Political Activities of Federal Officers and Employees* (Washington, D.C.: Government Printing Office, May 1966).

10. See Philip L. Martin, "The Hatch Act in Court: Some Recent Developments," *Public Administration Review*, 33 (September/October 1973), 443–447.

11. Philip L. Martin, "The Constitutionality of the Hatch Act: Second-class Citizenship for Public Employees," *University of Toledo Law Review*, 6 (Fall 1974), 78–109.

12. In *U.S. Civil Service Commission* v. *National Association of Letter Carriers*, 93 S.Ct. 2880 (1973). Also see Martin, "The Hatch Act in Court," for an analysis of this and other relevant decisions.

13. See Dalmas H. Nelson, "Political Expression under the Hatch Act and the Problem of Statutory Ambiguity," *Midwest Journal of Political Science*, 2 (February 1958), 82–85; and his "Public Employees and the Right to Engage in Political Activity," *Vanderbilt Law Review*, 9 (December 1955), 27–50, especially 35.

14. Ferrel Heady, "American Government and Politics, The Hatch Act Decisions," *American Political Science Review*, 41 (August 1947), 687–699, at 689–699.

15. Lest it be thought the suggestion is only that of a casual observer, readers should see Charles O. Jones, "Reevaluating the Hatch Act: A Report on the Commission on Political Activity of Government Personnel." *Public Administration Review*, 29 (May/June 1969), 249–254. Jones was a member of the Commission.

16. For a good review of Supreme Court action in recent terms, see Carl F. Goodman, "Public Employment and the Supreme Court's 1975–76 Term," *Public Personnel Management*, 5 (September/October 1976), 287–302, and his article of the same title for 1976–77 in *Public Personnel Management*, 6 (September/October 1977), 283–293.

17. See *Kelly* v. *Johnson*, 425 U.S. 238 (1976), in which the Supreme Court ruled that grooming regulations for police officers were legitimate in that the Constitution does not guarantee the right of police officers to choose their own life style when it could affect their jobs. *McCarthy* v. *Philadelphia*, 96 U.S. 1154 (1976), sanctioned residency requirements.

18. *Kelly* v. *Johnson*, 425 U.S. 238 (1976).

19. For a good review of the changing levels of interest and the problem generally, see Susan Wakefield, "Ethics and the Public Service: A Case for Individual Responsibility," *Public Administration Review*, 36 (November/December 1976), 661–666.
20. See James S. Bowman, "Ethics in the Federal Service: A Post-Watergate View," *Midwest Review of Public Administration*, 11 (March 1977), 3–20.
21. The American Society for Public Administration, Professional Standards and Ethics Committee, *Professional Standards and Ethics: A Workbook for Administrators* (Washington, D.C.: ASPA, 1979), is a monograph based on the belief that ethics comes from one's internal values and self-evaluation.
22. Carl J. Friedrich, "Public Policy and the Nature of Administrative Responsibility," *Public Policy*, 1940, 3–24, presents the case for professional and peer-group control.
23. Wakefield, "Ethics and the Public Service," 662.
24. Bowman, "Ethics in the Federal Service," 18–20. Herman Finer, "Administrative Responsibility in Democratic Government," *Public Administration Review*, 1 (1941), 335–350, presents the argument for the formal legal controls.
25. Executive Order 11222, May 8, 1965.
26. See David Rich, "Ethics," *Civil Service Journal*, 18 (January/March 1978), 24–26.
27. The material on the states through 1975 can be found in Council of State Governments, *Ethics: State Conflict of Interest/Financial Disclosure Legislation, 1972–1975* (Lexington, KY: The Council of State Governments, 1975), and *OPM News*, March 31, 1979.
28. AP Story, *Lubbock Avalanche-Journal*, April 3, 1979, p. A-20.
29. Philip L. Martin, "The Improper Discharge of a Federal Employee by a Constitutionally Permissible Process: The OEO Case," *Administrative Law Review*, 28 (Winter 1976), 27–39.
30. Richard L. Epstein, "The Grievance Procedure in the Nonunion Setting: Caveat Employer," *SPEER Newsletter* (Special Supplement, February 1978), 1–4.
31. Ronald L. Miller, "Grievance Procedures for Nonunion Employees," *Public Personnel Management*, 7 (September/October 1978), 302–311. The following discussion is based on his study.
32. Epstein, "The Grievance Procedure."
33. *Lindsay* v. *Kissinger*, D.D.C. (1973), is an interesting case in which the judge ruled that the "selection out" process of the State Department violates due process.
34. Joseph Shane, "Indirect Functions of the Grievance Procedure," *Public Personnel Management*, 2 (May/June 1973), 171–178.

SUGGESTED READINGS

American Society for Public Administration. *Professional Standards and Ethics: A Workbook for Administrators.* Washington, D.C.: ASPA, 1979.

Bolton, John R. *The Hatch Act: A Civil Libertarian Defense.* Washington, D.C.: American Enterprise Institute for Policy Research, 1976.

Bowman, James S. "Ethics in the Federal Service: A Post-Watergate View." *Midwest Review of Public Administration,* 11 (March 1977), 3–20.

Council of State Governments. *Ethics: State Conflict of Interest/Financial Disclosure Legislation, 1972–1975.* Lexington, KY: The Council of State Governments, 1975.

Donahue, Robert J. "Disciplinary Actions in New York State Service: A Radical Change." *Public Personnel Management,* 4 (March/April 1975), 110–112.

Dwoskin, Robert P. *Rights of the Public Employee.* Chicago: American Library Association, 1978.

Heisel, W.D., and Richard M. Gladstone. "Off-the-Job Conduct as a Disciplinary Problem. *Public Personnel Review,* 29 (January 1968), 23–28.

Martin, Philip L. "The Constitutionality of the Hatch Act: Second-class Citizenship for Public Employees." *University of Toledo Law Review,* 6 (Fall 1974), 78–109.

Martin, Philip L. "The Hatch Act in Court: Some Recent Developments." *Public Administration Review,* 33 (September/October 1973), 443–447.

———. "The Improper Discharge of a Federal Employee by a Constitutionally Permissible Process: The OEO Case." *Administrative Law Review,* 28 (Winter 1976), 27–39.

———. "Return to the Privilege-Right Doctrine in Public Employment." *Labor Law Journal,* June 1977, pp. 361–368.

Rose, Henry. "A Critical Look at the Hatch Act." *Harvard Law Review,* 75 (January 1962), 510–526.

Rosenbloom, David H. "The Constitution and the Civil Service: Some Recent Developments, Judicial and Political." *Kansas Law Review,* 18 (June 1970), 839–869.

Timmins, William. *Long Hair in a Merit System: An Appeal from Utopia Avenue.* Syracuse: The Inter-University Case Program, 1972.

Wakefield, Susan. "Ethics and the Public Service: A Case for Individual Responsibility." *Public Administration Review,* 36 (November/December 1976), 661–666.

Homespun Politics

Homespun County is a rural county with one large town which serves as the center of economic enterprise and is the county seat. The county is predominantly Democratic in political party affiliation, although the Republican party is beginning to show strength in local elections. It even succeeded in winning one of the county commissioner positions in the last election.

Jim Easterly is a data processing technician in the county tax-assessor collector's office and spends all his time working with data processing activities. His job does not call for any direct contact with anyone outside the office.

Jim, a Republican, decided to attend his precinct caucus. The caucus elected him as a delegate to the county convention, where he was elected to the state Republican convention as a delegate. In each of these conventions Jim said very little and never spoke out in a public forum. He did, however, work with the leadership, and he voted on convention business.

Tom West, a Democratic county commissioner, learned of Jim Easterly's activities. Because the state has a little Hatch Act prohibiting political activity by civil service employees, he has asked the director of data processing to terminate Easterly's employment. The director does so, but Jim Easterly decides to appeal to the personnel appeals board, which handles cases where employees feel they have been mistreated.

You are a member of the appeals board and you must vote on whether the action against Easterly was valid and, if so, whether the severity of the punishment was warranted.

1. What information will you want to have before deciding how to vote?
2. How would the nature of the information affect your vote?
3. Outside of the specific decision which must be made, how do you feel about the kind of regulation at issue? Why?

CASE 9.2

Mary Hinson

Klink Air Force Base is an installation which monitors sensitive defense information. It uses sophisticated technology and maintains top security over all its activities.

A new contract was signed with Top Clean, a custodial firm, to provide for routine custodial services. Under terms of the contract, all employees of the firm must clear security checks and must present a special identification card when they come to work on the base.

Mary Hinson has worked for Top Clean for fifteen years and is one of their best employees. She asked to work on the base as it was convenient to her home.

A few days after working on the base, she was asked by the security officer, Major Alert, to turn in her identification card. He refused to tell her why, and she appealed to the Air Force hearing examiner, who ruled that the revocation of the identification was valid. The base commander affirmed that decision.

Mary hires you as her attorney. She wants to continue working at the base even though Top Clean wants her to work at one of its other locations.

1. As her attorney, what action might you take?
2. Do you expect to be successful in helping her? Explain.

Chapter 10

Labor-Management Relations

It has frequently been noted in this book that many differences exist between public and private-sector personnel management. None, however, has been more clear-cut than the experience with collective bargaining. While the private sector has had a long history of collective bargaining, the public sector until recently has been characterized by an almost total absence of effective collective bargaining. Many public administrators reflect the opposition to collective bargaining by insisting on using the term labor-management relations.

This book uses the two terms more or less interchangeably, although labor-management relations generally refers to all aspects of the interchange between labor and management, while collective bargaining refers more specifically to the process by which labor and management participate in mutual decision making regarding the work situation. In such decision-making, employees organize and select a representative to work on their behalf with management. In the absence of collective bargaining, employees are on their own. They must negotiate individually with their employers over aspects of the work situation; what normally occurs is that management decides unilaterally.

While much of the growth in public-sector collective bargaining has been recent, some public employees have had a long history of unionization. Craftsmen in naval installations, for example, have been organized since the early part of the nineteenth century, and the

National Association of Letter Carriers came into existence in the late nineteenth century as an affiliate of the American Federation of Labor. Some state and local employees have also been unionized for a relatively long period of time. The International Association of Fire Fighters, an AFL-CIO affiliate, started in the 1880s as local social clubs and fire-men's benefit societies. Similarly, the American Federation of State, County, and Municipal Employees (AFSCME) began in 1936 under the auspices of the American Federation of Labor. The American Federation of Labor (AF of L) and Congress of Industrial Organizations (CIO) were national umbrella organizations which provided financial, political, and technical support to individual affiliates and local organizations. Originally one organization, they split in 1937 over internal disagreements about approaches to collective bargaining and because of personality conflicts among some of the leaders. After many years of spirited competition, the two groups merged again in 1955 to form the AFL-CIO.

Unionization, however, does not necessarily entail collective bargaining. It was not until the 1960s that collective bargaining played an important role in public personnel administration.[1] President John Kennedy's Executive Order 10988 in 1962 was a major force in stimulating public-sector bargaining activity. It granted federal employees the right to organize and engage in collective bargaining. Executive Orders 11491 (1969) and 11616 (1971) by President Richard Nixon and 11838 by President Gerald Ford clarified and formalized the bargaining process for federal employees. The Civil Service Reform Act of 1978 brought about further changes, which are discussed later in the chapter. One of the most significant features of the reform act was to spell out in statute the right to collective bargaining so that presidents no longer have the authority to regulate the process on their own. The process by which personnel decisions are made reflects the influence of labor organizations since the early 1960s.

Government Resistance

Several factors account for the lack of public-sector collective bargaining in the past. Among them were an unfavorable legal environment; legal doctrines of government sovereignty and privilege; an essentiality-of-service argument; the professional status of many public employees; the pay and fringe benefit levels of some employees; and the availability of other means by which employees could obtain their objectives. Additionally, the negative reaction of the public to collective bargaining among government employees constrained development of the process.

In general, the public has not looked favorably on public-sector employee bargaining, although in the 1960s and 1970s attitudes changed somewhat.[2] Many are afraid that unions already have too much power and would only gain more if they were permitted to bargain with government. Because unions help elect public officials who are supposed to represent the public, many critics feel an undue advantage would be accorded public employees if they also had unions bargaining for them.[3]

The power of unions may be exaggerated. Public employee unions, especially at the federal level, are restricted from engaging in partisan political activity and cannot negotiate for union security agreements guaranteeing that the employees they represent join the union or pay dues.[4] There are also numerous restrictions on what items can be bargained: pay and fringe benefits are excluded in federal bargaining and in some state and local jurisdictions. As some writers point out, public employee unions are also at a disadvantage because they have no natural allies in the political process, as most organized political interests find them easy targets for attack.[5] Management often uses the fear of union power to justify denying collective bargaining to public employees.

The political climate contributed to a legal framework in which bargaining was made difficult. Government employees were specifically exempted from the protections of the Wagner and Taft-Hartley acts, which spelled out the rights and responsibilities of parties in private-sector bargaining. Additionally, prior to 1960 courts consistently held that public employees had no constitutional right to join or organize unions, and public employers were under no obligation to bargain with employees. Starting in 1954, when by executive order Mayor Robert Wagner granted New York City employees the right to organize, the legal environment underwent rapid change. The collective bargaining apparatus was established in 1958, and the city began its bargaining process. In 1959 Wisconsin became the first state to authorize collective bargaining for public employees; however, only local government employees were affected since state employees were exempted from the law. With the aforementioned Kennedy order, the 1960s saw a flourishing of unionization and bargaining at all levels of government.

Prior to the Kennedy order, collective bargaining was nonexistent in the federal government service, although the Lloyd-LaFollette Act of 1912 granted employees the right to join labor organizations and to petition Congress without fear of reprisal. Before passage of that act, federal employees were subject to mandatory discharge and forfeiture of civil service status for union activity. Similarly, legislation in 1955 declared that a strike against the federal government was a felony and disqualified the participant from federal employment. The Kennedy Executive Order, however, signalled a turning point in labor relations. While it changed federal policy on bargaining with federal government employees, it also stimulated state and local governments to reexamine and change many of their policies.

There is no common legal framework under which state and local government labor relations are governed. Thus the fifty states have their own policies or nonpolicies, and many other variations are seen in the approximately eighty thousand local government jurisdictions across the country. Labor relations take place under policies made through common law doctrines, judicial decisions, executive orders, and statutes and ordinances.

Some forty-three states have statutes which govern collective bargaining among public employees, but there the similarity ends. States such as Michigan, Indiana, New York, and Hawaii have comprehensive laws covering all public employees. Other states such as Texas and Georgia have legislation governing certain groups of employees such as police, fire fighters, or teachers. Still others—for example, North Carolina and Tennessee—prohibit state and local entities from bargaining with their employees. Finally, in the absence of legislation in some states, Colorado and Arkansas among them, policy has been established by court decisions or opinions of the attorney general. Only Mississippi has no stated policy on the issue.[6]

Part of the legal environment used to preclude public employees from the bargaining process involved governmental doctrines. One is the sovereignty-of-government doctrine. This concept holds that government is the agent of the people and cannot delegate authority to others —such as employee organizations—without violating the trust the people placed in government. In other words, the authority is not the government's to delegate. In recent years the doctrine has waned in significance as governments have found it necessary to delegate power in a variety of areas and as courts have weakened the doctrine in many decisions.[7]

The privilege doctrine is another legal device which has been used to discourage public-sector collective bargaining. This doctrine holds that some benefits which governments confer are privileges and not rights. Education, welfare, and the like have been adjudged to be privileges. Similarly, public employment is viewed as a privilege extended to employees by government. Government can place restrictions on that privilege; prohibition of collective bargaining has been one such restriction. As with the sovereignty doctrine, the courts have greatly modified the privilege doctrine, and it no longer restricts bargaining in the public sector.[8]

Services performed by governments have ordinarily been characterized as essential, and bargaining has been denied public employees because of this essentiality of services. Particularly because collective bargaining is often equated with strikes, the prohibition of bargaining has been justified as a way of preventing the interruption of services. This argument has been weakened of late because many of the services that government provides are not viewed as essential. In fact, many private-sector services—the telephone, for example—would be more difficult to do without than many government services such as education or highway maintenance. Experience with loss of services such as sanitation, police, and education through strikes has demonstrated that people can cope with the situation and has lessened the fears surrounding collective bargaining. It must also be remembered that collective bargaining does not necessarily mean strikes will occur.

Public employees themselves have often been hesitant to engage in collective bargaining. Until the 1960s, unions and other labor organizations were not held in high esteem by public employees. Much public-sector labor is white collar, and there has been a tendency for employees to think of labor organizations as typically blue collar. Teachers in particular have been split over whether it is professional to belong to a union and engage in collective bargaining. Finding that unions could bring them gains, public employees have been changing their views, and many professional associations are becoming bargaining agents for public employees.

While pay and fringe benefits of state and local government employees are often poor, federal employees have very good fringe benefits; compensation, while not excessive, has also been relatively good. As a result, federal employees have been slower to see a need for collective bargaining than were some of their state and local counterparts. Nonetheless, federal workers are now more highly unionized than any other governmental sector.

Finally, public employees have had other means at their disposal for gaining their objectives. Because the decision makers are elected politicians, public employees have been able to gain access through participation in the election process. Employee groups can be effective forces in areas where they are highly concentrated. Because legislative bodies often retain control over pay and fringe benefits, lobbying is also an important method for gaining influence. Lack of centralized authority in the political system permits interests to gain in one place what they could not get in another. Thus if the executive does not satisfy the group, the group can go to the legislative body or a competing board or agency. Public employee groups have been effective in taking advantage of fragmented political structures—particularly at the local level.[9]

Politics and the Bargaining Process

Most experts agree that the major factor which differentiates public and private-sector collective bargaining is the political nature of the decision-making process in public-sector bargaining.[10] As Theodore Clark notes, collective bargaining is premised on the idea that the two parties to the bargaining process are adversaries who seek their own interests, and each party selects its representative without being influenced by the other party.[11] In the public sector, however, political considerations serve to violate these premises. In particular, public employee organizations participate in the selection of management through involvement in interest-group politics and through the election process. In short, employee organizations have special access to the decision-making process of management, thus enhancing the power of the organizations vis à vis management. A lot of the literature on public-sector bargaining decries the special position enjoyed by the public employee labor organizations and suggests that unions and the like dominate the process as a result.[12]

Summers, on the other hand, believes public employees need that special access because they face formidable opposition from all other interests in the political process.[13] Because tax revenues have to be raised or levels of service reduced to finance public employee demands, the political opposition to employee demands can be intense. The taxpayer revolts symbolized by California's Proposition 13 in 1978, and its stimulation of similar efforts in other jurisdictions, attest to the impact an aroused electorate can have. Similarly, public employees in San Francisco bore the brunt of taxpayer discontent with some of the employee gains in 1974 and 1975. Through referenda, salaries were rolled back and limits were established regarding how and what could be bargained. Thus abuses by employee organizations can be cited, but active citizen participation in the political process can also dwarf the influence of public employee organizations.

The political nature of public-sector collective bargaining is also reflected in the way management selects its representatives and decides on the policy it will bring to the bargaining table. Again, as Summers points out, citizens have an interest in these issues, whereas in the private sector, management makes such decisions without public involvement.[14] Because decisions on how management will select a representative and on what the bargaining position will be are matters of public concern, employee organizations have input into them, again augmenting their influence. On the other hand, management is normally prohibited from attempting to influence employee selection of bargaining agents and positions.

Additionally, it is difficult for management to send someone to the bargaining table who can bind public management. There are many other decision makers to whom the employee organizations can appeal if they do not get satisfaction in the actual bargaining process. Many times city councils or other legislative bodies need to ratify agreements and are hesitant to give up any authority to change elements of the agreement. Similarly, legislative bodies retain control over many aspects of the work situation, either mandating or setting restrictions on personnel practices. For local governments the issue is even more complicated by the fact that state legislation can mandate practices for all governmental bodies. If a state minimum salary or other requirement is imposed, the local jurisdiction has little flexibility. The costs normally have to be borne by the local government even though the policy comes from above. Public employee organizations use their access to elected political leaders to influence the decision-making process and participate in the election of such officials.

Another political aspect of public-sector bargaining is that personnel issues have larger policy implications. They are part of the policy-making process to the extent that the political representatives make the decisions in many cases and affect such issues as tax policy, budgeting, and level of services.[15] The political representatives are influenced by what will gain them votes. Such concerns often lead to problems if the political leader does not own up to the consequences of trying to curry favor with employee organizations for the purpose of gaining elective office. Officials in some cities, such as New York City, agreed to contracts whose costs were borne by future administrations. Pension plans in particular are often subject to such political manipulation. In the short run the politician gains, but the taxpayers and succeeding officials are then faced with bearing the long-term cost. Unless the public is made fully aware of the ultimate cost, it is difficult to prevent opportunistic politicians from taking advantage of the situation.

As a result of these problems, the "fish bowl" approach to public-sector bargaining has many advocates. The fish-bowl approach means that bargaining is done in public. In the private sector, closed-door sessions are almost universal. The public sector, however, runs into problems when it conducts closed negotiation sessions. In a democratic society, people are supposed to know what is going on so that they may retain control over the system. If bargaining is conducted in private, they can have no input into the process and hence relinquish control to the participants of the negotiation. On the other hand, when negotiation takes place in open meetings, participants may find themselves pushed into corners on the issues. Once people state a position publicly, it becomes difficult to change it because they may be perceived as backing down. Since negotiation requires compromise, it becomes exceedingly difficult to bargain effectively in public sessions. There is no easy way of reconciling the need for openness in democratic government and the need for frankness and compromise in collective bargaining.

The Bargainers and Their Selection

To have negotiations it is necessary to have representatives from each party. Management chooses a bargaining team, and employees decide on a representative or bargaining agent.

THE MANAGEMENT TEAM

As noted earlier, management often finds it difficult to organize for bargaining because of the fragmentation of political authority in government units. Moreover, because a great deal of energy has been expended in earlier attempts to resist collective bargaining, management has been ill-prepared to negotiate with employees. However, the situation has been changing rapidly, as many public managers have enrolled in special training programs and are becoming bargaining specialists.

To prepare for bargaining it is necessary to develop a management philosophy and make sure that people involved understand it fully. Management must anticipate the demands of its employees as much as possible so that it can prepare specific positions and be ready to offer alternatives.

A bargaining team must be selected with one individual usually assigned responsibility to speak for management. Labor relations specialists are employed in large jurisdictions. The bargaining team also normally includes personnel managers and legal counsel, although how formally organized such a team is depends upon the jurisdiction.

In addition to the actual negotiators, government has agencies supervising the bargaining process. The national government, under the Civil Service Reform Act of 1978, created a Federal Labor Relations Authority (FLRA) to oversee bargaining unit determination, supervise elections, and coordinate agency labor-management activities. The FLRA consists of three bipartisan presidential appointees with one designated as chairperson. Also appointed is a general counsel who investigates unfair labor practices, while the Federal Service Impasses Panel resolves impasses in the negotiation process.

At the state and local levels, the supervision of the collective bargaining process is varied. Some states create an agency whose sole purpose is to supervise public employee labor relations—usually including local governments. Maine, New York, and Hawaii are examples of such states. Another approach is to assign the responsibility to personnel departments, departments of labor, or personnel boards, as is done in Alaska, Massachusetts, Montana, and Wisconsin. A combination of approaches may be used in which a state board may oversee collective bargaining generally but individual departments have the specific responsibility for bargaining in their areas. Thus it is common to see departments of education or local boards of education having responsibility for supervising bargaining in their areas.

THE EMPLOYEE TEAM

Employees choose representatives to bargain for them. The selection process usually requires an election in which employees decide whether to adopt collective bargaining and, if so, who will bargain for them. The two actions may be taken at the same or separate elections. Representatives of employees fall into three main categories: unions, employee associations, and professional associations. All have become active in public-sector bargaining.[16]

Unions, of course, are most readily recognized as participants in collective bargaining, as they have been the traditional agents of employees in the private sector. Unions in the public sector may have members from that sector only or may have members from both the public and private sector. In late 1978 federal government employees were represented by seventy-eight different unions and associations, and the number at the state and local levels was even larger.[17]

The largest union is the American Federation of State, County and Municipal Employees (AFSCME) with a membership of over a million. Membership tells only part of the story, however. Unions in the public sector represent everyone in the bargaining unit even though they cannot require all employees in the unit to be dues-paying members. AFSCME represents well over 1.5 million employees at the local, state, and national levels. Very few, roughly 5,500, are federal government employees.

Representing mostly federal government employees are three other relatively large unions. The American Federation of Government Employees (AFGE) represents approximately 680,000 employees and has about 265,000 members, while the National Federation of Federal Employees (NFFE) represents 139,000 and has about 35,000 members. The National Treasury Employees Union (NTEU) represents approximately 99,000 and has about 65,000 members. Interestingly enough, the NTEU is gaining membership while other federal employee unions are having difficulty retaining members. One reason given for the loss of membership is that employers do not believe that unions and collective bargaining can help on the most important issues of wages and fringes. Other reasons cited are the cutbacks in civilian public employment and the constant rivalry from largely private-sector unions for membership.[18] While individual unions are losing membership, the total number of employees at the federal level reached an all-time high in 1978 at 2.1 million, with 1,228,136 civilian employees, other than those in the Postal Service, being represented by unions.[19] Thus about 60 percent of federal civilian employees are represented. Postal employees represented by unions numbered approximately 576,000.

The uniformed services are also represented by unions with almost exclusively public-sector membership. Police are represented by two major organizations, the Fraternal Order of Police (FOP) and the International Conference of Police Associations (ICPA). Some other unions such as AFSCME and the Teamsters also represent police in some jurisdictions. Because police protection is one of those essential services people are afraid of losing, these unions have been successful in obtaining their demands. Police unions usually play up the professional nature of their work and organizations rather than the union image which normally goes with such employee organizations. In recent years strike activity has increased—as in Albuquerque, San Francisco, Memphis, New Orleans—but sick-ins and slowdowns are more common techniques used by police employee unions.

The tactics are not always successful, however, as the experience of the New Orleans police in 1979 demonstrated. The strike, timed to occur during Mardi Gras, the city's busiest tourist season, was calculated to bring the pressure of business and the community to bear on the public officials. The union expected that such pressure would make management settle quickly to the benefit of the police. The actual result was that much of the Mardi Gras celebration was curtailed; the police union lost credibility with, and support of, the community; management held out until the police were willing to settle for what was essentially management's original offer. The New Orleans experience demonstrates the growing frustration of the taxpayer and shows that unions do not necessarily get what they want. Similarly, Atlanta Mayor Jackson's firing of 900 sanitation workers in 1977 and similar action in San Antonio in 1978 led to breaking of public-sector strikes. More and more public employee unions will see management taking a tougher stand as taxpayers become more militant in their demands.

Firefighters also have a long tradition of collective bargaining in an essential-service area. They are almost unique among public employees to the extent that the International Association of Firefighters (IAFF) exercises virtually exclusive jurisdiction over them. In contrast to the police organizations, the 170,000-member IAFF has traditionally stressed its union image and is associated with the AFL-CIO. While the national union does not officially sanction strikes, it does provide assistance to striking locals. Memphis and Chattanooga, Tennessee, and Manchester, New Hampshire, are cities where firefighters have recently been engaged in strikes or work actions.

As noted earlier, some unions consist of membership from both the public and private sectors. During the late 1950s many private-sector unions experienced declining membership and looked to the growing public sector to increase their rolls. These unions tend to seek members from all levels of government rather than from just one level. The AFL-CIO now has a department devoted entirely to public-sector collective bargaining. Reflecting the tradition of the private sector, these unions tend to be more occupationally segregated and more likely to favor strikes. Among these mixed-membership unions are the Service Employees International Union with a membership over 500,000, of whom more than 200,000 are public employees; the International Brotherhood of Teamsters with approximately 75,000 public employee members; and the Amalgamated Transit Union with approximately 70,000 public employee members. Many other unions have mixed membership. The mixed-membership unions have their interests divided between the private- and public-sector contingents, thus leading to some concern about how strongly they will represent public employee interests. However, they have the vast resources of the parent union behind them and are effective in marshalling support in the political process.

The second category of employee representation is the public employee association. Some associations on the state and local levels have existed for many years. Although originally organized to improve employee opportunities and the status of public employees, the associations have redirected their activities toward collective bargaining.[20] Because of their original purposes, they tend to be less in favor of strike activity and rely heavily upon public relations and lobbying. They are becoming increasingly militant, however, as competition for membership develops between them and the unions.

The Assembly of Government Employees is a loosely organized nationwide federation of independent, mostly state employee associations. Its associations have a membership of more than 700,000 public employees, but because of the independence of its affiliates it is not as strong a force as some smaller bargaining organizations. A similar but separate organization is the American Association of Classified School Employees.

Professional associations, the third category, have also been organized for a long time to better the status of their professions and members.

However, membership is much more limited than that of public employee associations in that educational or occupational criteria are imposed for membership. They have generally resisted joining the bargaining movement because they viewed bargaining as nonprofessional behavior. However, the success of unions and employee associations in recruiting members and in gaining benefits for members has stimulated professional groups to organize for collective bargaining.

Among the more active professional associations are the American Nurses Association (ANA), the National Association of Social Workers (NASW), and the American Association of University Professors (AAUP). The National Education Association (NEA) is the largest, with a membership of over 1.5 million, and is also one of the most active in the bargaining process. Its state affiliates decide on how deeply involved they wish to be in the bargaining process. The NEA and its affiliates provide some of the clearest evidence of the conflict in professional organizations over the collective bargaining issue. It has been pushed further and further into the bargaining process by the success of the American Federation of Teachers (AFT) in recruiting members and winning benefits for its members. To retain its membership, NEA feels the necessity to engage in bargaining. The AAUP has faced similar conflict at the higher education level and finds pressures for becoming more active in bargaining constantly increasing.

The variety of employee organizations in the bargaining process creates numerous approaches to issues in labor-management relations. Unions tend to be the most militant, although they vary greatly from one to another. Those unions associated with private-sector as well as public-sector employees are usually more likely to support the right to strike, but police and firefighter unions have certainly been involved in such activity in recent years. Employee and professional associations usually prefer public relations and lobbying to accomplish their objectives but have been pushed to more militant positions by the success of unions in bargaining efforts. Additionally, some organizations, particularly employee associations, stress the independence of their affiliates, while unions stress the resources their national organizations provide them.

The Negotiating Process

An essential element of the bargaining process is a determination of what can be bargained—in other words the scope of bargaining. Depending on the legal provisions under which bargaining takes place, a few or a wide range of items may be negotiated. The national government policy is fairly restrictive in that pay and fringe benefits are excluded from collective bargaining, while state and local situations vary greatly. Commonly states which have collective bargaining permit bargaining on wages and fringe benefits. California is an example of a state in which virtually all personnel activities are open to bargaining, as is the case in the cities of Los Angeles and San Francisco. Some states such as Hawaii, Maine, and Pennsylvania exclude issues such as merit systems policies, personnel direction, or items subject to managerial discretion from the bargaining table. Occasionally a state will make it mandatory to bargain on issues such as pay (Nevada). The law tends to be less explicit in most states, but generally when bargaining is authorized, states and their local governments must bargain with their employees if the employees so wish.[21] Some items may be mandatory bargaining issues, for example, wages, while others such as training programs or counseling services may be bargained on a voluntary basis. Some issues are prohibited as well; thus discriminatory provisions could not be included in an agreement.

Once it is determined what can be bargained and the employees have decided to use collective bargaining procedures and have selected a representative, the process may begin. Ordinarily the employees will express the desire to bargain an issue or issues by presenting proposals covering whatever items they wish to consider.[22] A meeting is then held at which the procedures or "ground rules" are decided upon by the employee and management representatives.

Of course, management is also working on its own positions in order to be prepared for the substantive negotiations and normally presents the employees its proposals. After each side makes and explains its proposals, each has to study the other's positions so that reactions and counterproposals can be made. These reactions and counterproposals become the focus of the negotiating process.

In negotiations the behavior of the parties becomes extremely important. One or the other party may decide to take an aggressive, challenging, hard-line approach on every item, hoping to wear down the other side. Or, the strategy may be to focus on a few issues that are of particular importance and make concessions on other issues. The strategy chosen normally depends on how far apart the parties are and on how important the issues are to the party. Relative political power also becomes a factor in the public sector, as has been illustrated by some of the examples cited earlier, particularly in New York City where employee organizations can bring other political forces into play. In New Orleans and Atlanta, however, the employee organizations miscalculated their power to influence management through appeals to citizens and the business community.

Most collective bargaining ends in agreement at the negotiating table. Then each side has to take the agreement back to its constituency for approval. The members of the employee organization vote on ratification of the agreement. If they vote no, more negotiation is necessary. If yes, management then usually has to go to the relevant legislative body for approval and funding of the cost elements of the agreement. Occasionally a city council rejects an agreement, in which case new negotiations have to be started, but ordinarily the agreement wins approval. At the state and national levels, specific legislative approval is not usually required, but in states where salary and fringe benefits are bargained, funding for the provisions does require legislative appropriations, thus indirect approval.

If the parties do not reach agreement at the negotiating table, there are several alternatives to attempt to resolve the impasse. These alternatives are called impasse procedures and include mediation, fact-finding, arbitration, and referendum. All involve outside parties.

Mediation is the most common form of impasse resolution and is used by most jurisdictions which permit bargaining. In mediation a neutral individual—usually trained in labor negotiations—attempts to get the two parties to resolve their differences through compromise. While they cannot impose decisions on the parties, mediators meet with each party and discuss the points of disagreement and how they might be reconciled. Thus they recommend solutions to the parties in hopes that the parties will work out the differences themselves. Mediation appears to be effective in resolving most impasses in the public sector.[23]

Fact-finding is a variation on the mediation process. In fact-finding, a neutral third party works with both parties to the dispute and conducts a formal investigation of the issues separating them. The fact-finder issues a formal report stating the "facts" of the situation. The intent is that by formally pinpointing the differences, the report will bring pressure to bear on the parties to resolve their differences. In some instances, such as New York and Wisconsin, the reports must be made public in hopes public opinion and pressure will cause the parties to settle. Fact-finding is usually employed if mediation fails, and the majority of states which permit bargaining permit its use.

If fact-finding fails, the next step is more controversial. Because public jurisdictions generally prohibit strikes, some form of final, binding decision becomes attractive. The alternative normally available is arbitration. In arbitration a neutral third party has the authority to impose a settlement or, in the case of advisory arbitration, is called on to recommend a solution. Conventional arbitration is binding in the sense that if parties go to arbitration, they are bound to accept the arbitrator's decision. In the process of arbitration the arbitrator does much the same work as a mediator or fact-finder, evaluates the situation, and decides on an equitable resolution.

In some instances, final-offer arbitration is used. Each party presents the arbitrator with its final offer for settlement, and the arbitrator then selects the best of the two. The logic behind this approach is that the parties can be expected to offer the most reasonable solution possible out of fear that a worse settlement proposed by the other party might be selected by the arbitrator. The evidence on the effects of this tactic seems to be mixed. Some studies suggest that it does create better results in getting agreements at the negotiating table, and others indicate that it leads to less equitable decisions.[24] Connecticut and Indiana use forms of final-offer arbitration.

The fourth impasse procedure is voter referendum, in which either party may take contested issues to the public. Colorado uses this method. The experience with such a procedure is not extensive enough to have provided much evidence concerning its effect. Of particular interest to students of collective bargaining will be how bargainers react to the use of referenda. Perhaps representatives of each side will fear the response of voters. In these days of public demands for tax cuts, employee organizations may feel particularly constrained in their positions. As with final-offer arbitration, the referendum approach could bring pressure to get the decision made early in the bargaining process so as to avoid potentially harsher agreements imposed from outside.

The impasse procedures outlined here progress from the least to the most coercive in terms of outside parties being able to impose settlements. However, there is interaction among the processes. The developments in mediation and fact-finding provide part of the basis for the arbitration process if it gets that far. Variations in each of the procedures may also combine elements from one or more of the "pure" impasse procedures noted.

If the procedures outlined above are not available or do not lead to resolution of the impasse, employees may decide they have no alternative but to strike. While most jurisdictions prohibit strikes by public employees, there has been no dearth of strikes in recent years (see Table 10–1). As was noted at the beginning of the chapter, much of the opposition to collective bargaining for public employees was based on opposition to strikes, especially in essential services. Opposition to strikes is still evident to the extent that all but seven states prohibit strikes; and where they are permitted, they are generally very limited in that only certain types of employees may engage in them. Police, fire, hospital and correctional facility personnel are usually excluded. While public opinion and legislation during the late 1960s and early 1970s shifted toward greater acceptance of public employee strikes,

Table 10–1   Work Stoppages by Level of Government 1942–1977 (workers and days idle in thousands)

Year	Total[1]			Federal government			State government			Local government[2]		
	Number of Stoppages	Workers Involved	Days Idle During Year	Number of Stoppages	Workers Involved	Days Idle During Year	Number of Stoppages	Workers Involved	Days Idle During Year	Number of Stoppages	Workers Involved	Days Idle During Year
1942										39	6.0	23.7
1943										51	10.2	48.5
1944							2	0.4	8.0	34	5.3	57.7
1945										32	3.4	20.0
1946							1	(3)	(3)	61	9.6	51.0
1947										14	1.1	7.3
1948										25	1.4	8.8
1949										7	2.9	10.3
1950										28	4.0	32.7
1951										36	4.9	28.8
1952										49	8.1	33.4
1953										30	6.3	53.4
1954							1	(3)	.8	9	1.8	9.6
1955							1	.2	.5	16	1.3	6.7
1956										27	3.5	11.1
1957										12	.8	4.4
1958	15	1.7	7.5	—	—	—	1	(3)	(3)	14	1.7	7.4
1959	25	2.0	10.5	—	—	—	4	.4	1.6	21	1.6	57.2

Year	Total: Stoppages	Workers	Days idle	Federal: Stoppages	Workers	Days idle	State: Stoppages	Workers	Days idle	Local: Stoppages	Workers	Days idle
1960	36	28.6	58.4	—	—	—	3	1.0	1.2	33	27.6	67.7
1961	28	6.6	15.3	—	—	—	—	—	—	28	6.6	15.3
1962	28	31.1	79.1	5	4.2	33.8	2	1.7	2.3	21	25.3	43.1
1963	29	4.8	15.4	—	—	—	2	.3	2.2	27	4.6	67.7
1964	41	22.7	70.8	—	—	—	4	.3	3.2	37	22.5	57.7
1965	42	11.9	146.0	—	—	—	—	—	[4]1.3	42	11.9	145.0
1966	142	105.0	455.0	—	—	—	9	3.1	6.0	133	102.0	449.0
1967	181	132.0	1,250.0	—	—	—	12	4.7	16.3	169	127.0	1,230.0
1968	254	201.8	2,545.2	3	1.7	9.6	16	9.3	42.8	235	190.9	2,492.8
1969	411	160.0	745.7	2	.6	1.1	37	20.5	152.4	372	139.0	592.2
1970	412	333.5	2,023.2	3	155.8	648.3	23	8.8	44.6	386	168.9	1,330.5
1971	329	152.6	901.4	2	1.0	8.1	23	14.5	81.8	304	137.1	811.6
1972	375	142.1	1,257.3	—	—	—	40	27.4	273.7	335	114.7	983.5
1973	387	196.4	2,303.9	1	.5	4.6	29	12.3	133.0	357	183.7	2,166.3
1974	384	160.7	1,404.2	2	.5	1.4	34	24.7	86.4	348	135.4	1,316.3
1975	478	318.5	2,204.4	—	—	—	32	66.6	300.5	446	252.0	1,903.9
1976	378	180.7	1,690.7	1	(3)	(3)	25	33.8	148.2	352	146.8	1,542.6
1977	413	170.2	1,765.7	2	.4	.5	44	33.7	181.9	367	136.2	1,583.3

[1] The Bureau of Labor Statistics has published data on strikes in government in its annual reports since 1942. Before that year, they had been included in a miscellaneous category—other nonmanufacturing industries. From 1942 through 1957, data refer only to strikes in administrative, protective, and sanitary services of government. Stoppages in establishments owned by governments were classified in their appropriate industry; for example, public schools and libraries were included in education services, not in government. Beginning in 1958, stoppages in such establishments were included under the government classification. Stoppages in publicly owned utilities, transportation, and schools were reclassified back to 1947 but a complete reclassification was not attempted. After 1957, dashes denote zeros.

[2] Includes all stoppages at the county, city, and special district level.

[3] Fewer than 100.

[4] Idleness in 1965 resulted from 2 stoppages that began in 1964.

Note: Because of rounding, sums of individual items may not equal totals.

SOURCE: Reprinted from U.S. Department of Labor, Bureau of Statistics, Work Stoppages in Government, 1979, p. 4.

the mood is shifting again. As a Louis Harris poll in late 1978 indicates, people are becoming less tolerant of such activity by public employees.[25] While the public supported the right of sanitation workers and garbage collectors to strike by a 52–45 percent margin, the margin was way below the 56–37 majority in 1974. A shift from a 58–36 majority to a mere 50–48 percent majority opposing teachers' right to strike had taken place. The public also shifted from slight support of to slight opposition to police strikes and opposed firefighters striking compared to an even split in 1974. Clearly the public is concerned about strikes, and the general negative reaction to government bureaucracy and costs is probably taking its toll on public employees.

States such as Vermont, Pennsylvania, and Hawaii permit limited rights to strike by public employees, but more common are strict prohibitions. Even where prohibited, however, strikes have become a way of life. The strikes in Dayton, New Orleans, Memphis, and Kansas City in recent years were clearly against the law. But implementing the law is not an easy undertaking. Officials, including judges, are usually reluctant to enforce no-strike legislation by jailing strikers because of the possible martyr effect. The people jailed become heroes to other employees and strikes are likely to grow, along with public sympathy for employees willing to go to such lengths for their cause. Dealing with strikes—even illegal ones—is a risky affair.

As noted earlier, however, some jurisdictions have been very effective in handling them. In Atlanta, San Antonio, and Orlando, Florida, management resolved the issue and broke the strikes by firing employees. Yet such a response may damage the morale of other employees and the credibility of management with its work force. In Massachusetts in the summer of 1976, a state court justice ordered a fine of $250,000 per day for a striking state employee union, resulting in a rapid return to work by the employees. While such drastic action accomplishes management's desired results, questions must be raised concerning the long-term impact. The question of balance of power between management and employee organizations is clearly still open. While many fear the power of employee unions, the examples cited here certainly suggest that management is not without its own resources; taxpayer concerns over cost often bolster the employer's position.

Contract Administration

Once an agreement is reached, it then must be implemented; the process for doing so is contract administration. This process gives meaning to the agreement and is thus an important part of collective bargaining. Implementation is generally the responsibility of management, but the employees react to what they perceive to be mis-interpretations of the agreement by management. Many provisions in a contract may be vague, causing problems in interpretation. Parties may disagree on what is meant by such terms as, say, "reasonable time." Similarly, unanticipated situations develop and must be dealt with under the terms of the contract.

Normally the governmental jurisdiction has an office or individual responsible for the overall labor relations program. This person or office has the responsibility of coordinating the implementation of the agree-ment and the particular duty to see that the agreement is well under-stood by the rest of management. Interpretations of provisions can be made consistent through coordination by this office. The first line super-visor, however, is the key management person in contract administration. The supervisor must be carefully instructed about the provisions of the contract if problems are to be avoided in the day-to-day carrying out of the contract.

Employees may react through complaint over the way a part of the agreement is or is not implemented, and normally one individual is chosen as the shop steward. The steward represents the employee and tries to resolve complaints. The steward also monitors implementation to insure compliance with the agreement and raises objections as appro-priate.[26] Most of management's contact with employees concerning contract administration is through the steward.

Despite efforts to implement the agreement correctly, problems often develop, and disagreements as to specific provisions become unresolv-able by the parties. In the vast majority of bargaining agreements this eventuality is provided for by grievance arbitration. The process normally calls for the employee with a complaint to file a written grievance to the immediate supervisor. The complaint may be settled at this level, but usually the issue can be appealed up through top management for resolu-tion. If the parties are still unable to resolve the issue, arbitration is invoked. The process is essentially the same as in the arbitration pro-cedure for resolving impasses. If there is no grievance arbitration clause in the collective bargaining agreement, personnel or civil service rules will provide for dealing with complaints over implementation of the agreement.

Impact of Public-sector Bargaining

The effects of collective bargaining are felt in all areas of management and service delivery. There are clear implications for financial manage-ment, budgeting, personnel, and planning, and for the roles of em-ployees and managers in the system.

In the area of financial management and budgeting, collective bargaining agreements often lock the jurisdiction into positions from which it cannot easily extricate itself. As the effects of taxpayer demands clearly illustrate, voters believe collective bargaining adds to the cost of government. The empirical evidence continues to be rather confusing, however. Recent studies suggest that the impact has been to increase the cost of government but that the overall increases have been relatively small.[27] Because personnel costs typically make up 70 to 90 percent of a jurisdiction's budget, it is inevitable that increased personnel costs will affect the cost of government unless there is a reduction in personnel and services. As a result, as noted in chapter 8, the jurisdiction attempts to offset costs for personnel by calling for increased productivity. Clearly, more attention will be paid to this issue as experience with the bargaining process continues. The bargaining process puts the costs under constant scrutiny, thus providing the potential for containment and the elimination of unnecessary items.

The budgeting process is affected as well. Negotiation and agreement typically take place before the budget is developed. As a result, flexibility in budgeting may be reduced. If management or the legislative body refuses to provide funds to cover the costs of the agreement, including salaries and wages, problems with the employee organization are certain to develop. While legislative bodies have the power to adopt governmental budgets, the bargaining process actually reduces that authority and effectively places it in the hands of the bargaining parties. Budgeting and planning become very difficult when the flexibility of the decision makers is hampered.

An aspect of compensation involves the use of comparability pay in which jurisdictions pay according to salaries and wages for similar jobs in other government units or in the private sector. Collective bargaining often results in such provisions for employee groups and can have the effect of continually escalating the pay scale as each jurisdiction tries to stay in line with the others. It is quite possible that such provisions will become obsolete, however, since both parties to the bargaining process will be well aware of what the prevailing wage is if they are prepared for bargaining.

The personnel function is greatly affected by the bargaining process because it is very difficult to limit the scope of bargaining. Given the many states which permit bargaining on all aspects of the employment situation, all elements of the personnel system become bargainable. It seems clear that merit system principles and personnel rules and regulations will increasingly become the subject of negotiation and will change in the process.[28]

For management the effects of collective bargaining are many. Traditionally management has taken the position that bargaining would be detrimental to its ability to manage. There is no question that with collective bargaining, management must share its power to govern and has much less discretion. However, management can and does reap benefits from the bargaining process if it is willing to do so. Lanning S. Mosher points out that management can be improved through the bargaining process in that bargaining focuses attention on it as a team. By identifying weakness and negotiating training needs of management, the bargaining process provides leverage for obtaining the resources necessary to be well prepared for negotiating and working with labor organizations.[29] Management is also under pressure to do a good job when it knows its activities will be under scrutiny in the bargaining process.

Collective bargaining has the potential of creating a wide variety of types of working conditions as each group of employees bargains with management. However, with a standard general policy under which agreements are bargained, the process can produce decisions which reflect a general perspective rather than the particular concerns of the moment or situation. In other words, it helps establish a general policy within which decisions can be made.

For employees, bargaining also has many effects, not the least of which is the ability to participate in deciding what the working conditions are to be. Workers often find that unionization and bargaining help them develop a consciousness; this was particularly true of employees in jobs such as sanitation and garbage collection. During the 1960s racial minorities who were relegated to these positions found unionization to be both a way of gaining dignity as human beings and a force for racial and social justice.[30] Generally, employees consider that collective bargaining protects them against arbitrariness in personnel and managerial decisions.[31] Additionally, because employees participate in the decision-making processes, they are likely to be more committed to the organization than when management unilaterally dictates policy. In fact, management often has an ally in the employee representative in getting its policies across. Employees are much more receptive to decisions that are explained by one of their own.[32] Otherwise, they may be obstacles to change and accommodation to management's desires.[33]

Summary

Most experts in public-sector collective bargaining believe that it will continue to expand. However, the constraints under which it takes place will also cause it to change. The political environment in the period of the early 1980s is likely to require restraint on the part of the employee organizations lest they become counterproductive by further arousing the voters against them. Limited resources of governments will create greater emphasis on productivity improvement and thus on productivity bargaining. Trade-offs in increased productivity for increased employee benefits will become a more and more common aspect of public-sector bargaining.

Greater experimentation with alternatives to strikes will also be likely. The referendum method of dealing with impasses, used in Colorado, will be watched closely and possibly will be emulated in other jurisdictions. Multi-jurisdictional bargaining, in which more than one jurisdiction bargains with a union, is likely to increase as well. Especially in large urban areas, where many governmental units exist, governments will find area-wide contracts helpful in avoiding a whipsawing effect as one jurisdiction grants a benefit only to have it used in the next as a basis for changes in agreements or the like.

Clearly collective bargaining is a factor with which governments and the public must deal. How well the differences between the parties involved in the process are reconciled will determine the level and quality of service the general public can expect.

NOTES

1. See Thomas R. Brooks, *Toil and Trouble*, 2nd ed. (New York: Dell, 1971), for an excellent history of the labor movement and ch. 23 for specific review of the public sector.
2. D.S. Chauhan, *Public Labor Relations: A Comparative State Study*, a Sage Professional Paper (Beverly Hills: Sage Publications, 1976), p. 8.
3. See Sara Silbiger, "The Missing Public: Collective Bargaining in Public Employment," *Public Personnel Management*, 4 (September/October 1975), 290–299; and Clyde W. Summers, "Public Bargaining: A Political Perspective," *Yale Law Journal*, 83 (May 1974), 1156–2000, at 1160–1164.
4. See James W. Singer, "The Limited Power of Federal Worker Unions," *National Journal*, 39 (September 32, 1978), 1547–1551.
5. Summers, "Public Bargaining," 1166–1168.
6. See *Summary of Public-sector Labor Relations Policies* (Washington, D.C.: U.S. Department of Labor, Labor-Management Services Administration, 1976).
7. The sovereignty issue is discussed fully by Louis V. Immundo, Jr., "Federal Government Sovereignty and Its Effect on Labor-Management Relations," *Labor Law Journal*, March 1975, pp. 146–151; and delegation is examined by Robert S. Lorch, *Democratic Process and Administrative Law* (Detroit: Wayne State University Press, 1969).

8. For excellent analyses of the privilege doctrine, see Philip L. Martin, "Return to the Privilege-Right Doctrine in Public Employment," *Labor Law Journal*, June 1977, pp. 361–368, and David H. Rosenbloom, "Public Personnel Administration and the Constitution: An Emergent Approach," *Public Administration Review*, 35 (January/February 1975), 52–59.

9. See John F. Burton, "Local Government Bargaining and Management Structure," *Industrial Relations*, 11 (May 1972), 123–140.

10. This discussion is based on the conflicting ideas of two of the most knowledgeable experts on the issue, Clyde W. Summers, "Public-sector Bargaining: Problems of Governmental Decision Making," *Cincinnati Law Review*, 44 (1975), 668–679, and R. Theodore Clark, Jr., "Politics and Public Employee Unionism: Some Recommendations for an Emerging Problem," *Cincinnati Law Review*, 44 (1975), 680–689.

11. Ibid., 684.

12. For example, Silbiger, "The Missing Public"; George Bennett, "The Elusive Public Interest in Labor Disputes," *Labor Law Journal*, 25 (November 1974), 678–681; and Raymond D. Horton, *Municipal Labor Relations in New York City* (New York: Praeger, 1973).

13. Summers, "Public-sector Bargaining," 674–677.

14. Ibid., 670.

15. Ibid., provides an excellent analysis of the policy implications.

16. Jack Stieber, *Public Employee Unionism: Structure, Growth, and Policy* (Washington, D.C.: Brookings, 1973), provides in-depth review of alternative organizations, especially pp. 1–9.

17. See Singer, "The Limited Power of Federal Worker Unions," 1547–1549.

18. Ibid.

19. *OPM News*, April 3, 1979.

20. See James F. Marshall, "Public Employee Associations: Roles and Programs," *Public Personnel Management*, 3 (September/October 1974), 415–424, for a review of such organizations.

21. A good but slightly dated review of state, local, and national policies on this and other issues is found in *Public-sector Labor Relations Policies*.

22. An excellent step-by-step outline of the process is provided in Florida Department of Community Affairs, *Collective Bargaining*, rev. (Tallahasse: State of Florida Department of Community Affairs, November 1977). This publication is part of an excellent series published by the department with IPA grant support.

23. See Thomas P. Gilroy and Anthony U. Sinicropi, "Impasse Resolution in Public Employment: A Current Assessment," *Industrial and Labor Relations Review*, 25 (July 1972), 496–511.

24. Peter Feuille, "Final-offer Arbitration and the Chilling Effect," *Industrial Relations*, 14 (October 1975), 302–310; and Charles Feigenbaum, "Final Arbitration: Better Theory than Practice," *Industrial Relations*, 14 (October 1975), 311–317.

25. Chicago Tribune-N.Y. News Syndicate, November 1978.

26. For an excellent discussion of the whole contract administration process, see *Questions and Answers on Contract Administration* (Bloomington, IN: School of Public and Environmental Affairs, 1978), and Mollie H. Bowers, *Contract Administration in the Public Sector* (Chicago: International Personnel Management Association, 1976).
27. For a comprehensive review of the studies of the issue, see Ralph Jones, *Public-Sector Labor Relations: An Evaluation of Policy-related Research* (Cambridge, MA: Ballinger, 1977).
28. These issues are discussed in detail in Muriel M. Morse, "The Impact of Collective Bargaining on the Merit System," *Public Service*, 5 (June 1978), 1–4.
29. Lanning S. Mosher, "Facing the Realities of Public Employee Bargaining," *Public Personnel Management*, 7 (July/August 1978), 243–248.
30. Gus Tyler, "Why They Organize," *Public Administration Review*, 32 (March/April 1972), 97–101.
31. Louis V. Immundo, Jr., "Why Federal Government Employees Join Unions: A Study of AFGE Local 916," *Public Personnel Management*, 2 (January/February 1973), 23–28, and David T. Stanley, "The Effect of Unions on Local Government," *Proceedings of the Academy of Political Science*, 28 (December 1970), 42–54.
32. David Lewin, "Public Employment Relations: Confronting the Issues," *Industrial Relations*, 12 (October 1973), 309–321, at 311.
33. For an example of a case in which management's directives were not accepted, see Wes Uhlman, "Standing Up to Union Pressures," *Nation's Cities*, 13 (November 1975), 12–14.

SUGGESTED READINGS

Bent, Alan Edward, and T. Zane Reeves. *Collective Bargaining in the Public Sector*. Menlo Park, CA: Benjamin/Cummings, 1978.

Bowers, Mollie H. *Contract Administration in the Public Sector*. Chicago: International Personnel Management Association, 1976.

Burton, John F. "Local Government Bargaining and Management Structure." *Industrial Relations*, 11 (May 1972), 123–140.

Clark, Theodore R., Jr. "Politics and Public Employee Unionism: Some Recommendations for an Emerging Problem." *Cincinnati Law Review*, 44 (1975), 680–689.

Feigenbaum, Charles. "Final Arbitration: Better Theory than Practice." *Industrial Relations*, 14 (October 1975), 311–317.

Feuille, Peter. "Final-offer Arbitration and the Chilling Effect." *Industrial Relations*, 14 (October 1975), 302–310.

Gilroy, Thomas P., and Anthony U. Sinicropi. "Impasse Resolution in Public Employment: A Current Assessment." *Industrial and Labor Relations Review*, 25 (July 1972), 496–511.

Horton, Raymond D. *Municipal Labor Relations in New York City: Lessons of the Lindsay-Wagner Years*. New York: Praeger, 1973.

Jones, Ralph. *Public-sector Labor Relations: An Evaluation of Policy-related Research.* Cambridge, MA: Ballinger, 1977.

Loewenberg, Joseph J., and Michael H. Moskow. *Collective Bargaining in the Public Service: Readings and Cases.* Englewood Cliffs, NJ: Prentice-Hall, 1972.

Midwest Center for Public Sector Labor Relations. *Questions and Answers on Fact-finding.* Bloomington, IN: Indiana University, School of Public and Environmental Affairs, 1978.

————. *Questions and Answers on Collective Bargaining.* Bloomington, IN: Indiana University, School of Public and Environmental Affairs, 1977.

————. *Questions and Answers on Unfair Labor Practices.* Bloomington, IN: Indiana University, School of Public and Environmental Affairs, 1977.

————. *Sources of Information in Public-sector Labor Relations.* Bloomington, IN: Indiana University, School of Public and Environmental Affairs, 1977.

————. *Questions and Answers in Public-sector Labor Relations.* Bloomington, IN: Indiana University, School of Public and Environmental Affairs, 1976.

————. *Terms in Public-sector Labor Relations.* Bloomington, IN: Indiana University, School of Public and Environmental Affairs, 1976.

————. *Primer in Public-sector Labor Relations.* Bloomington, IN: Indiana University, School of Public and Environmental Affairs, 1976.

————. *Public-sector Rules and Regulations in the Midwest.* Bloomington, IN: Indiana University, School of Public and Environmental Affairs, 1975.

————. *Public-sector Labor Legislation in the Midwest.* Bloomington, IN: Indiana University, School of Public and Environmental Affairs, 1975.

Morse, Muriel M. "The Impact of Collective Bargaining on the Merit System." *Public Service,* 5 (June 1978), 1–4.

Stieber, Jack. *Public Employee Unionism: Structure, Growth, and Policy.* Washington, D.C.: Brookings, 1973.

Summary of Public-sector Labor Relations Policies. Washington, D.C.: U.S. Department of Labor, Labor-Management Services Administration, 1976.

Summers, Clyde W. "Public Bargaining: A Political Perspective." *Yale Law Journal,* 83 (May 1974), 1156–2000.

————. "Public-sector Bargaining: Problems of Governmental Decision Making." *Cincinnati Law Review,* 44 (1975), 668–679.

Wellington, Harry H., and Ralph K. Winter, Jr. *The Unions and the Cities.* Washington, D.C.: Brookings, 1971.

Zagoria, Sam, ed. *Public Workers and Public Unions.* Englewood Cliffs, NJ: Prentice-Hall, 1972.

CASE 10.1

The Sanitation Strike

Verde Cliffs is a city of 500,000 in a state which prohibits collective bargaining between cities and their employees. A strike by employees is grounds for dismissal. Pay for sanitation workers is very low, and 80 percent of them are minority group members. The city is run by a five-person council and a city-manager form of government. All city council members are upper-middle-class white males.

On August 4, the sanitation workers present a petition to the council requesting a 20 percent pay increase. After a two-week delay, the manager recommends a 7 percent increase, but the council approves a 3 percent hike. The sanitation workers are unwilling to accept the 3 percent and decide to go on strike. For three days there is a stalemate, and the manager orders the strikers to return to work. They refuse. Citizens are getting angry, and the city council holds an emergency meeting and instructs the manager to get the situation resolved immediately.

1. What are the manager's options?
2. What are the consequences of each option?
3. What would you do if you were the manager? Why?

CASE 10.2

Flexitime

The director of the state Department of Forestry had been reading a lot about innovations in work schedules. In consultation with her assistants, she decided that she would adopt a system whereby employees could choose the time they came to and left work. The only stipulation was that they had to be present for an eight-hour period sometime between 6:00 A.M. and 6:00 P.M. Additionally, arrangements would have to be worked out so that the office was staffed between 9:00 A.M. and 5:00 P.M. each day.

The Department of Forestry was operating under a union contract with the Foresters Union Local 106. The contract provided that working conditions were negotiable items. When the flexitime program was announced, the union representative immediately objected, but the program was instituted anyway. The union then went to the state Labor Relations Authority with a complaint and asked that the program be rescinded.

---

1. What should the Labor Relations Authority do? Why?
2. Even if the union was not concerned about flexitime per se, why would it object?
3. Explain how you would have handled the situation if you were the department director.

Chapter 11

Public Personnel and Democratic Values

In recent years much controversy has surrounded the relationship of the personnel process to democracy. At a time when government, through such means as the Civil Rights Act of 1964, insists that other employers democratize personnel processes, it is imperative that it set an example. Not the least of the controversy is what is meant by democracy in personnel administration.

In reference to the public service, democracy may be thought of in terms of accountability and responsibility. As a matter of course the public service is expected to be accountable and responsible to the general public and its representatives. Earlier discussions of the environment in which public personnel administration operates outlined some of the means by which the activities of governments are overseen. This chapter will focus on how the personnel system and its employees function to foster accountability and responsibility.

Democracy in personnel systems has to do with (1) representative bureaucracy, including equal employment opportunity/affirmative action; (2) equity in dealing with clientele; (3) the democratic values of public employees; and (4) advocacy administration and citizen participation. Each of these will be examined in turn.

Representative Bureaucracy

The issue of representative bureaucracy has generated extensive concern and activity by public personnel administrators. As Rosenbloom has pointed out, the meaning of representative bureaucracy is fraught with ambiguity and numerous interpretations.[1] The Jeffersonians and Jacksonians felt that government positions should be filled by people who reflected the public or at least that part of the public which elected them. Political leaders at all levels of government have based staffing patterns on this basic approach to representativeness, even though it is not a very refined concept. In more recent years, students of the public service have attempted to analyze representation more rigorously and have been examining the implications of a representative bureaucracy.

Basic discussion of representative bureaucracy revolves around the distinction between active and passive representation, as suggested by Mosher.[2] In active representation a representative is expected to act in the interest of all sectors of society regardless of what group the representative belongs to. In passive representation one is assumed to represent the interests of the group from which one comes. Thus in passive representation the personal characteristics and social background of the representatives are of importance, and advocates of such representation believe the bureaucracy should be a mirror image of the society as a whole. Passive representation is exemplified by the goals and timetables that affirmative action plans use to make the public service an accurate reflection of the population.

There are grave differences, however, in the ways in which people perceive the linkage between active and passive representation. The assumption underlying equal employment opportunity/affirmative action programs is that passive representation will eventually lead to active representation of those groups who are becoming members of the bureaucracy. That assumption is the subject of much study and disagreement.[3] Despite these differences of opinion, government acts on the premise that the various groups in our society should all be represented and will influence the public service in its actions. Another important consideration is that citizens of minority groups are more likely to feel comfortable in dealing with bureaucrats from their own groups. Affirmative action has as one of its intended effects making bureaucracies and their programs more accessible to groups previously denied such access. Thus, as Rosenbloom and Kinnard note, representative bureaucracy is advocated for two main reasons: (1) to provide distributive justice and equal opportunity and (2) to allow for input from all social and economic groups.

DEVELOPMENT OF AN UNREPRESENTATIVE BUREAUCRACY

Although the Jeffersonians and Jacksonians "democratized" the public service in many ways, the United States public service has never really been representative of the society as a whole.[4] Among the many reasons for this situation are political considerations and traditions. It is also argued by some that bureaucracy, by its nature, requires skills that are not distributed throughout the population.[5] As a result, bureaucracies often discriminate in favor of middle-class people because they have the necessary skills. The reasons that many people do not acquire such skills are often political and social, and they will be the focus of this analysis.

Jacksonian Democracy opened the public service to a new element in the political system; but even while it permitted the common man to participate, it must be recalled that the new participants were men— and white men at that. Blacks and women were still excluded for the most part. The reign of the spoils system entrenched the white male in the public service by insuring that the friends and relatives of those already holding political power reaped the rewards. By the time minorities and women achieved some political influence, the spoils system had been fairly well destroyed as a means of staffing the federal bureaucracy and was on the way out in many state and local jurisdictions as well. With the blanketing-in procedures used for extending civil service protection, the white male was more or less assured of control over the bureaucracy and the selection of new members. Consequently, the newly emerging groups had few opportunities for entry into the system.

Although the Civil War emancipated the slaves, the political power of the black population was minimal until recently. A gradual process of judicial and legislative extension of rights to minorities and women took place during the late nineteenth century and the first half of the twentieth. Of course, passage of the Nineteenth Amendment to the Constitution was supposed to open the doors for women, but they, like the blacks, found that constitutionally guaranteed rights do not automatically translate into rights in practice. Instead, much effort is required for the realization of those rights.[6]

The middle years of the twentieth century witnessed a concern for the rights of minorities and individuals alike. The Warren Court and its libertarian and civil rights orientation jolted the consciences of citizens and political leaders. Many court decisions and much legislation prohibiting discrimination against minorities, and eventually women, resulted. In the employment area particularly, it became illegal to discriminate on the basis of race, religion, sex, and so on. Still, women and minorities experienced discrimination. To get around nondiscrimination orders and legislation, employers could often note that few women and minority applicants had the credentials required for the positions available, and such was often the truth. Unmentioned was the fact that credentials irrelevant to performance of the job were often used to avoid opening the doors too widely. The courts, however, have been instrumental in assuring that only qualifications relevant to the job are allowable.[7]

On the other hand, technological development created demand for highly skilled technicians in most of governmental bureaucracy. Most minorities and women did not, in fact, have such skills. Either they were discriminated against in access to education, or they were socialized in such a way as to deter them from acquiring such skills. Thus as minority groups and women finally gained the political strength to force an opening of the doors to public employment, they found that the demand for unskilled workers had dropped drastically and there was little need for their capabilities. Although nondiscrimination laws and rules helped, they fell far short of actually providing equality of opportunity, particularly in high-level positions.[8]

FROM NONDISCRIMINATION TO AFFIRMATIVE ACTION

Because nondiscrimination laws and regulations failed to achieve the expected results, government leaders decided a new approach was needed. President Kennedy, who owed his election in part to strong minority-group support, began emphasizing positive action to promote the well-being of those who had previously been discriminated against. Efforts were made to bring blacks in particular into prominent places in the public bureaucracy. President Johnson, who was eager to shed his Texas and southern identification for a national constituency, increased the pressure for employment of blacks. In doing so, of course, he increased his attractiveness to black voters. Minority-group support was a concern of President Nixon as well, and he took a special interest in Chicanos. Similarly, President Carter appealed to blacks, Chicanos, and women. The political strength of various minorities has thus been translated into specific actions taken by political leaders to increase employment opportunities. As women developed greater political consciousness in the late 1960s and the 1970s, leaders of both parties and at all levels of government have been eager to demonstrate their concern for women's rights (and votes) by making efforts to increase public employment of women.

There are two main approaches in opening up more public-sector jobs to women and minorities: equal employment opportunity and affirmative action. Equal employment opportunity does not necessarily result in greater opportunities; it merely requires that all groups have the same chance to compete for positions and are treated equally once employed. Of particular concern is that personnel decisions be made on the basis of criteria which are pertinent to the work. Equal opportunity requires neutrality on issues other than merit or ability in the personnel process. The Civil Rights Act of 1964 provides the basic requirements for equality of opportunity. The act applies to private-sector employers, and it was amended to cover public employees of state and local governments through what is known as the Equal Employment Opportunity Act of 1972.

Although guarantees of equal employment opportunity through legislation are important, they do not take effect on their own. Enforcement agencies and monitoring mechanisms have therefore been created to insure that the acts are implemented. The Equal Employment Opportunity Commission and the Civil Rights Commission are the major agencies at the national level which have enforcement responsibilities. Each department or agency which distributes grants or services, or has contracts with other employers including state and local governments, has some type of compliance office to insure that equal employment opportunity exists. Revenue-sharing funds now also come with the provision that they can be suspended if a court or administrative agency finds discrimination in services or employment of the recipient jurisdiction.

Monitoring agencies have difficulty in gaining compliance because they are usually inadequately staffed and often are on the periphery of the functional agencies. Standards of what constitutes equal opportunity also tend to be vague and hard to enforce. As a result of these problems, the concept of affirmative action developed.

Affirmative action requires employers to make a conscious effort to eliminate from their personnel system intended and unintended discrimination as well as the effects of past discrimination. Thus it calls for an examination of all personnel functions to identify possible barriers to equal employment opportunity so that they can be removed. The key to determining whether discrimination exists is to be found not in the intent of the policy but rather in what occurs as a result of the policy.

Before reviewing the steps required in affirmative action, it should be noted that affirmative action plans are not mandatory. Rather, granting agencies may require such plans, or compliance agencies or courts may require plans from those jurisdictions in which a complaint of discrimination has been found valid. Of course, many jurisdictions voluntarily develop plans. One reason they do so is to avoid costly and time-consuming litigation which is likely to occur if affirmative action is not practiced. Another reason is that the remedies imposed by courts and compliance agencies are likely to be tempered if voluntary action to correct problems is being taken.[9] Additionally, morale and productivity are likely to be higher, and employee skills are put to better use, when personnel decisions are made on the basis of competence and performance.

The first step in the affirmative action process is to go through all personnel policies to see if there are any potentially discriminatory features. Often the wording of a provision may dissuade some potential employees, and many provisions may actually have differential impact on groups. Any provision which has differential impact based on non-job-related factors should be suspect.

Next, a step-by-step evaluation of all personnel processes should be made. Classification plans, compensation policies, qualification requirements, recruitment and selection procedures, performance evaluation systems, training and promotional opportunities, grievance procedures, and fringe-benefit packages all need to be examined to insure that barriers to women and minorities are eliminated or that there is no differential impact on them. The focal point of much affirmative action is in the recruitment and selection phase of personnel actions, although pay, promotion, and fringe-benefit policies are also paid close attention (see Table 11–1).

Recruitment and selection processes provide the means by which target groups can first enter public employment and thus are seen as keys to expanding opportunities. In the recruitment effort the responsibility of the employer is to insure that minority groups and women are made aware of employment opportunities. Governments thereby need to seek out organizations of women and minorities to inform them of openings. Employers must also publicize employment opportunities widely. Internal promotion can be used to fill positions as long as all qualified employees have the chance to compete for the position. Most governmental jurisdictions should have little difficulty in satisfying recruitment requirements under affirmative action if they make a good-faith effort.

It is much more difficult to fulfill affirmative action requirements in the selection process. State and local governments find themselves under constant pressure to insure that their selection procedures are not discriminatory. The criteria used for judging among candidates must be job related, and if exams are used, they may be challenged by those who feel they are discriminatory. Many governments have been forced to abandon or modify exams which courts have found discriminatory. (See chapter 7.)

While affirmative action theoretically calls for the use of strict merit procedures by requiring that only job-relevant factors be considered,

Table 11–1   Establishing an Affirmative Action Plan

The most important measure of an affirmative action program is its *results*. Extensive efforts to develop procedures, analyses, data collection systems, report forms, and fine written policy statements are meaningless unless the end product will be *measurable yearly improvement in hiring, training, and promotion of minorities and females in all parts of your organization.* The only realistic basis for evaluating a program to increase opportunity for minorities and females is its actual impact upon these persons.

The essence of your affirmative action program should be:
• Establish strong agency policy and commitment.
• Assign responsibility and authority for the program to a top agency official.
• Analyze your present work force to identify jobs, departments, and units where minorities and females are underutilized.
• Set specific, measurable, attainable hiring and promotion goals, with target dates, in each area of underutilization.
• Make every manager and supervisor responsible and accountable for helping to meet these goals.
• Reevaluate job descriptions and hiring criteria to assure that they reflect actual job needs.
• Find minorities and females who qualify or can become qualified to fill goals.
• Review and revise all employment procedures to assure that they do not have discriminatory effects and that they help attain goals.
• Focus on getting minorities and females into upward mobility and relevant training pipelines where they have not had previous access.
• Develop systems to monitor and measure progress regularly. If results are not satisfactory to meet goals, find out why, and make necessary changes.

SOURCE: Adapted from U.S. Equal Employment Opportunity Commission, *Affirmative Action and Equal Employment: A Guidebook for Employers*, vol. 1, 1974, p. 3.

critics have complained that in practice affirmative action results in reverse discrimination. In other words, minorities and females are being given advantages to the detriment of white males.[10] The charge usually arises because of the use of "goals" for achieving balance in employment. Goals are established for the hiring, promotion, and so forth of females and minorities to bring them into the employment structure on a basis representative of their presence in the labor pool. In the view of many, goals are nothing more than quotas which must be met by employers to avoid being branded as discriminatory.

Enforcement or compliance agencies avoid the use of the term quotas and argue that goals are different. Theoretically, goals are targets the employer attempts to attain. However, circumstances may mean that those goals cannot be reached. If they are not met, the employer normally has to explain why. As a result, many employers feel under pressure to achieve the goals regardless of how they do so. They often then feel justified in hiring lesser-qualified minorities and females to meet their goals. It should be emphasized that affirmative action does not require such reverse discrimination in most cases. Compliance agencies are frequently at fault for their single-minded concern with meeting goals, but most such agenices recognize that circumstances do not always permit employers to meet all their anticipated goals and make their judgments on the basis of good-faith efforts.

Because employers often feel pressured to discriminate in favor of minorities and women, critics of affirmative action argue that merit and competence are sacrified to meet goals and timetables. Most critics believe that the quality of public service suffers from affirmative action efforts and base their opposition on that belief. Certainly there are also critics who have a self-interest in maintaining the status quo. Many employees and employee groups have been in the forefront of battles to protect their turf from intrusion by minorities and women. Teachers and university faculty, who many think should be the most open-minded, are often the most adamant opponents of affirmative action programs. Of course, their opposition is normally based on the argument that education quality will be lowered by such plans.

Teachers have not been the only ones to resist demands of the poor and minorities for inclusion in the system, however.[11] Public employee unions often thwart affirmative action plans or other efforts at improving the lot of minorities. Labor leaders frequently resent those who demand the right to jobs when they themselves had to work their way up into their positions. They cannot see why special treatment should be accorded minorities and women. Overlooked is the fact that jobs are scarcer today than they were in the past and the doors to union membership increasingly narrow. With self-regulated selection, unions parcel membership out to relatives and friends. Affirmative action seems to be the most effective method of opening those doors to minorities and females.

While unions have resisted affirmative action in many instances, they also can be helpful in fostering it. In Tacoma, Washington, for example, City Manager William Donaldson enlisted the aid of the firefighters union in an affirmative action effort. Because the firefighters assumed responsibility for improving equal employment opportunity, the project was successful in recruiting minority applicants. Morale in the department was also much higher than in cases where outsiders imposed the action.[12] The point is that unions do not all react in the same way, and members respond as nonunion employees do to the opportunity to participate in decision-making processes.

The record so far does not indicate that the fears of the critics are well founded. While minorities and women are increasingly evident in government employment, they are not represented at all levels of employment in proportion to their existence in the general public. The higher levels of management are still essentially the preserve of white

males, although changes are being made.[13] Because of the dispropor-
tionate representation of females and minorities at the lower levels of
public bureaucracies, increasing attention is being focused on upward
mobility programs and possible discrimination in promotion policies.

The ultimate goal of affirmative action is to insure that factors
irrelevant to performance of duties are not considered in the employment process. In the short run, however, it may be necessary to consider
sex and race in order to equalize the balance and redress the discrimination that was built into the system. Obviously, the problem of discrimination goes far beyond employment practices and can only be
solved by insuring that all people have the opportunity to develop their
talents and abilities through education and training. However, until
society can achieve that goal, there will be a need for such policies as
affirmative action.

Representation of various groups in the public service has been
challenged as undermining the merit concept.[14] The argument is that
equality of opportunity requirements leads to the hiring of less-qualified
applicants, in other words, the reverse discrimination argument. The real
problem seems to center on the fact that the public service has not paid
enough attention to the relevance of its personnel processes to actual
performance on the job. Selection, examination, and evaluation of qualifications have too often been tied to credentialism and irrelevant
examination scores. Eugene McGregor suggests that the way out of the
dilemma is to develop a "pluralistic basis for judging people."[15] The
idea is to recognize that different criteria and approaches are necessary
for different occupations. Only by identifying the occupational field
can officials hope to establish criteria for evaluating and selecting the
people who are to serve in it.[16]

The public bureaucracy will surely never be a mirror reflection of
the larger society. But by eliminating artificial barriers to employment,
the bureaucracy will relate and respond to all sectors of society and
will have a greater chance of being considered legitimate by all the
public.

Equity

Advocates of the "New Public Administration" have elevated concerns
with social equity to the forefront of public administration study.[17]
However, there is still much disagreement about what social equity
means and who has responsibility for fostering it.[18] In public administration, social equity refers to the belief that administrators have the
responsibility to mitigate the unequal distribution of benefits which

results from our pluralistic political system. According to this view, many people are denied access, opportunity, and services because they do not have the political power which permits them to compete for the system's resources and benefits. Furthermore, it is the responsibility of administrators to redress the inequitable treatment meted out to minorities and the poor. The problem for the public administrator is that there are many publics to be served and one group is not willing to permit its claims to be slighted in order to provide equitable services to another.

There is not much evidence to suggest that public administrators have embraced the new public administration's attachment to the social equity issue. At least there is no formal espousal of the view. However, agencies at all levels of government do have more and more responsibility to respond to issues of concern to minorities and the poor. Through affirmative action and citizen participation programs, agencies are becoming more sensitized to the needs of these groups. As the courts continue to focus on the rights of minorities and the poor, it is likely that sensitivity to these issues will continue to be of concern. At any rate, a representative bureaucracy is likely to promote equity.

Democratic Values of Public Employees

Another approach to democracy in public personnel administration is to examine the extent to which the public service embodies democratic ideas and how it responds to the needs of the public as a result. In this approach it is assumed that the interests of varying groups may be represented without necessarily having members of the group actually part of the service.[19] In other words, democracy involves a commitment rather than a reflection of the makeup of a society.

The question of just how committed public bureaucrats are to democratic ideals is a difficult one, particularly because little real evaluation has been made of the issue. Bob Wynia, who has studied the issue, suggests that many bureaucrats do hold views quite inconsistent with democracy.[20] Of course, views vary from agency to agency and with the number of years in the public service. The human relations approach taught that people's attitudes are shaped by colleagues in an organization and that frequently differing ideas are just not welcome. Selection procedures, especially if developed by the agency itself, can help to insure that new members share the views of those already in the organization. Graham Allison's analysis of many federal agencies suggests contempt for the public on the part of many public servants.[21] The point is that people in public agencies (as in the private sector) may lose touch with the public. When that happens, public servants cannot be expected to be responsive to public needs.

William Pearson studied the attitudes of state bureaucrats toward a democratic ideology and reached conclusions somewhat different from those of Wynia.[22] He found that state administrators are strongly committed to democratic values, much more strongly, in fact, than were the federal executives in the Wynia study. As he suggests, his findings might indicate that decentralization would result in greater democratization of services. His study may support the belief that federal bureaucrats lose touch with the people because they are isolated from the "real world." It will be interesting to see whether local bureaucrats are more like their federal or state counterparts.

Advocacy and Participatory Administration

Some students of public administration feel that the only way to make the public service democratic is to democratize the decision-making processes within agencies and particularly to provide methods by which clientele and public interest groups can participate in administration.[23] Many programs of the Office of Economic Opportunity during the 1960s attempted to implement citizen participation, and such activities are required now under such programs as revenue sharing and the community development block grant program. Even where not required, citizen and public interest groups have become increasingly involved in pressing their interests.

Citizen participation affects job design and the response of public employees to community needs. Often citizen participation means that employees are selected from the community served. Additionally, members of the community may be placed on advisory monitoring boards. Because people from the community often lack appropriate skills, jobs may have to be redesigned or training programs developed. People from the community also tend to understand the community and have loyalty to it, thus tempering loyalty to the agency or supervisor.

The purposes of citizen participation are generally to make administration more responsive to the public and to enhance the legitimacy of government programs and agencies. As Stephen Cupps notes, citizen participation has been responsible for opening to public debate many issues which would otherwise have gone without public input.[24] Additionally, citizen and public interest groups have caused issues to be raised and considered by governments which would have been content to ignore them. With the participation generated by these activities, groups have been effective checks on governments and have stimulated greater public involvement in decision making at all levels of government.

While the benefits of citizen participation are many, there are also numerous difficulties.[25] As Cupps notes, citizen participation often encounters problems associated with (1) shortsightedness on the part of administrators trying to respond to citizen and public interest groups; (2) difficulties in representation and legitimacy; (3) style and tactics of participating groups; and (4) lack of effective measures for evaluating citizen group proposals. Administrators often respond quickly to demands of citizen groups in order to demonstrate their responsiveness and to generate greater public support for their programs and agencies. However, the short-term benefits of such response may lead to long-term problems, or the interests of a small vocal group may be satisfied to the detriment of the general public. Often the less visible, but equally necessary, activities of the agency get lost in the shuffle as more popular activities and efforts to maintain good public relations receive the attention and resources. The age-old problem of agencies becoming dominated by clientele groups is also of concern to administrators. Some employees feel compelled to continue supporting the interests of their clientele because of the influence the group has over the agency.

Another difficulty with citizen participation is determining how representative given groups are. Groups tend to suggest that they have a much wider constituency than is actually the case, and many become very self-righteous in their approach. Environmental and consumer interest groups often assume that their point of view is the only one representing the public interest.[26] Agency personnel must recognize that there are many perspectives and groups which have to be considered. While public interest organizations wish to portray themselves as serving no special interests, they normally are in fact devoted to some particular concern and are as likely as any other group to perceive issues narrowly. The important thing to remember is that the causes they represent are often attended to by public agencies because of the activism of the groups. Without such activism, consumer and environmental concerns and the like would probably receive little consideration.

Another approach to humanizing and democratizing the public service favors advocacy administration. The idea here is to develop agents of change who will redirect the way the public service carries out its mission.[27] Such a position is in stark contrast to the traditional approach to the merit system in which the public servant is to maintain a completely neutral stance on controversial issues and policy making in general. Those who favor advocacy administration believe that public policy ignores many people and groups because only those who have power or "know the rules of the game" can really participate. The poor and others cannot hope to compete with well-organized and economically powerful interests. The solution is to introduce change agents into the bureaucracy. Their function is to organize and mobilize those who now exist outside the political process. The proponents of change agents in the public service have met with much resistance, to say the least, but they have made a positive contribution insofar as they have induced the service to analyze itself and its role.

Participatory administration also involves participation by employees of the organization through democratized decision-making processes and collective bargaining. These issues are explored in chapters 8 and 10.

Summary

In a democratic society there must be concern with how democratic the public service is. The problem is that merit principles may be inconsistent with the democratization of the service. The concept of merit itself, however, is not precisely understood, and many practices have been justified under it.[28] For instance, veteran's preference has been a major element of our merit systems for many years, even though it works to undermine the concept of merit. When minorities and women demand equality or preference, the merit concept often becomes the major front of resistance, even by those who favor veteran's preference. Additionally, those who seek to participate in the administrative process often encounter resistance from those comfortable dealing with a familiar clientele and from the clientele itself which fears having to share the benefits it receives. The moral is that those who threaten the political interests of people already in power are going to have difficulty in achieving their demands. The solution has to be worked out in the political processes and, increasingly, in the courts. There is little doubt, however, that pressure for equality of opportunity will continue, as will resistance by those sensing a threat to their status and achievement.

Democracy and personnel management interact on a continuous basis. The personnel administrator must be concerned with efforts to democratize the public service through representation of groups in the service and through responsiveness of employees to the public. Equal employment opportunity and affirmative action can help administrators achieve these goals, as well as create a bureaucracy more sensitive to all interests. Many critics suggest that these approaches are passive in that the presence of a group in the organization is assumed to insure representation of its interest. These critics believe that bureaucrats should make active efforts to increase the access of groups previously excluded from decision making. In their view, public employees need to be committed to democratic values and should be advocates for the poor and minorities. Similarly, citizen participation in decision making is suggested as a way of improving responsiveness.

All these pressures for democratizing the public service require the personnel administrator's attention. These concerns, along with increasing demands by taxpayers for frugal use of tax dollars, put the personnel manager in a delicate situation.

NOTES

1. David H. Rosenbloom, *Federal Equal Employment Opportunity: Politics and Public Personnel Administration* (New York: Praeger, 1977); Rosenbloom and Jeannette G. Featherstonhaugh, "Passive and Active Representation in the Federal Service: A Comparison of Blacks and Whites," *Social Science Quarterly*, 57 (March 1977), 873–882, at 873–874; and Rosenbloom and Douglas Kinnard, "Bureaucratic Representation and Bureaucratic Behavior: An Exploratory Analysis," *Midwest Review of Public Administration*, 11 (March 1977), 35–42, at 35–36.
2. Frederick C. Mosher, *Democracy and the Public Service* (New York: Oxford University Press, 1968), pp. 11–13.
3. For instance, see Rosenbloom and Featherstonhaugh, "Passive and Active Representation"; Lee Sigelman and Robert L. Carter, "Passive and Active Representation in the Federal Service: A Reanalysis," *Social Science Quarterly*, 58 (March 1978), 724–726; and Rosenbloom and Featherstonhaugh's Response, pp. 726–728 of the same issue.
4. See Harry Kranz, *The Participatory Bureaucracy: Women and Minorities in a More Representative Public Service* (Lexington, MA: Lexington Books, 1976).
5. Samuel Krislov, *Representative Bureaucracy* (Englewood Cliffs, NJ: Prentice-Hall, 1974), pp. 49–51 and throughout the book, notes this important consideration. John Gardner, *Excellence: Can We Be Equal and Excellent Too?* (New York: Harper & Row, 1961), also bases much of his analysis on this point. Discussing negative implications of the issue is Nathan Glazer, *Affirmative Discrimination: Ethnic Inequality and Public Policy* (New York: Basic Books, 1975).
6. Thomas R. Dye, *The Politics of Equality* (Indianapolis: Bobbs-Merrill, 1971) provides an excellent history of the development of equal rights for blacks; pp. 230–235 deal specifically with how the control over institutions by Caucasians resulted in roadblocks for blacks. John Kenneth Galbraith, *Economics and the Public Purpose* (Boston: Houghton-

Mifflin, 1973), ch. 23, explains the reasons for lack of access by females and suggests some strong action to remedy the situation, as does Helene Markoff, "The Federal Women's Program," *Public Administration Review*, 34 (January/February 1974), 18–29.

7. See particularly the Supreme Court decision in *Griggs* v. *Duke Power Co.*, 401 U.S. 424 (1971). For an excellent analysis of the decision and its implications for the question of equity in public personnel administration, see Eugene B. McGregor, Jr., "Social Equity and the Public Service," *Public Administration Review*, 34 (January/February 1974), 18–20. Carl F. Goodman, "Public Employment and the Supreme Court's 1976–77 Term," *Public Personnel Management*, 6 (September/October 1977), 283–293, also evaluates more recent cases involving equal employment issues.

8. See Harry Kranz, "How Representative Is the Public Service?" *Public Personnel Management*, 2 (July/August 1973), 242–255; and Krislov, *Representative Bureaucracy*.

9. See Arthur L. Finkle, "Avoiding High Costs of Job Discrimination Remedies," *Public Personnel Management*, 5 (March/April 1976), 128–131.

10. See Glazer, *Affirmative Discrimination*, and Sidney Hook, "On Discrimination: Part One," in Lucy W. Sells, ed., *Toward Affirmative Action: New Directions for Institutional Research* (San Francisco: Jossey-Bass, 1974).

11. See Frances Fox Piven, "Militant Civil Servants in New York City," *Transaction*, 7 (November 1969), 24–28, 55, for an excellent evaluation of the issue. Also see William B. Gould, "Labor Relations and Race Relations," in Sam Zagoria, ed., *Public Work and Public Unions* (Englewood Cliffs, NJ: Prentice-Hall, 1972), pp. 147–159; and Ray Marshall and Arvil Van Adams, "Racial Negotiations: The Memphis Case," in J. Joseph Loewenberg and Michael H. Moskow, eds., *Collective Bargaining in Government: Readings and Cases* (Englewood Cliffs, NJ: Prentice-Hall, 1972).

12. A brief review of the Tacoma experience can be found in Ralph J. Flynn, *Public Work, Public Workers* (Washington, D.C.: The New Republic Book Company, 1975), p. 57.

13. Kranz, *The Participatory Bureaucracy*; Rosenbloom, *Federal Equal Employment Opportunity*; and Nesta M. Gallas, ed., "A Symposium: Women in Public Administration," *Public Administration Review*, 36 (July/August 1976), 347–389 deal with this issue. Statistical data is continually reported by the U.S. Civil Service Commission in its periodic publications, *Minority Group Employment in the Federal Government*; *Federal Civilian Personnel Statistics*; *and Study of Employment of Women in the Federal Government*.

14. For an exhaustive treatment of the issue, see Gardner, *Excellence*.

15. Eugene B. McGregor, Jr., "Social Equity and the Public Service," *Public Administration Review*, 34 (January/February 1974), 18–29, at 27.

16. Ibid.
17. H. George Frederickson, *Toward a New Public Administration* (Scranton, PA: Chandler, 1971), ch. 11.
18. David K. Hart, "Social Equity, Justice, and the Equitable Administrator," *Public Administration Review*, 34 (January/February 1974), 3–11, provides an excellent discussion of the definitional and conceptual problems.
19. V. Subramanian, "Representative Bureaucracy: A Reassessment," *American Political Science Review*, 61 (December 1967), 1010–1019, presents an excellent analysis of the meaning of representation.
20. Bob L. Wynia, "Federal Bureaucrats' Attitudes toward a Democratic Ideology," *Public Administration Review*, 34 (March/April 1974), 156–162.
21. Graham T. Allison, "Conceptual Models and the Cuban Missile Crisis," *American Political Science Review*, 63 (September 1969), 689–718.
22. William M. Pearson, "State Executives' Attitudes toward a Democratic Ideology," *Midwest Review of Public Administration*, 11 (December 1977), 270–280.
23. As suggested throughout Frank Marini, ed., *Toward a New Public Administration: The Minnowbrook Perspective* (San Francisco: Chandler, 1971). Also see Hazel Henderson, "Information and the New Movements for Citizen Participation," *Annals of the American Academy of Political and Social Science*, 412 (March 1974), 34–43.
24. D. Stephen Cupps, "Emerging Problems of Citizen Participation," *Public Administration Review*, 37 (September/October 1977), 478–487, at 479.
25. This discussion is based largely on Cupps, "Problems of Citizen Participation," which presents an excellent evaluation of citizen participation.
26. Henderson, "New Movements for Citizen Participation."
27. Marini, *Toward a New Public Administration*, is based on this position. For one of the best presentations of this position, see Louis C. Gawthrop, *Administrative Politics and Social Change* (New York: St. Martin's, 1971).
28. One of the early attempts at reconciling democracy and merit is Frederick C. Mosher, *Democracy and the Public Service* (New York: Oxford University Press, 1968). Also see Emmette S. Redford, *Democracy in the Administrative State* (New York: Oxford University Press, 1969).

SUGGESTED READINGS

Cupps, D. Stephen. "Emerging Problems of Citizen Participation." *Public Administration Review*, 37 (September/October 1977), 478–487.
Dye, Thomas. *The Politics of Equality*. Indianapolis: Bobbs-Merrill, 1971.
Frederickson, H. George. *Toward a New Public Administration*. Scranton, PA: Chandler, 1971.

Gardner, John. *Excellence: Can We Be Equal and Excellent Too?* New York: Harper & Row, 1961.

Glazer, Nathan. *Affirmative Discrimination: Ethnic Inequality and Public Policy.* New York: Basic Books, 1975.

Kranz, Harry. *The Participatory Bureaucracy: Women and Minorities in a More Representative Public Service.* Lexington, MA: Lexington Books, 1976.

Krislov, Samuel. *Representative Bureaucracy.* Englewood Cliffs, NJ: Prentice-Hall, 1974.

Marini, Frank, ed. *Toward a New Public Administration: The Minnowbrook Perspective.* San Francisco: Chandler, 1971.

Mosher, Frederick C. *Democracy and the Public Service.* New York: Oxford University Press, 1968.

Pearson, William M. "State Executives' Attitudes toward a Democratic Ideology." *Midwest Review of Public Administration,* 11 (December 1977), 270–280.

Rosenbloom, David H. *Federal Equal Employment Opportunity: Politics and Public Personnel Administration.* New York: Praeger, 1977.

Thompson, Frank J. "Minority Groups in Public Bureaucracies: Are Passive and Active Representation Linked?" *Administration and Society,* 8 (August 1976), 201–226.

Wynia, Bob L. "Federal Bureaucrats' Attitudes toward a Democratic Ideology." *Public Administration Review,* 34 (March/April 1974), 156–162.

The Water Meter Repairer

The town of Sandy Shores operated a municipal water system, and Harry Hork was the director of the Water Department. He always seemed to have difficulty finding qualified meter repair technicians. In his last effort, he had only one applicant. She was Jane Borden and had worked in another state with a small city in its water department, where she learned meter repair. That state, however, did not require meter repair workers to be licensed. Sandy Shores was in a state which required state certification. Harry informed Jane of the requirement and told her he could not hire her.

The position went vacant until Jim Hale applied. He had attended the state certification school but had not completed the program. He had no experience, but Harry hired him provided that he attend the training program and become certified.

Jane learned of the situation and complained to the Equal Employment Opportunity Commission that she was the object of discrimination.

1. What are the issues the EEOC hearing officer must consider?
2. What should the officer decide? Why?

Upward Mobility

The city of Uplands was very proud of its efforts to increase opportunities for minorities and females through its training program. The city provided that training would be available to any minority or female applicant in the lower third of the position classification system. They could take an aptitude test and then be eligible for training funds to support them while they learned skills preparing them for a higher-paying job available in the city and for which they had the aptitude.

Jim White believed that it was not fair that he, a white male, should not be eligible for the program. As a result, he filed a complaint with the EEOC.

1. How should the EEOC handle this case? Why?
2. What are the conflicting issues in this case?

Chapter 12

Forces For Change:
A Look Ahead

Public personnel management has been presented in this book as a number of processes, institutions, and policies shaped by a large number of forces in its environment. As with other activities in our political system, public personnel administration is an ever-changing activity. Change, however, tends to be incremental and gradual. Thus the current state of affairs in the field is a product of constant adjustment to changing technology, citizen and political demands, and changes in managers and employees. The years ahead will surely bring further accommodations. Predicting those changes is virtually impossible. A recent Delphi exercise involving a panel of personnel directors, other personnel officials, and academic experts resulted in little agreement concerning what personnel management in the public sector is now or is likely to be in the next twenty years.[1] Despite a lack of consensus on what will happen, it is possible to identify forces which are likely to affect the field and speculate on some of the effects these forces may have.

Some forces in the environment of public personnel management which will have effects on the process have been of concern for a long time. Others are relatively new concerns. There will be new advances in technology affecting all areas of personnel management. Citizen/taxpayer concerns will exert pressures to use new and old technology to provide services as cheaply as possible. These concerns will focus greater attention on productivity. Various interest groups in society will continue to pursue their interests through personnel systems as well as other means. Equity in the personnel system will thus continue to attract much attention. Concerns of employees and the continuation of collective bargaining activities are also likely to remain important issues as is the ever-expanding litigation of personnel matters.

Technological Advances

It is impossible to predict what sort of technological advances will develop in any society, but it is certain that new discoveries will continue to be made. With new technology come new expertise and ways of solving old problems. The public service has to change constantly to accommodate new technology. Governments depend more and more upon highly specialized individuals to perform their work. The recruitment and continued training of people in new skill areas will remain an important part of the personnel function. Thus training programs are likely to expand as skills of current employees become obsolete and new employees require training to be useful to the organization.

New management tools and technologies are certain to appear as they have in the past and will be applied with varying effectiveness in different organizations. Of particular interest to personnel managers will be improved methods of testing potential employees, evaluating performance, and measuring productivity. These and other improvements will permit personnel managers to do their jobs more effectively and to meet the demands placed upon them by other changes in society.

It is also likely that technological change will affect authority relationships within the public sector. As employees become more specialized, it becomes more difficult to direct the large number of highly skilled people and coordinate their activities toward a common objective. Managers often do not have the expertise to be able to intelligently question what the specialist does. As specializations narrow further, more authority will have to be shared through collegial or task-oriented work groups. In such situations, the traditional concerns of the personnel manager with orderly position classification, qualification requirements, and the like have to give way to more flexible and adaptive arrangements.

Technological changes tend to bring about changes among the practitioners of the technology as well. Professions and professional associations develop around the new technology. Professional associations seem to be exerting greater influence over various personnel operations, and increased specialization opens the door for professional associations to develop standards of conduct and minimum levels of training and competence of members. While such guidelines may help improve the quality of the service, they also limit the discretion of personnel agencies in developing personnel policy. Professional associations can possibly dictate what are acceptable qualifications for given jobs. It is likely that intensified professionalization will increase the conflicts.

As public agencies become more professionalized and develop greater expertise, their ability to affect political decisions grows. Thus the power of Congress and the president over bureaucrats may diminish. Because Congress and the president have limited time, they tend to defer to experts in much of the policy-making process. Since it is often difficult for the nonexpert to understand what the professionals are talking about, it grows more likely that the experts make the decisions.[2] Congress and legislative bodies in general view such developments with some alarm because they see more and more power flowing to the executive branch. Many also fear that the human element may be ignored as professional skills and technical expertise become the bases for decision. What is technically most efficient may not always work to the benefit of the public.

Professionalism also affects the loyalty of employees. With increasing professionalism, loyalty may shift to professional norms and organizations and away from the employing agency. Employees will have more independence and mobility, decreasing the authority of their supervisors over their activities. Agencies may benefit by gaining new ideas and perspectives, which will enable them to improve the quality and responsiveness of their services, but personnel policies will also have to recognize that professional competence may take priority over agency loyalty. It is likely that there will be even greater interchange of personnel between government and the private sector than exists now.

Professional organizations will probably increase their political activities on behalf of members. Such activity is particularly important in the public sector because the interests of the profession could become more important than the interests of the public at large. On the other hand, professionalism also may lead to greater clientelism, especially if the clientele is powerful and supportive of the profession. As noted earlier, however, professionalism may also work to the detriment of efforts aimed at improving opportunities of minorities and women. Professional credentials are often barriers to employment for those who lack the necessary education or symbols of expertise. Those people see professionalism as locking them out of the system.

Citizen/Taxpayer Concerns

Public personnel administrators will continue to have limited resources. As inflation eats away at the finances of taxpayers, they become less willing to support expensive government. All across the country efforts to limit spending and reduce taxes continue to gain momentum. There is nothing to suggest that this trend will reverse itself in the near future. As a result, the personnel administrator must find ways of making limited resources stretch and buy even more than they did in the past. It will not be an easy task, since government costs of doing things go up with inflation just as others do.

There are many ways in which personnel managers will be able to try to cope with shrinking resources. First, productivity improvement efforts will continue to grow in scope and in kind. Greater emphasis will be put on measuring and improving productivity in collective bargaining agreements and management policy and experimentation. If some of the costs of providing the service can be recovered through improved productivity of the employees, the governmental unit can operate with fewer resources. Pay increases are increasingly likely to be tied to increased productivity of employees, units, or organizations.

Jurisdictions may also conserve resources by cooperating in various aspects of personnel administration. Cooperative arrangements for recruiting, examining, and certifying are certain to attract more attention in the future. For smaller jurisdictions such efforts can help improve their ability to perform personnel functions without adding greatly to their expenditures. While the initial benefit to the larger jurisdictions will not be as apparent, they will be able to save resources by sharing the costs of such operations with other units of government using the services. The use of cooperative bargaining arrangements is also likely to increase. They may stabilize some of the cost factors for personnel management, but could be hard on smaller jurisdictions in terms of higher wages. If such jurisdictions are to attract qualified personnel, however, they will have to pay competitive salaries and wages. Thus the benefits in reducing the probability of whipsawing will probably outweigh the drawbacks.

Contracting out for services may also help jurisdictions satisfy demands for less costly government service. Smaller jurisdictions often find that large capital investments are needed to offer many services and that they can contract with private firms or with other jurisdictions for the services for less cost. Some cities, for example, have found that they can contract with private water companies or fire protection services more cheaply than they can provide the services on their own. Contracting with other jurisdictions for water, health, and computer services is also common practice now among local governments. Personnel managers will probably have to be concerned with insuring that such services can be contracted for. They will be responsible for overseeing policies which enforce nondiscrimination and other rules and regulations related to personnel. It is likely that contracting for services will expand in the future. Private companies or large jurisdictions have the resources to make the necessary investments without jeopardizing the operating functions of their organizations. The contracting for services may further blur the lines between private- and public-sector management.

Related to citizen/taxpayer concerns is the image of the public service. Public personnel administrators must be attentive to public attitudes toward their employees. Because the image is somewhat tarnished of late, efforts must be made to improve it. Greater attention is being paid to the ethical conduct of public employees, and it is likely that more and more restrictions will be placed on their behavior. Ethical behavior will probably be increasingly emphasized in public employee training programs. If the public is convinced that employees are performing their duties with integrity, the image of the public service will improve.

Equity and Interest Group Demands

Both the public and private sectors will be under continuing pressure to be fair in their personnel processes. They will need to demonstrate that they are not discriminating against women, minorities, and other target groups. At the same time attempts must be made to avoid reverse discrimination as well. Personnel managers will be charged with developing effective tools for reaching target group individuals and with providing mechanisms and programs through which they can gain just consideration. Equality of opportunity and affirmative action will continue to be an integral part of the merit concept, and public personnel agencies will probably have to step up their efforts to make progress in the area.

Affirmative action plans are necessary to redress the imbalance that has resulted from past discrimination against a number of groups. It is likely that in the coming years the public bureaucracy will become more representative of the society it serves. It is unlikely, however, that there will ever be an end to discrimination. Racial discrimination continues to diminish in the employment arena, and women increasingly find more opportunity; but as soon as progress is made by one group, another develops the consciousness to challenge the discrimination it suffers. American Indians, for example, have been somewhat successful in calling attention to their plight in recent years. Older workers and the handicapped have also been successful in obtaining protective legislation, but their efforts have not yet led to much real change in personnel activities. The immediate future is likely to produce an intensification of their demands for equitable treatment in the personnel process. Personnel administrators will have the complex task of dealing with the rules and regulations now being developed pursuant to the federal legislation relating to age and the handicapped.

Perhaps the most controversial demands of the coming years are those being made by homosexual groups. Although a few states and localities have extended protection to gays in the employment process and other areas, it is still an emotional issue, and it will probably be a long time before they are granted the same equality of opportunity that other groups have achieved. The intensity of the reactions to gay rights can create many problems for personnel managers. The extent of the emotionalism is illustrated by the demands of at least one straight police officer in San Francisco. He does not want a homosexual officer viewing his body and is insisting on separate facilities as the department implements its recruitment of gays. While this complaint is rather trifling, it will not be easily resolved given the strength of the feelings involved. Groups must have political power before their demands are granted, and few gay groups command that kind of influence. In some places they have been successful, and those successes are likely to build confidence nationwide; thus efforts at gaining protection are likely to increase. The general public has not been very sympathetic, but voters in the state of California and other places have approved protection of gays. Public personnel systems may well become the focal point of gays and other groups which seek protection of employment rights. As with other groups, they are asking that they be judged on the basis of their work performance and not on external considerations.

Employee Demands

Another facet of equity will be demands to protect the rights of employees. As our society becomes more complex and impersonal, legal and institutional means will be used to insure human dignity in the personnel process. One effect may be stricter rules and regulations governing the manager's control over employees, thus weakening management's position. It is more likely that managers and supervisors will become more aware of the need for dealing with people as individuals. The rights of employees in the appeals and grievance processes will probably lead to more training in labor relations for supervisory personnel.

Participation by employees in personnel activities and policies will undoubtedly increase as time passes. Employees will continue to demand a greater voice in policies affecting their jobs as they become increasingly concerned with meaningful work. No longer content to do repetitious and boring jobs, they are demanding the opportunity to use their abilities as much as possible. Organizations will have to spend more time redesigning and redefining the work units and will have to give employees more say in decisions affecting their jobs.

Employee participation is enhanced by the well-established trend toward collective bargaining in the public service. Collective bargaining will continue to grow in the public sector, but the rate of growth will slow down. Much of the public sector now engages in collective bargaining and there are fewer areas in which to expand. Additionally, the negative public reaction to public service costs and to some collective bargaining agreements or actions of employee organizations have helped curb expansion of the process. Collective bargaining means that managers have to share authority with employee organizations, and many activities previously seen as management prerogatives will now be subject to negotiation. Rights of employees will also be protected through the bargaining process, and personnel agencies will need to monitor the process to insure that responsiveness to the public is not impaired. Abuses in the process will be corrected, and management will continue to increase its ability to bargain effectively. All levels of management will be undergoing training in labor relations so that the process can proceed smoothly.

Collective bargaining will continue to cause changes in the merit concept. The issue of management prerogatives has already been mentioned. Other issues such as seniority as a basis for promotion and employee organization involvement in performance evaluation and discipline will present continued challenges to merit as it has been known in the past. To accommodate the bargaining process, changes will have to be made. Collective bargaining means that personnel policy is not dominated by management but is determined by cooperative interaction between management and employees.

Employees will probably make more demands for services from the employer. Counseling programs on alcohol and drug abuse are already fairly common, and other programs on a range of personal problems are likely to develop as well. Such programs mean that personnel managers have to deal with the employee as a whole person and not only in terms of his or her performance on the job.

Groups outside the public service will also be demanding more participation in organization activities. As employees demand more control over selection, pay, and promotion policies, minorities, women and members of the community will be seeking assurance that they are protected in the processes. The desire of employees to protect their rights and status often conflicts with the interests of minority groups and women, especially regarding equality of opportunity. Personnel agencies will be at the center of the controversy and must develop procedures to encourage the opening of union ranks to more minorities and women at the same time that they protect current employee rights.

Participation of employees goes beyond the job situation. In our society, where everyone demands a right to be heard, public employees will maintain their pressure to be given their rights as citizens in a democracy. Assaults on the Hatch Acts and on other restrictions against public employees will continue. The right to dissent will be claimed ever more strongly as people realize that the only way they can control bureaucracy and keep it responsive is to know as much as possible about its activities. Thus public employees are likely to want to share more information, and their professional mobility probably will make their demands for political participation rights more potent.

Litigation

Today everyone seems to believe that the way to solve a problem is to take it to court. Personnel managers have not escaped the trend. Litigation on almost every aspect of the personnel process is becoming common. Equal employment opportunity has spawned the most activity and has led to challenges of examinations, promotions, pay, and evaluations, as well as many other aspects of the personnel function. Litigation is also common in the areas of labor relations, employment of the handicapped and elderly, and safety. These challenges can only be expected to increase.

The increasing number of lawsuits necessitates new expertise in the personnel field. Personnel managers have not been noted for their legal training, and legal staff have not been particularly well trained in the public personnel field. That condition is changing rapidly as personnel offices need people to represent them in all facets of employee relations. Thus legal staffs are being added to personnel departments, or legal departments are employing people with specialization in personnel law.

Summary

Many changes can be expected to occur in the personnel field. In addition to those already mentioned, reform movements are likely to bring about a new alignment of the personnel organization. It is likely that there will be a separation of the implementation and review processes of personnel as is done at the national level under the Civil Service Reform Act of 1978. The old approach of having a civil service commission which developed policy, implemented it, and then sat in judgment over the departments is giving way to a new arrangement. It consists of a personnel agency which develops and administers the personnel program and policy, and a separate review board or commission which deals with complaints and compliance issues. The personnel agency needs to be closely tied to the overall management function and should not be as independent as has been the case in the past. The independent civil service model served its purpose of separating personnel from political influence; but now that this goal has been achieved, priorities need to be reordered. Personnel must be seen as a tool of management and ultimately must be fully integrated into the management process. At the same time employees need to feel that there is a place they can go where their problems will be impartially resolved. The independent board or commission with appeals authority does just that.

The personnel function is likely to be conceived of in terms of total human resource management in the future. If it is to become fully integrated into management, it must deal with all aspects of the employment situation. Thus it will increasingly respond to the needs of all employees in the organization while it also works to improve the way in which organizations are managed. No longer can it afford to be a narrow policing function.

While there are certain to be many changes in the personnel function, one part of the process will not change. The unpredictability of the individual human being and the political process will continue to make the job of personnel administrators a challenging one.

NOTES

1. Lyle J. Sumek and Gail Elias, *Human Resources Management in the Future* (Denver: University of Colorado Graduate School of Public Affairs, n.d.).
2. Guy Benveniste, *The Politics of Expertise* (Berkeley: Glendessary Press, 1972), deals with the acquisition and use of power by experts.

SUGGESTED READINGS

Dempsey, John R. "Carter Reorganization: A Midterm Appraisal." *Public Administration Review*, 39 (January/February 1979), 74–78.
Foster, Gregory D. "The 1978 Civil Service Reform Act: Post-mortem or Rebirth?" *Public Administration Review*, 39 (January/February 1979), 78–85.

Gallas, Edward C., and Nesta M. Gallas. "General Problems of the Public Service." *Public Personnel Management*, 8 (March/April 1979), 64–73.

Knudsen, Steven, Larry Jakus, and Maida Metz. "The Civil Service Reform Act of 1978." *Public Personnel Management*, 8 (May/June 1979), 170–181.

Rainey, Hal G. "Perceptions of Incentives in Business and Government: Implications for Civil Service Reform." *Public Administration Review*, 39 (September/October 1979), 440–448.

Sumek, Lyle J., and Gail Elias. *Human Resources Management in the Future*. Denver: University of Colorado Graduate School of Public Affairs, n.d.

U.S. Civil Service Commission. *Conference Report on Public Personnel Management Reform*. Washington, D.C.: Bureau of Intergovernmental Personnel Programs, 1978.

Index